D1297595

ADVANCES
IN CHILD DEVELOPMENT
AND BEHAVIOR

VARIETIES OF EARLY EXPERIENCE: IMPLICATIONS FOR THE DEVELOPMENT OF DECLARATIVE MEMORY IN INFANCY

VOLUME 38

Contributors to This Volume

Patricia J. Bauer

Melissa M. Burch

Carol L. Cheatham

Dante Cicchetti

Michael K. Georgieff

Megan R. Gunnar

Dana E. Johnson

Maria G. Kroupina

Marina Larkina

Charles A. Nelson

Tracy Riggins

Jennifer A. Schwade

Heather Whitney Sesma

Sheree L. Toth

ADVANCES IN CHILD DEVELOPMENT AND BEHAVIOR

VARIETIES OF EARLY EXPERIENCE:
IMPLICATIONS FOR THE DEVELOPMENT OF
DECLARATIVE MEMORY IN INFANCY

edited by

Patricia J. Bauer
Department of Psychology
Emory University
Atlanta, GA 30322, USA

VOLUME 38

AMSTERDAM • BOSTON • HEIDELBERG • LONDON
NEW YORK • OXFORD • PARIS • SAN DIEGO
SAN FRANCISCO • SINGAPORE • SYDNEY • TOKYO
Academic Press is an imprint of Elsevier

ELSEVIER

Academic Press is an imprint of Elsevier
32 Jamestown Road, London NW1 7BY, UK
Radarweg 29, PO Box 211, 1000 AE Amsterdam, The Netherlands
30 Corporate Drive, Suite 400, Burlington, MA 01803, USA
525 B Street, Suite 1900, San Diego, CA 92101-4495, USA

First edition 2010

Library of Congress Cataloging-in-Publication Data
A catalogue record for this book is available from the Library of Congress

British Library Cataloguing in Publication Data
A catalog record for this book is available from the British Library

ISBN: 978-0-12-374471-5
ISSN: 0065-2407 (Series)

For information on all Academic Press publications
visit our website at elsevierdirect.com

Transferred to Digital Printing 2011

Contents

Declarative Memory Performance in Infants of Diabetic Mothers

TRACY RIGGINS, PATRICIA J. BAUER, MICHAEL K. GEORGIEFF, AND CHARLES A. NELSON

The Development of Declarative Memory in Infants Born Preterm

CAROL L. CHEATHAM, HEATHER WHITNEY SESMA, PATRICIA J. BAUER, AND MICHAEL K. GEORGIEFF

Institutional Care as a Risk for Declarative Memory Development

MARIA G. KROUPINA, PATRICIA J. BAUER, MEGAN R. GUNNAR, AND DANA E. JOHNSON

Declarative Memory in Abused and Neglected Infants

CAROL L. CHEATHAM, MARINA LARKINA, PATRICIA J. BAUER, SHEREE L. TOTH, AND DANTE CICCHETTI

Declarative Memory in Infancy: Lessons Learned from Typical and Atypical Development

PATRICIA J. BAUER

Contributors

PATRICIA J. BAUER
Department of Psychology, Emory University, Atlanta, Georgia, USA
MELISSA M. BURCH
School of Cognitive Science, Hampshire College, Amherst, Massachusetts, USA
CAROL L. CHEATHAM
Department of Psychology, and Nutrition Research Institute, University of North Carolina at Chapel Hill, Chapel Hill, Kannapolis, North Carolina, USA
DANTE CICCHETTI
Institute of Child Development, University of Minnesota, Minneapolis, Minnesota, USA
MICHAEL K. GEORGIEFF
Department of Pediatrics and Center for Neurobehavioral Development, University of Minnesota, Minneapolis, Minnesota, USA
MEGAN R. GUNNAR
Institute of Child Development, University of Minnesota, Minneapolis, Minnesota, USA
DANA E. JOHNSON
Department of Pediatrics, University of Minnesota, Minneapolis, Minnesota, USA
MARIA G. KROUPINA
Department of Pediatrics, University of Minnesota, Minneapolis, Minnesota, USA
MARINA LARKINA
Department of Psychology, Emory University, Atlanta, Georgia, USA
CHARLES A. NELSON
Harvard Medical School, Children's Hospital Boston, Massachusetts, USA
TRACY RIGGINS
Department of Psychology, University of Maryland, College Park, Maryland, USA
JENNIFER A. SCHWADE
Department of Psychology, Cornell University, Ithaca, New York, USA

HEATHER WHITNEY SESMA
Institute of Child Development, University of Minnesota, Minneapolis, Minnesota, USA
SHEREE L. TOTH
Mt. Hope Family Center, University of Rochester, Rochester, New York, USA

Preface

A hallmark of the *Advances in Child Development and Behavior* series has been timely review, analysis, and critique of the many fields and sub-fields that make up the study of child development and behavior. With Volume 38 of the series, the publishers introduce a new format for the collection, namely, thematic collections. The purpose of the thematic collections is to permit more in-depth treatment of timely and important topics. The tradition volumes and thematic collections will coexist, providing the field with the best of both worlds.

As implied by the subtitle of this volume, this first thematic collection brings together work that addresses how the development of declarative (or explicit) memory in infancy is influenced by a number of different types of early experiences. Declarative memory is the type of memory that most of us have in mind when we think "memory." It is the capacity for rapid, even one-trial, learning of novel facts and events. For much of the history of research in developmental psychology, it was thought that infants and very young children lacked this important capacity. We knew that infants learned and otherwise benefited from past experience. However, because declarative memory is typically assessed verbally, and because infants are unable to speak, it was widely believed that infants were incapable of explicitly or consciously recalling past experiences.

The perspective on infants' memory abilities began to change with the development of a nonverbal means of assessing declarative memory, namely, elicited and deferred imitation. The paradigm is introduced in Chapters 1 and 2 of this volume. Briefly, in elicited and deferred imitation, props are used to demonstrate a novel action or multistep sequence of actions that the infant is invited to imitate. Differences between infants' production of the target actions and sequences before versus after the demonstration are the index of memory. Using this technique, we have learned a great deal about declarative memory in typically developing infants and young children. Some of the major changes in declarative memory over the first two years of life as revealed by this paradigm are summarized in Chapters 1–3.

Simultaneous with work on the typical course of development of declarative memory in infants was work demonstrating that the nonverbal technique of elicited and deferred imitation was sensitive to lesion and disease of one of the major neural structures that supports declarative memory, namely, the medial–temporal lobe structure of the hippocampus. The evidence came in the form of demonstrations that adults with hippocampal lesions, in whom declarative memory processes are disrupted, performed poorly on an adult version of the task. Deficits were apparent whether the lesion was inflicted in adulthood (McDonough, Mandler, McKee, & Squire, 1995) or in infancy or early childhood (Adlam, Vargha-Khadem, Mishkin & de Haan, 2005). This research suggested the utility of the elicited/deferred imitation task as a means of assessing the integrity of the hippocampus in infancy. In this thematic volume, my colleagues and I report the results of some initial investigations that capitalize on this suggestion.

The motivation for examining "varieties of early experience" stems from two facts: the declarative memory network is slow to develop (see Chapter 1, this volume) and for reasons that are not entirely clear, the hippocampus is a structure that is especially vulnerable to insult (Nelson & Carver, 1998). The combination of a slow course of development and an integral structure that is especially open to environmental influence leads to the possibility that there may be populations in whom the early development of declarative memory is compromised. In this volume, we bring together results from four populations of children in whom my colleagues and I have investigated this possibility: infants of mothers with gestational diabetes, infants born prior to term, infants adopted from institutional care, and infants maltreated by their caregivers. In each case, we have reason to expect that the hippocampus has been compromised by early experience and that as a result, children will evidence deficits in declarative memory.

For all populations, we used a common methodology to examine declarative memory function in the second year of life, namely, imitation-based tasks that measure immediate and delayed recall memory. Additional measures were also used for some, but not all, populations. Use of the same methodology with different populations permits relatively direct comparisons which in turn will inform our understanding of the effects of early experience on development of the fundamental capacity of declarative memory. As will become apparent throughout Chapters 4 through 7, which are dedicated to each of the special populations in turn, each population showed impaired declarative memory performance, though the levels and patterns of impairment differed. The final chapter of the collection is devoted to a summary of the patterns and discussion of their implications.

The approach of application of the same methods and tasks to typically developing infants and infants in each of four special populations was facilitated by physical proximity and a climate of collaboration among faculty and graduate students at the University of Minnesota's Institute of Child Development, Department of Pediatrics, and Center for Neurobehavioral Development. Most of the work reported in this collection was initiated while the authors were at the University of Minnesota. Several of the authors have since left the land of 10,000 lakes, yet remained in collaborative contact. Ironically, one of the collaborators (Dante Cicchetti) on the only study that was not conducted at the University of Minnesota, namely, infants maltreated by their caregivers (Chapter 7), since moved to the University of Minnesota. He made the move even as other members of the then-faculty (Patricia Bauer and Charles Nelson) moved elsewhere. This large-scale collaboration provided an unprecedented opportunity for comparison across studies without concerns that methodological differences might compromise interpretation.

This thematic collection provides a unique perspective on a question of major interest and significance to developmental and cognitive psychologists, developmental and cognitive scientists, and developmental cognitive neuroscientists, as well as to clinicians who work with children from the special populations on whom much of the research is focused. It informs normative development and also sheds new light on the processes involved in declarative memory, and some of the determinants of its typical and atypical developmental course.

Patricia J. Bauer
Department of Psychology,
Emory University,
Atlanta, Georgia, USA

REFERENCES

Adlam, A.-L. R., Vargha-Khadem, F., Mishkin, M., & de Haan, M. (2005). Deferred imitation of action sequences in developmental amnesia. *Journal of Cognitive Neuroscience*, *17*, 240–248.

McDonough, L., Mandler, J. M., McKee, R. D., & Squire, L. R. (1995). The deferred imitation task as a nonverbal measure of declarative memory. *Proceedings of the National Academy of Sciences*, *92*, 7580–7584.

Nelson, C. A., & Carver, L. J. (1998). The effects of stress and trauma on brain and memory: A view from developmental cognitive neuroscience. *Development & Psychopathology*, *10*(4), 793–809.

DECLARATIVE MEMORY IN INFANCY: AN INTRODUCTION TO TYPICAL AND ATYPICAL DEVELOPMENT

Patricia J. Bauer

DEPARTMENT OF PSYCHOLOGY, EMORY UNIVERSITY, ATLANTA, GEORGIA, USA

Memory is a fundamental cognitive process. Without it, we would not be able to recognize familiar faces, find our car in the parking lot at the end of the day, or share with a friend tales of our adventures on a recent vacation. How and when memory develops, and the reasons why it develops as it does, have been topics of speculation at least since Freud's (1905/1953) observations of the "great intellectual accomplishments" (p. 64) of which infants and young children are capable. Yet, much of what we know about early memory has been learned since the 1980s. Until that time, it was generally assumed that infants were unable to encode, store, and subsequently retrieve memories of specific past events. This perspective held sway for both conceptual and methodological reasons.

1

Advances in Child Development and Behavior
Patricia Bauer : Editor

As in so many areas of cognitive developmental science, the study of the development of memory got its start with Piaget (1952, 1962). Among the tenets of Piaget's theory of genetic epistemology was the suggestion that for the first 18–24 months of life, infants lacked symbolic capacity and thus, the ability to mentally *represent* objects and events. Instead, they were thought to live in a world of physically present entities that had no past and no future. Even as tenets attributed to Piagetian theory were being challenged on multiple fronts (e.g., Gelman & Baillargeon, 1983), the suggestion that infants were unable to remember the events of their lives went unexamined for want of suitable methodology. In older children and adults, memory is examined primarily through verbal report. For infants and young children, this is not a viable alternative: It is not until age 3 that children become reliable informants about the past. It was seen as more than coincidence that age 3 marks the end of the period of infantile amnesia (i.e., the relative paucity among adults of verbally expressible memories of specific events from the first years of life). Indeed, that the average age of earliest memory among adults is 3½ (see Bauer, 2007; West & Bauer, 1999, for reviews), and that age 3–3½ marks the beginning of children's abilities to share past experiences verbally, "conspired" to create the impression that age 3 marked the onset of the ability to remember.

In this chapter, I summarize some of the research that has contributed to revision of the perspective that infants are unable to remember the past. Because questions of whether infants are able to create, retain, and later retrieve accessible memories of specific past experiences has been the focus of much of the research attention, this type of memory (i.e., declarative memory for specific events or episodes) is featured.

As will be discussed, declarative memory is dependent on a particular neural system that is slow to develop. These facts lead to speculation that there may be populations of infants in whom the substrate for declarative memory is impaired, with the result that performance on declarative memory tasks also is impaired. The logic for this speculation is that a memory system that is slow to develop is a system that is vulnerable to perturbation. Moreover, for reasons that are not entirely known, the lynchpin neural structure in the declarative memory system, namely, the hippocampus, is especially vulnerable to early insult (Nelson & Carver, 1998). The combination of a slow course of development and an integral structure that is especially open to environmental influence leads to the suggestion that there may be populations in whom the early development of declarative memory is compromised. In this volume, we bring together results from four populations of children in whom my colleagues and I have investigated this possibility: infants of mothers with gestational diabetes, infants born prior to term, infants adopted from institutional care, and infants maltreated by their caregivers. In each case, we have reason to expect that the hippocampus has been compromised by early experience and that as a result, children will evidence deficits in declarative memory. We report the results of tests of this hypothesis.

I. Assessing Memory in Infancy

It has long been clear that infants learn and otherwise benefit from past experience and thus, evidence memory of some sort. In fact, DeCasper and Spence (1986) suggest that even prenatal experiences later may manifest themselves in changes in behavior toward stimuli: Mere hours after birth, infants distinguish between a novel story passage and one that their mothers read aloud during the last weeks of pregnancy. These results and those from other infant paradigms have revealed evidence of strikingly robust memory from very young infants. Yet as discussed in Bauer (2006a, 2007), these findings were not what prompted revision of the suggestion that the first years of life were devoid of the ability to mentally represent objects or events and thereby recall them. That distinction is reserved for findings from a memory paradigm that is an accepted nonverbal analogue to verbal report, and thus, a measure of declarative memory, namely, *elicited* and *deferred imitation*. Before summarizing some of the major findings from this paradigm used with typical infants, I elaborate the definition of declarative memory and develop the argument that imitation-based tasks can be used to investigate its development.

A. DISTINGUISHING DECLARATIVE AND NONDECLARATIVE MEMORY

It is widely believed that memory is not a unitary trait but comprised of different systems or processes, which serve distinct functions, and are characterized by fundamentally different rules of operation (e.g., Squire, 1992). The type of memory termed *declarative* (or explicit) captures most of what we think of when we refer to "memory" or "remembering" (Zola-Morgan & Squire, 1993). It involves the capacity for explicit recognition or recall of names, places, dates, events, and so on. In contrast, the type of memory termed *nondeclarative* represents a variety of nonconscious abilities, including the capacity for learning habits and skills, priming, and some forms of conditioning (see Lloyd & Newcombe, 2009; Parkin, 1997, for reviews). A defining feature of nondeclarative memory is that the impact of experience is made evident through a change in behavior or performance, but that the experience leading to the change is not consciously accessible (Zola-Morgan & Squire). Declarative memory is characterized as fast (e.g., supporting one-trial learning), fallible (e.g., memory traces degrade, retrieval failures occur), and flexible (i.e., not tied to a specific modality or context). Nondeclarative memory is characterized as slow (i.e., with the exception of priming, it results from gradual or incremental learning), reliable, and inflexible (Squire, Knowlton, & Musen, 1993).

The distinction between different types of memory originally was derived from the adult cognitive and neuroscience literatures. Yet it is vitally important for developmental scientists, because declarative and nondeclarative memory rely on different neural substrates that have different courses of development. Declarative memory, in particular, is potentially vulnerable to insults from a variety of pre- and postnatal conditions, four of which are the subjects of reports in this volume. A variety of brain regions are implicated in support of nondeclarative memory, including neocortex (priming), striatum (skill learning), and cerebellum (conditioning; see Toth, 2000, for review). These regions are thought to develop early and as a result, to support early emergence of nondeclarative memory (see Nelson, 1997, for review). In contrast, as described in more detail later, declarative memory depends on a multicomponent neural network including temporal and cortical structures (e.g., Zola & Squire, 2000). Whereas most (*although not all*) of the medial temporal lobe components of declarative memory develop early, other aspects of the network undergo a protracted developmental course. The entire circuit begins to coalesce near the end of the first year of life and continues to develop for years thereafter, contributing to pronounced changes in declarative memory (see Bachevalier & Mishkin, 1994; Bauer, 2007, 2009a,b; Nelson, de Haan, & Thomas, 2006; Richman & Nelson, 2008, for reviews).

B. ELICITED AND DEFERRED IMITATION

Deferred imitation originally was suggested by Piaget (1952, 1962) as a hallmark of the development of symbolic thought. Beginning in the mid 1980s, the technique was developed as a test of memory ability in infants and young children (e.g., Bauer & Mandler, 1989; Bauer & Shore, 1987; Meltzoff, 1985). It involves using props to produce a single action or a multistep sequence and then, either immediately (elicited imitation), after a delay (deferred imitation), or both, inviting the infant or young child to imitate.

As discussed in detail elsewhere (e.g., Bauer, 2007; Bauer, DeBoer, & Lukowski, 2007; Carver & Bauer, 2001; Mandler, 1990; Meltzoff, 1990; Squire *et al.*, 1993), the conditions of learning and later testing in elicited and deferred imitation are conducive to formation of declarative memories but not nondeclarative memories, and the resulting mnemonic behaviors share characteristics of declarative memories. First, although performance is facilitated by multiple experiences (e.g., Bauer, Hertsgaard, & Wewerka, 1995), infants learn and remember on the basis of a single experience (e.g., Bauer & Hertsgaard, 1993). Rapid learning is characteristic of declarative memory. Second, the contents of memories formed in imitation-based tasks are accessible to language. Once children acquire the language capacity to do so, they talk about multistep sequences they experienced as preverbal infants (e.g., Bauer, Kroupina, Schwade, Dropik, & Wewerka, 1998; Cheatham & Bauer, 2005; although see Simcock & Hayne, 2002, for a suggestion to the contrary, and Bauer *et al.*, 2004, for discussion of possible reasons for the negative findings in Simcock & Hayne).

Third, the memory traces formed in imitation-based tasks are flexible. Infants show that they remember even when (a) the objects available at the time of retrieval differ in size, shape, color, and/or material composition from those encountered at the time of encoding (e.g., Bauer & Dow, 1994; Bauer & Fivush, 1992; Bauer & Lukowski, 2010; Lechuga, Marcos-Ruiz, & Bauer, 2001), (b) the appearance of the room at the time of retrieval is different from that at the time of encoding (e.g., Barnat, Klein, & Meltzoff, 1996; Klein & Meltzoff, 1999), (c) encoding and retrieval take place in different settings (e.g., Hanna & Meltzoff, 1993; Klein & Meltzoff, 1999), and (d) the individual who elicits recall is different from the individual who demonstrated the actions (e.g., Hanna & Meltzoff, 1993). Evidence of flexible extension of event knowledge is apparent in infants as young as 9–11 months of age (e.g., Baldwin, Markman, & Melartin, 1993; Lukowski, Wiebe, & Bauer, in press; McDonough & Mandler, 1998).

Fourth, imitation-based tasks pass the "amnesia test." McDonough, Mandler, McKee, and Squire (1995) tested adults with amnesia (in whom declarative memory processes are impaired) and control participants in an imitation-based task using multistep sequences. Whereas normal adults produced the model's actions even after a delay, patients with amnesia did poorly, performing no better than control participants who had never seen the events demonstrated. Older children and young adults who were rendered amnesic as a result of pre- or perinatal insults also show decreased performance on imitation-based tasks (Adlam, Vargha-Khadem, Mishkin, & de Haan, 2005). These findings strongly suggest that although imitation-based tasks are behavioral rather than verbal, they tap declarative memory. As such, the technique is widely accepted as a nonverbal analogue to verbal report (e.g., Bauer, 2002; Mandler, 1990; Meltzoff, 1990; Rovee-Collier & Hayne, 2000; Schneider & Bjorklund, 1998; Squire *et al.*, 1993; Wheeler, 2000). Critical to the research reported in this volume, performance on the paradigm also reflects the integrity of the underlying neural system with which it is associated.

II. Declarative Memory Development: The Typical Case

There are numerous behavioral changes relevant to memory that occur across infancy and very early childhood. I focus on a subset of three salient changes (see Bauer, 2007, for a more extensive review). Other changes are summarized in detail in Chapters 2 and 3 of this volume.

A. CHANGES IN TEMPORAL EXTENT

The length of time infants retain declarative memories increases dramatically over the first 2 years of life. Importantly, because like any complex behavior, the length of time an episode is remembered is multiply determined, there is no "growth chart" function that specifies that children of a given age will remember for a particular length of time. Nevertheless, by comparing across studies, it is possible to discern that with increasing age, infants tolerate lengthier retention intervals. For example, at 6 months of age, infants remember an average of one action of a three-step sequence (taking a mitten off a puppet's hand, shaking the mitten which, at the time of demonstration, held a bell that rang, and replacing the mitten) for 24 h (Barr, Dowden, & Hayne, 1996). Collie and Hayne (1999) found that 6-month-olds remembered an average of one out of five possible actions over a 24-h delay.

By 9–11 months of age, the length of time over which memory for laboratory events is apparent has increased substantially. Nine-month olds remember individual actions over delays from 24 h (Meltzoff, 1988) to 5 weeks (Carver & Bauer, 1999, 2001). By 10–11 months, infants remember over delays of 3 months (Carver & Bauer, 2001; Mandler & McDonough, 1995). Thirteen- to fourteen-month olds remember actions over delays of 4–6 months (Bauer, Wenner, Dropik, & Wewerka, 2000; Meltzoff, 1995). By 20 months of age, children remember the actions of event sequences for as many as 12 months (Bauer *et al.*, 2000). Thus, over the first 2 years of life, there are steady age-related increases in the length of time events are remembered.

B. CHANGES IN ROBUSTNESS

The first 2 years of life also are witness to changes in the robustness of memories. As noted earlier, infants demonstrate memory even when the materials, contexts, and examiners change between encoding and test. Yet there also are reports of developmental changes in the extent to which infants and very young children are sensitive to these types of contextual changes. For example, in research by Hayne, MacDonald, and Barr (1997), when 18-month olds experienced the puppet sequence (see above) demonstrated on a cow puppet and then were tested with the same puppet, they showed robust retention over 24 h. However, when they experienced the sequence modeled on a cow puppet and then were tested with a duck puppet, they did not show evidence of memory. Twenty-one-month olds remembered the sequence whether tested with the same or a different puppet (see also Hayne, Boniface, & Barr, 2000; Herbert & Hayne, 2000). Taken as a whole, this literature indicates that whereas from an early age, infants' memories survive changes in context and stimuli, flexible extension becomes more apparent with age.

Another index of the robustness of memory is an age-related reduction in the number of exposures to an event required for an infant to remember. Early in the first year, long-term recall seems dependent on multiple experiences. For example, in Barr *et al.* (1996), 6-month olds who saw actions modeled six times remembered them for 24 h, whereas infants who saw the actions modeled only three times did not. By 9 months, three demonstrations are sufficient to support recall of individual actions over 24 h (Meltzoff, 1988) and 1 week (Bauer, Wiebe, Waters, & Bangston, 2001). By early in the second year, a single exposure is sufficient for infants to recall it as many as 4 months later (Meltzoff, 1995). At least by 20 months of age, infants remember not only the individual actions but also the temporal order of actions months later, after only a single experience of them (Bauer, unpublished data). These developments are critical to the ability to remember unique episodes and events.

C. CHANGES IN SPECIFICITY

Another aspect of children's memory that increases across infancy and early childhood is the specificity with which events are remembered. Some of the findings reviewed in the section on the robustness of memory already suggested that infants remember the specific details of the objects used to produce events in elicited and deferred imitation paradigms. For example, the fact that 18-month-olds' recall can be disrupted by changes to the objects used to produce events (e.g., changing the puppet from a cow to a duck: Hayne *et al.*, 1997), indicates that infants encode specific features. More direct evidence of memory for specific features in infancy comes from studies in which forced-choice selection procedures are used to test recognition of the props used to produce events. In Bauer and Dow (1994), 16- and 20-month olds showed above-chance levels of selection of the props used to produce events, even when tested with functionally equivalent distracter props. By 20 months of age, memory for the specific objects used to produce multistep sequences predicts how well the events will be remembered 1 month later (Bauer & Lukowski, 2010).

III. Explaining Age-Related Changes

Ultimately, several sources of variance will be implicated in the explanation of age-related changes in declarative memory. They will range from changes in the neural systems and basic mnemonic processes that permit memories to be formed, retained, and later retrieved, to the social forces that shape what children come to view as important to remember and even how they express their memories. In this section, I illustrate some of these mechanisms of change. I begin with a brief review of the neural network thought to subserve declarative memory in the adult and what is known about its development. I then examine the basic mnemonic processes of encoding, consolidation, storage, and retrieval, and evaluate their contributions to age-related changes in declarative memory in infancy (see Bauer, 2004, 2006b, 2007, 2008, 2009b, for expanded versions of this discussion).

A. THE NEURAL SUBSTRATE OF DECLARATIVE MEMORY AND ITS DEVELOPMENT

In adult humans, the formation, maintenance, and retrieval of declarative memories depend on a multicomponent neural network involving temporal and cortical structures (e.g., Eichenbaum & Cohen, 2001; Markowitsch, 2000; Zola & Squire, 2000). Upon experience of an event, sensory and motor inputs from multiple brain regions distributed throughout the cortex converge on parahippocampal structures within the temporal lobes (e.g., entorhinal cortex). The work of binding the elements together to create a durable, integrated memory trace is carried out by another temporal lobe structure, the hippocampus. Cortical structures are the long-term storage sites for memories. Prefrontal structures are implicated in their retrieval after a delay. Thus, long-term recall requires multiple cortical regions, including prefrontal cortex, temporal structures, and intact connections between them.

In humans, aspects of the temporal structures in the temporal–cortical declarative memory network develop early. For instance, as reviewed by Seress and Abraham (2008), the cells that make up most of the hippocampus are formed in the first half of gestation and virtually all are in their adult locations by the end of the prenatal period. The neurons in most of the hippocampus also begin to connect early in development, with the adult number and density of synapses reached by approximately 6 postnatal months. Lagging behind in development is the dentate gyrus of the hippocampus (Seress & Abraham). At birth, this critical bridge between cortex and the hippocampus includes only about 70% of the adult number of cells and it is not until 12–15 postnatal months that the morphology of the structure appears adultlike. Maximum density of synaptic connections in the dentate gyrus also is delayed. Synaptic density increases dramatically (to well above adult levels) beginning at 8–12 postnatal months and reaches its peak at 16–20 months. After a period of relative stability, excess synapses are pruned until adult levels are reached at about 4–5 years of age (Eckenhoff & Rakic, 1991). As discussed elsewhere (e.g., Bauer, 2007, 2009a; Nelson, 1995, 1997, 2000), development of the dentate gyrus of the hippocampus may be a rate-limiting variable in declarative memory early in life. Even beyond the preschool years, there are increases in hippocampal volume and myelination that continue into adolescence (e.g., Arnold & Trojanowski, 1996; Benes, Turtle, Khan, & Farol, 1994; Gogtay *et al.*, 2004; Utsunomiya, Takano, Okazaki, & Mistudome, 1999).

The association areas also undergo a protracted course of development. It is not until the seventh prenatal month that all six cortical layers are apparent. The density of synapses in prefrontal cortex increases dramatically at 8 postnatal months and peaks between 15 and 24 months. Pruning to adult levels does not begin until late childhood; adult levels are not reached until late adolescence or early adulthood (Huttenlocher, 1979; Huttenlocher & Dabholkar, 1997; see Bourgeois, 2001, for discussion). In the years between, in some cortical layers there are changes in the size of cells and the lengths and branching of dendrites (Benes, 2001). There also are changes in glucose utilization and blood flow over the second half of the first year and into the second year (Chugani, Phelps, & Mazziotta, 1987). Other maturational changes in prefrontal cortex, such as myelination, continue into adolescence, and adult levels of some neurotransmitters are not seen until the second and third decades of life (Benes, 2001).

B. CHANGES IN BASIC MNEMONIC PROCESSES

Developmental changes in the declarative memory network have implications for the efficacy and efficiency with which information is encoded and stabilized for long-term storage, in the reliability with which it is stored, and in the ease with which it is retrieved. Late development of prefrontal cortex can be expected to impact all phases of the life of a memory trace from its initial encoding through consolidation to retrieval. Late development of the dentate gyrus is significant because it may lead to less effective and efficient consolidation of new information. As discussed in Bauer (2006a, 2009a, 2009b), the consequences of less effective and efficient early-stage processing are profound: If encoding is compromised, there is less to be consolidated. If consolidation is compromised and/or the information available for consolidation is degraded, less information will be stored. If less information is stored, there will be less to retrieve. Differences in the amount available for retrieval will become more apparent with the passage of time as interference and decay take their toll, further depleting the already degraded trace.

1. Encoding

Developmental changes in prefrontal cortex in particular may be expected to contribute to age-related changes in the efficiency with which young children encode information. Consistent with this suggestion, 3-month-old infants require more time to encode a stimulus than 6-month-old infants (Rose, Gottfried, Melloy-Carminar, & Bridger, 1982). Researchers also have used event-related potentials (ERPs) to assess age-related changes in encoding processes. ERPs are electrical oscillations in the brain that are time-locked to presentation of a stimulus. Differences in the activity recorded to different classes of stimuli (e.g., familiar and novel stimuli) can be interpreted as differential neural processing and recognition. In a longitudinal study of relations between encoding and long-term recall, Bauer *et al.* (2006) recorded infants' ERPs as they looked at photographs of props used in multistep sequences to which they had just been exposed interspersed with photographs of props from novel sequences. The amplitudes of responses to newly encoded stimuli at 10 months were larger than those of the same infants at 9 months; there were no differences in responses to novel stimuli. The differences at encoding were related to differences at recall. One month after each ERP, imitation was used to test long-term recall of the sequences. The infants had higher rates of recall of the sequences to which they had been exposed at 10 months, relative to the sequences to which they had been exposed at 9 months.

Age-related differences in encoding do not end at 1 year of age. Relative to 15-month olds, 12-month olds require more trials to learn multistep events to a criterion (learning to a criterion indicates that the material was fully encoded). In turn, 15-month olds are slower to achieve criterion, relative to 18-month olds (Howe & Courage, 1997).

2. Consolidation and Storage

Age-related differences in encoding are not the sole source of age trends in long-term declarative memory. Even with levels of encoding controlled statistically (Bauer *et al.*, 2000), by matching (Bauer, 2005), or by bringing children of different ages to the same learning criterion (Howe & Courage, 1997), older children have higher levels of long-term recall relative to younger children. This suggests that for younger children in particular, even once a memory has been successfully encoded, it remains vulnerable to forgetting. Greater vulnerability likely stems from the relative immaturity of the structures and connections required to consolidate memories for long-term storage (see Bauer, 2006a, 2009b, for discussion).

A clear indication that consolidation and storage processes are a source of variance in long-term recall in the first year comes from research in which behavioral and ERP measures were combined to assess memory in 9-month-old infants (Bauer, Wiebe, Carver, Waters, & Nelson, 2003). In this study, encoding was tested via immediate ERP, consolidation and storage were assessed 1 week later via ERP, and long-term recall was tested 1 month later through deferred imitation. As a group, the infants showed evidence of encoding (differential responses to the old and new stimuli), yet there was differential long-term recall that in turn related to differential consolidation and storage. Infants who did not recall the events after 1 month also did not recognize the familiar props after 1 week. Conversely, infants who recalled the events after 1 month showed successful consolidation and storage after 1 week. The two subgroups of infants did not differ at encoding, and individual variability in encoding was not a significant predictor of long-term recall. In contrast, successful consolidation and storage over 1 week accounted for 28% of the variance in recall 1 month later. Consolidation and storage processes continue to account for individual difference in recall in the second year of life. For infants 20 months of age, the amount of information retained after 48 h after exposure to events explained 25% of variance in recall after 1 month (Bauer, Cheatham, Cary, & Van Abbema, 2002).

3. Retrieval

Retrieval of memories from long-term storage is thought to depend on prefrontal cortex, a neural structure that undergoes a protracted developmental course. In part for this reason, traditionally, retrieval processes have been considered to be the major source of developmental differences in long-term recall (e.g., Hayne *et al.*, 2000; Liston & Kagan, 2002). However, there actually are few data with which to evaluate the contribution of retrieval processes because in most studies, there are alternative candidate sources of age-related changes. For instance, as implied earlier, unless the contributions of the early-stage processes of encoding and consolidation are evaluated, it is not appropriate to implicate retrieval-related processes as the major explanation for age-related differences in long-term recall (see Bauer, 2006a, 2009b, for discussion). Moreover, on the basis of a single recall test, it is difficult if not impossible to know whether a memory representation remains intact but is inaccessible given the cues provided (retrieval failure) or whether the trace has lost its integrity (consolidation/storage failure).

In the infant literature, one study in which measures of encoding and multiple recall tests are available is Bauer *et al.* (2000). Children of multiple ages (13, 16, 20 months) were tested over a range of delays (1–12 months). To eliminate encoding processes as a potential source of developmental differences in long-term recall, subsets of 13- and 16-month olds and subsets of 16- and 20-month olds were matched for levels of encoding (Bauer, 2005). In addition, at the time of test, the children were given two recall trials and also tested for relearning, thus allowing for assessment of the possibility of test-related increases in retrieval. Even under these conditions, the younger children remembered less than the older children. They also had lower levels of relearning. Together, the findings strongly implicate consolidation and storage as opposed to retrieval processes as the major source of developmental change (see Bauer, 2006a, 2007, 2009b, for further discussion).

IV. Declarative Memory Development: Atypical Cases

In this section, I introduce the possibility of impairments in declarative memory in infancy as a result of a variety of insults that may be expected to affect medial temporal structures in general and the hippocampus in particular. By virtue of the fact that development of the neural substrate of long-term declarative memory is protracted, there is ample opportunity for it to be perturbed by a number and variety of forces. Indeed, scholars have proposed that the hippocampus, in particular, is open to postnatal environmental influence (e.g., Webb, Monk, & Nelson, 2001). The hypothesized susceptibility of this neural structure, coupled with evidence that its major role, namely, consolidation and storage of memory traces, is a primary source of developmental change in the first years of life, suggests that there may be developmental populations in whom consolidation and/or storage functions are compromised. In this section, I introduce four populations of infants in which we may expect atypical development of declarative memory: infants born to mothers with gestational diabetes, infants born prior to term, infants adopted from institutional care, and infants who have been neglected, abused, or both, by their caregivers. In each case, there is reason to suspect compromised medial temporal function. As is clear in chapters of this volume devoted to each population (Chapters 4–7, respectively), in each case, evidence of deficits in declarative memory consolidation are apparent. By observing the development of declarative memory in populations for whom the construction process may be different from that typically observed, we gain insight into the factors that affect development more broadly.

A. GENERAL METHOD

The data from each of the three target populations were collected in different studies. Nevertheless, across studies, my colleagues and I used common methods to evaluate declarative memory processes. In each study, using imitation-based techniques, the children were tested for immediate imitation and imitation after a 10- to 15-min delay. In all cases, infants were tested for recall of multistep sequences. Multistep sequences are desirable because they provide information on infants' recall of temporal order. Temporal information is especially sensitive to lesions of the hippocampus (e.g., McDonough *et al.*, 1995; see Chapters 2 and 3 for elaboration). In two of the studies, infants also were tested for a task that demands that they integrate information presented over time.

Measures of immediate recall provide an opportunity to determine whether groups of children differ in encoding processes. Measures of performance after 10–15-min permit determination of whether groups of children differ in the formation of memory traces that would survive for long-term storage. Although 10 min may not seem a long time, we had three reasons to believe that performance after a 10-min delay would be diagnostic of consolidation processes. First, adults suffering from medial temporal lobe amnesia exhibit deficits in performance on tasks such as diagram recall, in which they are required to reproduce a diagram from memory after a 5–10-min delay (e.g., Reed & Squire, 1998). Second, medial temporal lesions inflicted on nonhuman primates produce deficits in declarative memory tasks after delays as brief as 10 min (e.g., Zola-Morgan, Squire, Rempel, Clower, & Amaral, 1992). Third, in normally developing human children, recall after a 10-min delay is correlated with recall after a 48-h delay (Bauer, Van Abbema, & de Haan, 1999). These observations suggest that performance after a 10-min delay provides information as to the integrity of medial temporal function. In the case of work with children at risk, a brief delay is preferable because it permits all testing to take place in a single session. In addition, because the delay is so short, retrieval processes are relatively untaxed, thereby permitting evaluation of consolidation processes. Finally, measures of temporal integration (available for two samples) provide insight into the ability to segment an ongoing stream of activity and integrate the relevant elements into a whole. This sort of "relational processing" is thought to be dependent on the hippocampus (e.g., Lloyd, Doydum, & Newcombe, 2009).

B. ATYPICAL POPULATIONS

Chapters 4–7 are devoted to discussion of declarative memory performance for infants born to mothers with gestational diabetes, children born prior to term, children adopted from institutional care, and children who have been neglected, abused, or both, by their caregivers, respectively. Here, I introduce each population, with a brief explanation of the basis for speculation that their declarative memory development may be atypical. The reader is referred to the relevant chapters for elaboration.

1. Infants Born to Mothers with Gestational Diabetes

Maternal diabetes is relatively common: Approximately 3–10% of pregnancies are affected with abnormal glycemic (sugar) control and 90% of those are diagnosed as gestational diabetes (Georgieff et al., 1990). Gestational diabetes occurs both when women who already have diabetes mellitus become pregnant and when otherwise healthy women develop blood sugar control problems during their pregnancies. Work with animal models has shown that infants of mothers with diabetes are exposed prenatally to chronic metabolic insults, including iron deficiency. It has been known for some time that deficiencies in iron are related to deficits in motor and cognitive function (see Georgieff & Rao, 2001, for a review). Whereas the motor impairments are reversible with iron replacement therapy, the cognitive impairments seem less amenable to treatment. As a result, even after iron levels have been restored, children who suffered iron deficiency prenatally may experience as much as a 10–12-point reduction in IQ, as measured by tests such as the *Bayley Scales of Infant Development* (Lozoff, 1990).

As discussed by Georgieff and Rao (2001), one possible reason for the persistent cognitive deficit associated with prenatal iron deficiency is that iron affects neurodevelopment. It is known that iron is essential for myelination (Larkin, Jarratt, & Rao, 1986). For reasons that are not clear at this time, the hippocampus is a region of the brain that is at particular risk for reductions in iron uptake (Erikson, Pinero, Connor, & Beard, 1997). This suggests that infants born to mothers with gestational diabetes may be a population in whom medial temporal function is impaired. This possibility is explored in research reported in Chapter 4.

2. Infants Born Prior to Term but Otherwise at Low Risk

Most infants are born after 38–40 weeks of gestation. However, a number are born preterm (i.e., at ≤ 37 weeks' gestation). There is an extensive literature documenting poor cognitive outcomes for preterm infants with medical risk factors (e.g., infants who had very low birth weight or experienced intraventricular hemorrhages). The patient Jon, tested by Vargha-Khadem and her colleagues (e.g., Gadian *et al.*, 2000), is a case in point. Jon was born at 26 weeks of gestation, weighing only 940 g. He suffered breathing problems that required intubation (i.e., insertion of a tube into his lungs). Whereas normal breathing was established within an hour of his birth, at the age of 3 weeks, his condition deteriorated and he required intubation and ventilation for 1 week (Gadian *et al.*). Jon suffers pronounced declarative memory impairments (see Bauer, 2007, for discussion). Because prematurity strikes disproportionally among populations who received poor prenatal care (though this apparently was not the case with Jon), preterm infants often are at social risk as well as medical risk (e.g., there is a high rate of preterm birth among young, single mothers of low socioeconomic status). Relatively less is known about the later developmental status of infants who survive prematurity sustaining no measurable neurological damage and with few to no social risk factors. These infants are of considerable theoretical interest because they provide a potential "experimental" model for investigating the relative importance of maturational and experiential factors in development of cognitive abilities (e.g., Jiang, 1995; Matthews, Ellis, & Nelson, 1996; van Hof-van Duin, Heersema, Groenendaal, Baerts, & Fetter, 1992).

Mounting evidence that experience plays a crucial role in shaping normative brain development suggests the possibility that the atypical timing and nature of postnatal experience in preterm infants may have lasting consequences for subsequent brain and behavioral development. As an example, in the domain of visual perception, visual acuity and visual form perception are not affected in healthy preterms (Seigal, 1994; van Hof-van Duin *et al.*, 1992), but visual–spatial processing is compromised even into the school age (Foreman, Fielder, Minshell, Hurrion, & Sergienko, 1997). This differential sensitivity of different aspects of visual processing to the effects of prematurity is argued to be due to the differences in timing of development of the dorsal visual pathway (spatial or "where" pathway) and ventral visual pathway (object or "what" pathway) that render them differentially sensitive to postnatal experience. Similarly, later and more slowly developing memory systems may be most vulnerable to variations in postnatal experience. The possibility of deficits in declarative memory as a result of preterm birth is explored in research reported in Chapter 5.

3. Infants Adopted from Institutional Care

There are a number of reasons to expect the possibility of compromised hippocampal development in children who spent their early months in an institutional care environment. Perhaps chief among them is deprivation, both cognitive and social. Thankfully, at the end of the twentieth century, conditions in most orphanages (almost all of which are in the developing world and Eastern Europe) are significantly better than those observed under the Ceaucescu regime in Romania (which fell in the early 1990s; see the report by Rutter and the English and Romanian Adoptees study team, 1998, for a description), for example. Nevertheless, relative to the "expected" environment, institutions invariably fall short. Even when adequate nutrition and health care are available, children rarely are provided with levels of stimulation and support sufficient to ensure normative development. Ratios of children to staff often are high; the staff frequently turns over; and due to concerns about transmission of disease, children are given few toys to manipulate and explore (see Gunnar, 2001, for discussion). These conditions virtually ensure that children receive suboptimal levels of social and cognitive interaction. As a consequence, institutionalized children frequently exhibit sensorimotor, cognitive, and language delays. The longer children remain institutionalized, the more pronounced the effects (see Gunnar, 2001, for a review).

Animal models of early deprivation provide some insight into one potential source of cognitive delay, namely, compromised hippocampal function. For example, primates deprived of normal rearing conditions exhibit elevated levels of glucocorticoids in response to stressors (e.g., Higley, Suomi, & Linnoila, 1992). High levels of glucocorticoids are not healthy for hippocampal neurons. In addition, there are suggestions that the licking and grooming that rodent mothers provide to their pups supports the development of the hippocampus (Caldji *et al.*, 1998). Removal of this source of stimulation results in levels of hippocampal cell death as much as 50% higher than normal (Zhang, Xing, Levine, Post, & Smith, 1997). The combination of these effects could be profound indeed: Infants deprived of social–emotional support and stimulation could be expected to mount exaggerated responses to stressors leading to cell death in a hippocampus that already has fewer than the expected number of neurons. Coupled with a lack of cognitive stimulation, compromised hippocampal function seems likely. The possible implications of these early living conditions for the development of declarative memory are explored in research reported in Chapter 6.

4. Infants Neglected, Abused, or Both by Their Caregivers

Infants who are neglected, abused, or both by their caregivers experience conditions that are not unlike those experienced by infants in institutional care. They typically are both socially and cognitively deprived. Even when basic physical needs are met, abused and neglected children are not provided with levels of positive stimulation and support sufficient to ensure normative development. As a result, abused and neglected children exhibit developmental delays at three times the typical rate (e.g., Scarborough, Lloyd, & Barth, 2009). There also are strong suggestions that the chronic stress that abused and neglected children experience has deleterious effects on the developing brain. For example, myelination (the fatty sheath that covers the axons of neurons and contributes to efficient neuronal communication) is susceptible to stress (Dunlop, Archer, Quinlivan, Beazley, & Newnham, 1997). Less than optimal myelination may contribute to the developmental delays apparent in maltreated children. Maltreatment also may contribute to chronically high cortisol levels, which in turn may contribute to damage and even death of cells in the hippocampus, thus contributing to deficits in declarative memory in particular. As above, we may expect that maltreated infants who are deprived of social–emotional support and stimulation might mount exaggerated responses to stressors leading to cell death in a hippocampus that already has fewer than the expected number of neurons. Coupled with a lack of cognitive stimulation, compromised hippocampal function seems likely. The possible implications of maltreatment early in life for the development of declarative memory are explored in research reported in Chapter 7.

V. Summary and Plan for the Volume

As is apparent from the brief reviews above, the development of declarative memory in infancy and early childhood is influenced by a number of different types of early experiences. For much of the history of research in developmental psychology, it was thought that infants and very young children lacked declarative memory capacity. We knew that infants learned and otherwise benefited from past experience. However, because declarative memory traditionally has been assessed verbally, and because infants are unable to participate in verbal paradigms, it was widely believed that infants were incapable of explicitly or consciously recognizing or recalling past experiences.

With the advent of development of a nonverbal analogue to verbal report, namely, elicited and deferred imitation (e.g., Bauer & Mandler, 1989; Bauer & Shore, 1987; Meltzoff, 1988), our perspective on the capacity of pre- and early-verbal children for declarative memory changed dramatically. Studies using this technique make clear that in the course of typical development, the capacity for even long-term recall of past events emerges and coalesces over the course of the latter half of the first year and throughout the second year of life (respectively). By some metrics, the course of construction of declarative memory is quite rapid: In the period of 6–20 months, children go from being able to remember individual actions for 24 h to being able to remember ordered sequences for 12 months. By other metrics, however, the course of development is extremely protracted: It takes 20 months of postnatal development to become reliable on tests of declarative memory, especially over a delay. Description of this developmental course is one of the two main purposes of this volume. We summarize what is known about the typical course of development of declarative memory in infancy, with special emphasis on what infants remember and on age-related and individual differences in declarative memory. In addition to the present chapter, this purpose is pursued in Chapters 2 and 3.

The second broad purpose of the volume is to examine a major implication of the slow course of development of declarative memory in infancy. A system that is slow to come together and has so many moving parts, is a system that is vulnerable to perturbation. Moreover, for reasons that are not entirely known, the hippocampus is a structure that is especially vulnerable to early insult (Nelson & Carver, 1998). The combination of a slow course of development and an integral structure that is especially open to environmental influence leads to the suggestion that there may be populations in whom the early development of declarative memory is compromised. We present data on declarative memory development in infancy for each of four special populations in which we have reason to expect compromised development of declarative memory: infants of mothers with gestational diabetes, infants born prior to term, infants adopted from institutional care, and infants maltreated by their caregivers. In each case, we have reason to expect that the hippocampus has been compromised by early experience and that as a result, infants will evidence deficits in declarative memory. As will become apparent, the different groups have different profiles of performance. The levels and patterns of performance are described in Chapters 4–7.

A unique feature of the collection is that for all four populations of infants, we have used a common methodology to examine declarative memory function in the second year of life, namely, imitation-based tasks that measure declarative memory immediately and after a delay. Application of the same general methods—and even the same tasks—permits direct comparisons of levels and patterns of performance in the different populations. Explicit comparison of the patterns of performance across the four atypical populations is the subject of the final chapter in the volume (Chapter 8). Consideration of the patterns of deficit and sparing and their presumed etiologies is expected to shed important new light on the mechanisms of early memory development. The comparisons will inform our understanding of the effects of early experience on development of the fundamental capacity of declarative memory.

Acknowledgment

The research summarized in this chapter was supported by grants from the NICHD (HD28425, HD42483) to Patricia J. Bauer.

REFERENCES

Adlam, A.-L. R., Vargha-Khadem, F., Mishkin, M., & de Haan, M. (2005). Deferred imitation of action sequences in developmental amnesia. *Journal of Cognitive Neuroscience, 17,* 240–248.

Arnold, S. E., & Trojanowski, J. Q. (1996). Human fetal hippocampal development: I. Cytoarchitecture, myeloarchitecture, and neuronal morphologic features. *The Journal of Comparative Neurology, 367,* 274–292.

Bachevalier, J., & Mishkin, M. (1994). Effects of selective neonatal temporal lobe lesions on visual recognition memory in rhesus monkeys. *The Journal of Neuroscience, 14,* 2128–2139.

Baldwin, D. A., Markman, E. M., & Melartin, R. L. (1993). Infants' ability to draw inferences about nonobvious object properties: Evidence from exploratory play. *Child Development, 64,* 711–728.

Barnat, S. B., Klein, P. J., & Meltzoff, A. N. (1996). Deferred imitation across changes in context and object: Memory and generalization in 14-month-old children. *Infant Behavior & Development, 19,* 241–251.

Barr, R., Dowden, A., & Hayne, H. (1996). Developmental change in deferred imitation by 6- to 24-month-old infants. *Infant Behavior & Development, 19,* 159–170.

Bauer, P. J. (2002). Early memory development. In U. Goswami (Ed.), *Blackwell handbook of childhood cognitive development.* Oxford, UK: Blackwell.

Bauer, P. J. (2004). New developments in the study of infant memory. In D. M. Teti (Ed.), *Blackwell handbook of research methods in developmental science.* Oxford, UK: Blackwell.

Bauer, P. J. (2005). Developments in declarative memory: Decreasing susceptibility to storage failure over the second year of life. *Psychological Science, 16,* 41–47.

Bauer, P. J. (2006a). Constructing a past in infancy: A neuro-developmental account. *Trends in Cognitive Sciences, 10,* 175–181.

Bauer, P. J. (2006b). Event memory. In D. Kuhn & R. Siegler (Vol. Eds.), *Cognition, perception, and language* (Vol. 2). In W. Damon & R. M. Lerner (Eds.-in-Chief), *Handbook of child psychology* (6th ed., pp. 373–425). Hoboken, NJ: Wiley.

Bauer, P. J. (2007). *Remembering the times of our lives: Memory in infancy and beyond.* Mahwah, NJ: Erlbaum.

Bauer, P. J. (2008). Toward a neuro-developmental account of the development of declarative memory. *Developmental Psychobiology, 50,* 19–31.

Bauer, P. J. (2009a). The cognitive neuroscience of the development of memory. In M. L. Courage & N. Cowan (Eds.), *The development of memory in infancy and childhood* (2nd ed., pp. 115–144). New York, NY: Psychology Press.

Bauer, P. J. (2009b). Neurodevelopmental changes in infancy and beyond: Implications for learning and memory. In O. A. Barbarin & B. H. Wasik (Eds.), *Handbook of child development and early education: Research to practice.* New York: The Guilford Press.

Bauer, P. J., Cheatham, C. L., Cary, M. S., & Van Abbema, D. L. (2002). Short-term forgetting: Charting its course and its implications for long-term remembering. In S. P. Shohov (Ed.), *Advances in psychology research.* Huntington, NY: Nova Science Publishers (Reprinted, In S. P. Shohov (Ed.), *Perspectives on cognitive psychology* (pp. 93–112). Huntington, NY: Nova Science Publishers.

Bauer, P. J., DeBoer, T., & Lukowski, A. F. (2007). In the language of multiple memory systems, defining and describing developments in long-term declarative memory. In L. M. Oakes & P. J. Bauer (Eds.), *Short- and long-term memory in infancy and early childhood: Taking the first steps toward remembering.* New York, NY: Oxford University Press.

Bauer, P. J., & Dow, G. A. A. (1994). Episodic memory in 16- and 20-month-old children: Specifics are generalized, but not forgotten. *Developmental Psychology, 30,* 403–417.

Bauer, P. J., & Fivush, R. (1992). Constructing event representations: Building on a foundation of variation and enabling relations. *Cognitive Development, 7,* 381–401.

Bauer, P. J., & Hertsgaard, L. A. (1993). Increasing steps in recall of events: Factors facilitating immediate and long-term memory in 13.5- and 16.5-month-old children. *Child Development, 64,* 1204–1223.

Bauer, P. J., Hertsgaard, L. A., & Wewerka, S. S. (1995). Effects of experience and reminding on long-term recall in infancy: Remembering not to forget. *Journal of Experimental Child Psychology, 59,* 260–298.

Bauer, P. J., Kroupina, M. G., Schwade, J. A., Dropik, P., & Wewerka, S. S. (1998). If memory serves, will language? Later verbal accessibility of early memories. *Development and Psychopathology, 10,* 655–679.

Bauer, P. J., & Lukowski, A. F. (2010). The memory is in the details: Relations between memory for the specific features of events and long-term recall in infancy. *Journal of Experimental Child Psychology*, (Ms. ID# NIHMS196588).

Bauer, P. J., & Mandler, J. M. (1989). One thing follows another: Effects of temporal structure on one- to two-year-olds' recall of events. *Developmental Psychology, 25*, 197–206.

Bauer, P. J., & Shore, C. M. (1987). Making a memorable event: Effects of familiarity and organization on young children's recall of action sequences. *Cognitive Development, 2*, 327–338.

Bauer, P. J., Van Abbema, D. L., & de Haan, M. (1999). In for the short haul: Immediate and short-term remembering and forgetting by 20-month-old children. *Infant Behavior & Development, 22*, 321–343.

Bauer, P. J., Van Abbema, D. L., Wiebe, S. A., Strand Cary, M., Phill, C., & Burch, M. M. (2004). Props, not pictures, are worth a thousand words: Verbal accessibility of early memories under different conditions of contextual support. *Applied Cognitive Psychology, 18*, 373–392.

Bauer, P. J., Wenner, J. A., Dropik, P. L., & Wewerka, S. S. (2000). Parameters of remembering and forgetting in the transition from infancy to early childhood. *Monographs of the Society for Research in Child Development, 65*, (4, Serial No. 263).

Bauer, P. J., Wiebe, S. A., Carver, L. J., Lukowski, A. F., Haight, J. C., Waters, J. M., et al. (2006). Electrophysiological indices of encoding and behavioral indices of recall: Examining relations and developmental change late in the first year of life. *Developmental Neuropsychology, 29*, 293–320.

Bauer, P. J., Wiebe, S. A., Carver, L. J., Waters, J. M., & Nelson, C. A. (2003). Developments in long-term explicit memory late in the first year of life: Behavioral and electrophysiological indices. *Psychological Science, 14*, 629–635.

Bauer, P. J., Wiebe, S. A., Waters, J. M., & Bangston, S. K. (2001). Reexposure breeds recall: Effects of experience on 9-month-olds' ordered recall. *Journal of Experimental Child Psychology, 80*, 174–200.

Benes, F. M. (2001). The development of prefrontal cortex: The maturation of neurotransmitter systems and their interaction. In C. A. Nelson & M. Luciana (Eds.), *Handbook of developmental cognitive neuroscience*. Cambridge, MA: The MIT Press.

Benes, F. M., Turtle, M., Khan, Y., & Farol, P. (1994). Myelination of a key relay zone in the hippocampal formation occurs in the human brain during childhood, adolescence, and adulthood. *Archives of General Psychiatry, 51*, 477–484.

Bourgeois, J.-P. (2001). Synaptogenesis in the neocortex of the newborn: The ultimate frontier for individuation? In C. A. Nelson & M. Luciana (Eds.), *Handbook of developmental cognitive neuroscience*. Cambridge, MA: The MIT Press.

Caldji, C., Tannenbaum, B., Sharma, S., Francis, D., Plotsky, P. M., & Meaney, M. J. (1998). Maternal care during infancy regulates the development of neural systems mediating the expression of fearfulness in the rat. *Proceedings of the National Academy of Sciences of the United States of America, 95*, 5335–5340.

Carver, L. J., & Bauer, P. J. (1999). When the event is more than the sum of its parts: Nine-month-olds' long-term ordered recall. *Memory, 7*, 147–174.

Carver, L. J., & Bauer, P. J. (2001). The dawning of a past: The emergence of long-term explicit memory in infancy. *Journal of Experimental Psychology: General, 130*, 726–745.

Cheatham, C. L., & Bauer, P. J. (2005). Construction of a more coherent story: Prior verbal recall predicts later verbal accessibility of early memories. *Memory, 13*, 516–532.

Chugani, H. T., Phelps, M., & Mazziotta, J. (1987). Positron emission tomography study of human brain functional development. *Annals of Neurology, 22*, 487–497.

Collie, R., & Hayne, H. (1999). Deferred imitation by 6- and 9-month-old infants: More evidence of declarative memory. *Developmental Psychobiology, 35,* 83–90.

DeCasper, A. J., & Spence, M. J. (1986). Prenatal maternal speech influences newborns' perceptions of speech sounds. *Infant Behavior & Development, 9,* 133–150.

Dunlop, S. A., Archer, M. A., Quinlivan, J. A., Beazley, L. D., & Newnham, J. P. (1997). Repeated prenatal corticosteroids delay myelination in the ovine central nervous system. *The Journal of Maternal-Fetal Medicine, 6*(6), 309–313.

Eckenhoff, M., & Rakic, P. (1991). A quantitative analysis of synaptogenesis in the molecular layer of the dentate gyrus in the rhesus monkey. *Developmental Brain Research, 64,* 129–135.

Eichenbaum, H., & Cohen, N. J. (2001). *From conditioning to conscious recollection: Memory systems of the brain.* New York: Oxford University Press.

Erikson, K. M., Pinero, D. J., Connor, J. R., & Beard, J. L. (1997). Regional brain iron, ferritin, and transferrin concentrations during iron deficiency and iron repletion in developing rats. *The Journal of Nutrition, 127,* 2030–2038.

Foreman, N., Fielder, A., Minshell, C., Hurrion, E., & Sergienko, E. (1997). Visual search, perception, and visual-motor skill in "healthy" children born 27-32 weeks' gestation. *Journal of Experimental Child Psychology, 64,* 27–41.

Freud, S. (1905). Three essays on the theory of sexuality. In J. Strachey (Ed.), *The standard edition of the complete psychological works of Sigmund Freud* (Vol. 7, pp. 135–243). London: Hogarth Press.

Gadian, D. G., Aicardi, J., Watkins, K. E., Porter, D. A., Mishkin, M., & Vargha-Khadem, F. (2000). Developmental amnesia associated with hear hypoxic-ischaemic injury. *Brain, 123,* 499–507.

Gelman, R., & Baillargeon, R. (1983). A review of some Piagetian concepts. In J. H. Flavell & E. M. Markman (Eds.), *Handbook of child psychology—Cognitive development* (Vol. III, pp. 167–230). New York: Wiley.

Georgieff, M. K., Landon, M. B., Mills, M. M., Hedlund, B. E., Faassen, A. E., Schmidt, R. L., et al. (1990). Abnormal iron distribution in infants of diabetic mothers: Spectrum and maternal antecedents. *The Journal of Pediatrics, 117,* 455–461.

Georgieff, M. K., & Rao, R. (2001). The role of nutrition in cognitive development. In C. A. Nelson & M. Luciana (Eds.), *Handbook of developmental cognitive neuroscience.* Cambridge, MA: The MIT Press.

Gogtay, N., Giedd, J. N., Lusk, L., Hayashi, K. M., Greenstein, D., Vaituzis, A. C., et al. (2004). Dynamic mapping of human cortical development during childhood through early adulthood. *Proceedings of the National Academy of Sciences of the United States of America, 101,* 8174–8179.

Gunnar, M. R. (2001). Effects of early deprivation: Findings from orphanage-reared infants and children. In C. A. Nelson & M. Luciana (Eds.), *Handbook of developmental cognitive neuroscience.* Cambridge, MA: The MIT Press.

Hanna, E., & Meltzoff, A. N. (1993). Peer imitation by toddlers in laboratory, home, and day-care contexts: Implications for social learning and memory. *Developmental Psychology, 29,* 702–710.

Hayne, H., Boniface, J., & Barr, R. (2000). The development of declarative memory in human infants: Age-related changes in deferred imitation. *Behavioral Neuroscience, 114,* 77–83.

Hayne, H., MacDonald, S., & Barr, R. (1997). Developmental changes in the specificity of memory over the second year of lie. *Infant Behavior & Development, 20,* 233–245.

Herbert, J., & Hayne, H. (2000). Memory retrieval by 18-30-month-olds: Age-related changes in representational flexibility. *Developmental Psychology, 36,* 473–484.

Higley, L. D., Suomi, S. J., & Linnoila, M. (1992). A longitudinal study of CSF monoamine metabolite and plasma cortisol concentrations in young rhesus monkeys: Effects of early experience, age, sex, and stress on continuity of individual differences. *Biological Psychiatry, 32,* 127–145.

Howe, M. L., & Courage, M. L. (1997). Independent paths in the development of infant learning and forgetting. *Journal of Experimental Child Psychology, 67,* 131–163.

Huttenlocher, P. R. (1979). Synaptic density in human frontal cortex: Developmental changes and effects of aging. *Brain Research, 163,* 195–205.

Huttenlocher, P. R., & Dabholkar, A. S. (1997). Regional differences in synaptogenesis in human cerebral cortex. *The Journal of Comparative Neurology, 387,* 167–178.

Jiang, Z. D. (1995). Maturation of the auditory brainstem in low risk-preterm infants: A comparison with age-matched full term infants up to 6 years. *Early Human Development, 42,* 49–65.

Klein, P. J., & Meltzoff, A. N. (1999). Long-term memory, forgetting, and deferred imitation in 12-month-old infants. *Developmental Science, 2,* 102–113.

Larkin, E. C., Jarratt, B. A., & Rao, G. A. (1986). Reduction of relative levels of nervonic to lignoceric acid in the brain of rat pups due to iron deficiency. *Nutrition Research, 6,* 309–314.

Lechuga, M. T., Marcos-Ruiz, R., & Bauer, P. J. (2001). Episodic recall of specifics and generalisation coexist in 25-month-old children. *Memory, 9,* 117–132.

Liston, C., & Kagan, J. (2002). Memory enhancement in early childhood. *Nature, 419,* 896.

Lloyd, M. E., Doydum, A. O., & Newcombe, N. S. (2009). Memory binding in early childhood: Evidence for a retrieval deficit. *Child Development, 80,* 1321–1328.

Lloyd, M. E., & Newcombe, N. S. (2009). Implicit memory in childhood: Reassessing developmental invariance. In M. L. Courage & N. Cowan (Eds.), *The development of memory in infancy and childhood.* New York, NY: Taylor & Francis.

Lozoff, B. (1990). Has iron deficiency been shown to cause altered behavior in infants? In J. Dobbing (Ed.), *Brain, behavior and iron in the infant diet.* London: Springer-Verlag.

Lukowski, A. F., Wiebe, S. A., & Bauer, P. J. (in press). Going beyond the specifics: Generalization of single actions, but not temporal order, at nine months. *Infant Behavior and Development.*

Mandler, J. M. (1990). Recall of events by preverbal children. In A. Diamond (Ed.), *The development and neural bases of higher cognitive functions.* New York: New York Academy of Science.

Mandler, J. M., & McDonough, L. (1995). Long-term recall of event sequences in infancy. *Journal of Experimental Child Psychology, 59,* 457–474.

Markowitsch, H. J. (2000). Neuroanatomy of memory. In E. Tulving & F. I. M. Craik (Eds.), *The Oxford handbook of memory.* New York: Oxford University Press.

Matthews, A., Ellis, A. E., & Nelson, C. A. (1996). Development of preterm and full-term infant ability on AB, recall memory, transparent barrier detour, and means-end. *Child Development, 67,* 2658–2676.

McDonough, L., & Mandler, J. M. (1998). Inductive generalization in 9- and 11-month-olds. *Developmental Science, 1,* 227–232.

McDonough, L., Mandler, J. M., McKee, R. D., & Squire, L. R. (1995). The deferred imitation task as a nonverbal measure of declarative memory. *Proceedings of the National Academy of Sciences of the United States of America, 92,* 7580–7584.

Meltzoff, A. N. (1985). Immediate and deferred imitation in fourteen- and twenty-four-month-old infants. *Child Development, 56,* 62–72.

Meltzoff, A. N. (1988). Infant imitation and memory: Nine-month-olds in immediate and deferred tests. *Child Development, 59*, 217–225.

Meltzoff, A. N. (1990). The implications of cross-modal matching and imitation for the development of representation and memory in infants. In A. Diamond (Ed.), *The development and neural bases of higher cognitive functions*. New York: New York Academy of Science.

Meltzoff, A. N. (1995). What infant memory tells us about infantile amnesia: Long-term recall and deferred imitation. *Journal of Experimental Child Psychology, 59*, 497–515.

Nelson, C. A. (1995). The ontogeny of human memory: A cognitive neuroscience perspective. *Developmental Psychology, 31*, 723–738.

Nelson, C. A. (1997). The neurobiological basis of early memory development. In N. Cowan (Ed.), *The development of memory in childhood*. Hove East Sussex: Psychology Press.

Nelson, C. A. (2000). Neural plasticity and human development: The role of early experience in sculpting memory systems. *Developmental Science, 3*, 115–136.

Nelson, C. A., & Carver, L. J. (1998). The effects of stress and trauma on brain and memory: A view from developmental cognitive neuroscience. *Development and Psychopathology, 10*(4), 793–809.

Nelson, C. A., de Haan, M., & Thomas, K. (2006). Neural bases of cognitive development. In D. Kuhn & R. Siegler (Vol. Eds.), *Cognition, perception, and language*, W. Damon & R. M. Lerner (Eds.-in-Chief). *Handbook of child psychology* (6th ed., pp. 3–57). Hoboken, NJ: Wiley.

Parkin, A. J. (1997). The development of procedural and declarative memory. In N. Cowan (Ed.), *The development of memory in childhood*. Hove, UK: Psychology Press.

Piaget, J. (1952). *The origins of intelligence in children*. New York: International Universities Press.

Piaget, J. (1962). *Play, dreams and imitation in childhood*. New York: W. W. Norton & Co.

Reed, J. M., & Squire, L. R. (1998). Retrograde amnesia for facts and events: Findings from four new cases. *The Journal of Neuroscience, 18*, 3943–3954.

Richman, J., & Nelson, C. A. (2008). Mechanisms of change: A cognitive neuroscience approach to declarative memory development. In C. A. Nelson & M. Luciana (Eds.), *Handbook of developmental Cognitive neuroscience*. (2nd ed., pp. 541–552). Cambridge, MA: The MIT Press.

Rose, S. A., Gottfried, A. W., Melloy-Carminar, P., & Bridger, W. H. (1982). Familiarity and novelty preferences in infant recognition memory: Implications for information processing. *Developmental Psychology, 18*, 704–713.

Rovee-Collier, C., & Hayne, H. (2000). Memory in infancy and early childhood. In E. Tulving & F. I. M. Craik (Eds.), *The Oxford handbook of memory*. New York: Oxford University Press.

Rutter, M., the English and Romanian Adoptees (ERP) study team. (1998). Developmental catch-up, and deficit, following adoption after severe global early privaion. *Journal of Child Psychology and Psychiatry, 39*, 465–476.

Scarborough, A. A., Lloyd, E. C., & Barth, R. P. (2009). Maltreated infants and toddlers: Predictors of developmental delay. *Journal of Developmental and Behavioral Pediatrics, 30*(6), 489–498.

Schneider, W., & Bjorklund, D. F. (1998). Memory. In D. Kuhn & R. S. Siegler (Vol. Eds.) *Cognition, perception, and language* (Vol. 2). In W. Damon (Ed.-in-Chief), *Handbook of child psychology* (5th ed., pp. 467–521). New York: Wiley.

Seigal, L. S. (1994). The long-term prognosis of pre-term infants: Conceptual, methodological and ethical issues. *Human Nature (Hawthorne, NY), 5*, 103–126.

Seress, L., & Abraham, H. (2008). Pre- and postnatal morphological development of the human hippocampal formation. In C. A. Nelson & M. Luciana (Eds.), *Handbook of developmental cognitive neuroscience.* (2nd ed., pp. 187–212). Cambridge, MA: The MIT Press.

Simcock, G., & Hayne, H. (2002). Breaking the barrier? Children fail to translate their preverbal memories into language. *Psychological Science, 13,* 225–231.

Squire, L. R. (1992). Memory and the hippocampus: A synthesis from findings with rats, monkeys, and humans. *Psychological Review, 99,* 195–231.

Squire, L. R., Knowlton, B., & Musen, G. (1993). The structure and organization of memory. *Annual Review of Psychology, 44,* 453–495.

Toth, J. P. (2000). Nonconscious forms of human memory. In E. Tulving & F. I. M. Craik (Eds.), *The Oxford handbook of memory.* New York: Oxford University Press.

Utsunomiya, H., Takano, K., Okazaki, M., & Mistudome, A. (1999). Development of the temporal lobe in infants and children: Analysis by MR-based volumetry. *AJNR. American Journal of Neuroradiology, 20,* 717–723.

van Hof-van Duin, J., Heersema, D. J., Groenendaal, F., Baerts, W., & Fetter, W. P. (1992). Visual field and grating acuity development in low-risk preterm infants during the first 2 1/2 years after term. *Behavioural Brain Research, 49,* 115–122.

Webb, S. J., Monk, C. S., & Nelson, C. A. (2001). Mechanisms of postnatal neurobiological development: Implications for human development. *Developmental Neuropsychology, 19,* 147–171.

West, T. A., & Bauer, P. J. (1999). Assumptions of infantile amnesia: Are there differences between early and later memories? *Memory, 7,* 257–278.

Wheeler, M. A. (2000). Episodic memory and autonoetic awareness. In E. Tulving & F. I. M. Craik (Eds.), *The Oxford handbook of memory.* New York: Oxford University Press.

Zhang, L. X., Xing, G. O., Levine, S., Post, R. M., & Smith, M. A. (1997). Maternal deprivation induces neuronal death. *Abstracts—Society for Neuroscience, October,* 1113.

Zola, S. M., & Squire, L. R. (2000). The medial temporal lobe and the hippocampus. In E. Tulving & F. I. M. Craik (Eds.), *The Oxford handbook of memory.* New York: Oxford University Press.

Zola-Morgan, S., & Squire, L. R. (1993). Neuroanatomy of memory. *Annual Review of Neuroscience, 16,* 547–563.

Zola-Morgan, S., Squire, L. R., Rempel, N. L., Clower, R. P., & Amaral, D. G. (1992). Enduring memory impairment in monkeys after ischemic damage to the hippocampus. *The Journal of Neuroscience, 9,* 4355–4370.

FINDING THE RIGHT FIT: EXAMINING DEVELOPMENTALLY APPROPRIATE LEVELS OF CHALLENGE IN ELICITED-IMITATION STUDIES

Melissa M. Burch, * *Jennifer A. Schwade,* [†] *and Patricia J. Bauer* [‡]

* SCHOOL OF COGNITIVE SCIENCE, HAMPSHIRE COLLEGE, AMHERST, MASSACHUSETTS, USA

[†] DEPARTMENT OF PSYCHOLOGY, CORNELL UNIVERSITY, ITHACA, NEW YORK, USA

[‡] DEPARTMENT OF PSYCHOLOGY, EMORY UNIVERSITY, ATLANTA, GEORGIA, USA

Over the last two decades, elicited and deferred imitation have emerged as widely used paradigms for the assessment of developmental changes in children's memory abilities. To be implemented effectively, the use of elicited imitation begins with the selection of to-be-remembered material that presents an appropriate level of challenge to the developmental abilities of the children participating. This has been implicit in the use of imitation in that older children are presented with longer sequences than are younger children. For example, 6-month-old infants are tested using one-step events (e.g., Meltzoff, 1988), 9-month olds are tested with two-step events (Carver & Bauer, 1999, 2001), 13-month olds are tested with three-step sequences, and 20-month olds are tested with four-step sequences (Bauer, Wenner, Dropik, & Wewerka, 2000). However, to date, children of varying ages have rarely been tested on comparable events, nor have children of one age been tested on events of a range of challenges. In this chapter, we present results from two studies examining the abilities of 16- to 32-month-old children to recall event sequences of a variety of lengths in an elicited-imitation paradigm. The results provide normative information on age-related

27

Advances in Child Development and Behavior
Patricia Bauer : Editor

immediate imitation abilities, and also can serve as a guide for researchers who plan to use elicited imitation with special populations or who use elicited imitation as a tool to study memory's relation to other developmental domains by establishing developmentally appropriate materials with which to test children across the second and third years of life.

Using imitation-based techniques, researchers have established that infants and very young children recall the past and that there are age-related changes in declarative memory in the first and second years of life (see Bauer, Chapter 1, this volume). Evidence that infants as young as 6 months of age recall past experiences was provided by Barr, Dowden, and Hayne (1996). They contrasted the performance of groups of infants who had been exposed to a puppet with a bell hidden in a mitten on its hand with that of groups of infants with no previous exposure to the puppet. Whereas the experienced infants later attempted to make the bell ring, the naïve infants did not (see also Meltzoff, 1988). At least by 9 months of age, infants successfully reproduce ordered sequences of action, with some infants remembering the sequences in the correct temporal order after a delay of as much as 1 month (e.g., Bauer, Wiebe, Waters, & Bangston, 2001; Carver & Bauer, 1999, 2001).

Over the course of the second- and into the third year of life, there appear to be developmental changes in the lengths of sequences that children can remember accurately. Although this suggestion has not been tested directly, developmental changes are implied by the fact that in studies of immediate and long-term recall, older children typically are tested on longer sequences, relative to younger children. For example, children 9–11 months of age have been tested on sequences two steps in length (e.g., Bauer & Mandler, 1992; Bauer *et al.*, 2001); children 13–16 months of age have been tested on sequences two and three steps in length (e.g., Bauer & Hertsgaard, 1993); children 16–20 months of age have been tested on sequences three and four steps in length (e.g., Bauer *et al.*, 2000); children 24 months of age have been tested on sequences four and five steps in length (Bauer & Travis, 1993); children 28 months of age have been tested on sequences five steps in length (Bauer, Hertsgaard, Dropik, & Daly, 1998); and children 30 months of age have been tested on sequences six and eight steps in length (Bauer, Dow, Bittinger, & Wenner, 1998; Bauer & Fivush, 1992, respectively).

Although the literature reviewed here provides a good guide to the sequence lengths that are appropriate for children of different ages, it does not contain a direct test of the question. That is, none of the studies was designed with the goal of establishing developmentally appropriate sequence lengths for children of different ages. Moreover, in none of the studies was there a within-subjects comparison of performance on more than one sequence length. In the present investigation, we tested children on sequences of different lengths, suggested by the existing literature, with the goal of determining sequence lengths that would be appropriate for children across the second and into the third year of life. We took this step in two experiments. For present purposes, the primary goal was to identify sequences that would present to children of different ages roughly comparable levels of challenge. Identifying developmentally appropriate sequence lengths for children of various ages can be expected to facilitate research in which the elicited-imitation paradigm is used to examine memory development in special populations of children (e.g., children born prematurely: e.g., de Haan, Bauer, Georgieff, & Nelson, 2000; see Chapters 4–7 in the present volume), or as a tool to study developments outside the domain of memory (e.g., use of elicited imitation to assess compliance with maternal requests: e.g., Kochanska, Tjebkes, & Forman, 1998).

In both experiments, we tested children on sequences the temporal orders of which were wholly or largely constrained by enabling relations. Enabling relations are said to exist when one step in a sequence is both temporally prior to and necessary for the next step (e.g., Bauer, 1992). We focused on this sequence type because previous research has shown that it is not until approximately 20–22 months that children reliably reproduce arbitrarily ordered sequences (i.e., sequences that lack enabling relations among the actions: Bauer, Hertsgaard *et al.*, 1998; Wenner & Bauer, 1999). Thus, in order to address the major questions, it was necessary to use sequences with enabling relations. In Experiment 1, we compared children's performance on two adjacent step lengths, one of which overlapped with a sequence length used with a younger age group, and one of which was also used with an older age group. In Experiment 2, we tested children on the entire set of sequence lengths from Experiment 1 to further examine how children respond to a range of challenges. Experiment 2 provides a broader examination of performance in the second year of life as 16-, 20-, and 24-month-olds recall sequences ranging from two to seven steps in length to examine the complexity of events that children can recall.

I. Experiment 1

A. METHOD

1. Participants

Sixty children participated in a cross-sectional study. Twelve of the children were 16 months of age ($M = 16$; 2, range $= 15$; 21–16; 10), 12 were 20 months of age ($M = 20$; 6, range $= 19$; 24–20; 15), 12 were 24 months of age

($M=24$; 5, range $=23$; 21–24; 16), 12 were 28 months of age ($M=28$; 5, range $=27$; 15–28; 23), and 12 were 32 months of age ($M=32$; 9, range $=31$; 27–32; 24). Children were recruited from an existing pool of volunteer parents who had expressed interest in participating in research at the time of their children's births. Although no data on the socioeconomic status of the participants were collected, the participant pool primarily includes families of middle- and upper-middle class status. All of the children were given an age-appropriate gift to acknowledge their participation.

2. Materials

The children in each age group were tested for immediate recall of one "short" sequence and one "long" sequence. Sequence lengths increased with age: at 16 months, children were tested on two- and three-step sequences; at 20 months, children were tested on three- and four-step sequences; at 24 months, children were tested on four- and five-step sequences; at 28 months, children were tested on five- and six-step sequences; and at 32 months, children were tested on six- and seven-step sequences. These sequence lengths were chosen on the basis of the literature reviewed earlier. The sequences were designed to maximize the number of enabling relations inherent in them. That is, as much as possible, in order to reach the desired end-state or goal of the sequence, the actions in the sequences had to be performed in a particular temporal order (see Bauer, 1992, for discussion). Although achievement of the desired end-state or goal of the sequence was dependent on production of the actions in the target order, each target action could be completed independent of the other. Because of the difficulties inherent in designing longer sequences that were completely constrained by enabling relations, the longer sequences contained a mixture of enabling and arbitrary temporal relations.

3. Procedure

Children were tested individually in a laboratory playroom. After a brief warm-up period, children were seated in a booster seat or on their parents' laps, across an adult-sized table from an experimenter. Two practice sequences were used to acquaint the children with the elicited-imitation procedure. The practice sequences consisted of (a) rolling a ball and placing it on top of a slinky, and (b) stretching the slinky to its full length and then letting go of one end. For each practice sequence in turn the children were allowed to manipulate the props. The experimenter then modeled the sequence two times in succession, with narration (e.g., "Roll the ball. Put it on top!"). She then returned the props to the children and encouraged their exact imitation (e.g., "Now you roll the ball and put it on top, just like I did"). Children's efforts were rewarded with social praise (e.g., hand clapping and "You did it!").

The procedure for the test sequences was identical to that for the practice sequences, except that the specific actions were not prompted. Children's performance prior to modeling provided a baseline measure of the spontaneous occurrence of the target actions and sequences. The period was "child controlled": it ended when the child pushed the props away, or engaged in repetitive exploratory behaviors (e.g., banging the objects on the table). After baseline, the experimenter modeled the sequence twice in succession, with narration. Immediately after modeling, she encouraged exact imitation with such statements as "Now its your turn to make/do X, just like I did." The imitation period also was child controlled. Children's postmodeling performance provided the measure of immediate recall.

In each age group, children were tested on the short sequence, followed by the long sequence. There were two sequences of each length. In each age group, half of the children were tested on one of the sequences and half on the other sequence. The sessions were videotaped for later scoring and analysis.

4. Scoring

The children's behavior was scored from videotapes of the sessions. For each sequence, we calculated the total number of individual target actions produced (maximum $= 2.0$, 3.0, 4.0, 5.0, 6.0, and 7.0, for two-, three-, four-, five-, six-, and seven-step sequences, respectively) and the total number of pairs of actions produced in the target order (maximum $= 1.0$, 2.0, 3.0, 4.0, 5.0, and 6.0, for two-, three-, four-, five-, six-, and seven-step sequences, respectively). For the latter measure, only the first occurrence of each target action was considered so as to reduce credit that might be received due to chance or trial and error, thereby providing a more conservative measure of memory ability. For example, on a four-step sequence, if children produced the string of target actions 4, 3, 1, 2, 3, 4, they would receive credit for four different target actions but for only one ordered pair of actions (i.e., 1–2). (Ordered pairs need not involve adjacent actions: actions 1 and 3, in that order, would be considered one correctly ordered pair.) They would not be credited with the correctly ordered pairs 2–3 or 3–4, because they would already have been credited with production of actions 3 and 4 (i.e., the first two actions produced); the second production of these actions would not be considered. This scoring procedure reduces the likelihood that children will receive credit for pairs of actions that are correctly ordered by chance or by trial and error.

B. RESULTS

At each age, the children were tested on sequences of two different lengths (i.e., one short and one long sequence). To permit direct comparisons of children's performance on sequences of different lengths, we converted their raw scores to proportions. Descriptive statistics on children's performance prior to and after modeling, on each sequence length, are provided in Table I, for each age group.

Table I

Experiment 1: Descriptive Statistics for Immediate Recall of the Individual Target Actions and Temporal Order of Actions (as Measured by Pairs of Actions in the Target Order), in Proportions

		Phase of Testing			
		Baseline		Immediate Recall	
Age Group	Sequence Length	Mean	(SD)	Mean	(SD)
Proportion of individual target actions produced					
16 months	Two steps	.08	(.19)	.79	(.26)
	Three steps	.14	(.22)	.56	(.41)
20 months	Three steps	.28	(.28)	.81	(.30)
	Four steps	.31	(.26)	.54	(.42)
24 months	Four steps	.25	(.26)	.88	(.29)
	Five steps	.15	(.17)	.78	(.34)
28 months	Five steps	.17	(.12)	.99	(.10)
	Six steps	.33	(.19)	.96	(.10)
32 months	Six steps	.32	(.25)	.97	(.10)
	Seven steps	.41	(.23)	.92	(.10)
Proportion of pairs of actions produced in the target order					
16 months	Two steps	.00	(–)	.58	(.51)
	Three steps	.00	(–)	.46	(.45)
20 months	Three steps	.13	(.23)	.75	(.34)
	Four steps	.14	(.22)	.42	(.47)
24 months	Four steps	.08	(.21)	.78	(.33)
	Five steps	.00	(–)	.56	(.23)
28 months	Five-steps	.02	(.07)	.81	(.16)
	Six steps	.10	(.16)	.75	(.12)
32 months	Six steps	.13	(.23)	.80	(.19)
	Seven steps	.21	(.24)	.74	(.11)

The first two questions to be addressed were whether the children evidenced immediate recall of the sequences of each length, and whether performance at any age differed as a function of sequence length. To address these questions, for each age group, we conducted 2 (phase: premodeling, postmodeling) × 2 (sequence length: short, long) within-subjects analyses of variance (ANOVAs) on the proportion of individual target actions produced and on the proportion of pairs of actions produced in the target order. At all ages, the children showed evidence of immediate recall of both the individual target actions and the temporal order of actions of the sequences. That is, at each age, there were main effects of phase, for both dependent variables: individual target actions, $Fs(1, 11) = 52.35$, 12.50, 86.22, 426.07, and 92.46, $ps < .005$; and pairs of actions in target order, $Fs(1, 11) = 25.00$, 15.08, 70.45, 743.16, and 79.27, $ps < .003$, for 16-, 20-, 24-, 28-, and 32-month olds, respectively. In all cases, the children's performance after modeling of the sequences was greater than their performance prior to modeling. This demonstration of immediate recall is a replication of several prior studies in which elicited imitation has been used to examine immediate recall memory in children in this age range (e.g., Bauer & Hertsgaard, 1993; Bauer, Hertsgaard *et al.*, 1998; Bauer & Travis, 1993).

Across phases, the 28-month-old children produced a larger proportion of the individual target actions of the long sequences ($M = .65$, $SD = .35$) relative to the short sequences ($M = .55$, $SD = .41$). Analysis of the interaction of phase × sequence length, $F(1, 11) = 5.07$, $p < .05$, revealed the difference only prior to modeling: $F(1, 11) = 6.22$, $p < .03$ (see Table I for means). After modeling, the proportion of individual target actions produced by the 28-month olds on the short and long sequences did not differ. Although there was a trend toward differential production of the individual target actions of the short and long sequences in the 24-month age group ($p < .07$), there were no other significant effects of sequence length on children's production of individual target actions.

For production of pairs of actions in the target order, the only reliable effect of sequence length was a main effect observed among the 24-month olds: $F(1, 11) = 6.87$, $p < .03$. However, once the trend toward differential levels of production of the individual target actions of the sequences by this age group was controlled via analysis of covariance (ANCOVA), the difference no longer remained significant. There were no other reliable effects of sequence length. Thus, after modeling, neither the proportion of individual target actions nor the proportion of pairs of actions in the target order produced by the children differed as a function of whether the children were tested on short or on long sequences.

The next question to be addressed was whether, on sequences of a given length, older children performed at higher levels, relative to younger children. To address this question we conducted separate one-way ANOVAs for each step length, comparing the performance of the younger and older children. Because it is clear that children in this age range perform at higher levels in the postmodeling relative to premodeling phase of testing, in order to maintain focus on children's postmodeling levels of performance, we did not include measures from the baseline phase in these analyses. The one-way analyses were conducted on sequences three, four, five, and six steps in length. We did not conduct these analyses for two-step and seven-step sequences because only one age group was tested on each sequence length (i.e., 16- and 32-month olds, respectively) and thus, no between-age-group comparisons were possible.

On the four-step sequences, the 20-month-old children produced a smaller proportion of the individual target actions, relative to the 24-month olds (see Table I for relevant means): $F(1, 22) = 5.03$, $p < .04$. On the three- and five-step sequences, there were nonsignificant trends suggesting higher levels of performance by the older relative to the younger children ($ps = .10$ and $.15$, for the three- and five-step sequences, respectively). On the six-step sequences, there was no suggestion of an age-related effect.

In terms of ordered reproduction of the sequences, the older children performed at higher levels than the younger children on three-, four-, and five-step sequences. On three-step sequences, the effect was at the level of a trend: $F(1, 22) = 3.23$, $p < .09$. On the four- and five-step sequences, the effects were statistically significant: $Fs(1, 22) = 4.72$ and 4.98, $ps < .04$, respectively. However, when the variance associated with differential levels of production of the individual target actions of the sequences was controlled via ANCOVA, the effects no longer were apparent. On the six-step sequences, there was no suggestion of an age-related effect. These analyses suggest that whereas on sequences of a given length, older children tend to produce a greater proportion of possible target actions, relative to younger children, the age effects are not large. Moreover, on sequences of a given length, after differential levels of production of the individual actions of the sequences are taken into account, older children do not appear to have better organized memory representations, relative to younger children.

Another means of assessing the organization of memory representations is to compare observed levels of production of pairs of actions in the target order to the levels of ordered reproduction that would be expected by chance. On any given trial, regardless of the number of target actions produced, by chance, one half of all pairs of actions would be correctly ordered. To determine whether children's levels of sequencing performance were reliably greater than chance, for sequences for which children performed at least two target actions (and thus had the potential to order their actions) we assigned children 1 point for each correctly ordered pair of actions produced. This resulted in total observed sequencing scores that could range 0–1, 0–2, 0–3, 0–4, 0–5, and 0–6 for the two-, three-, four-, five-, six-, and seven-step sequences, respectively. We then determined for each child the number of correctly ordered pairs of actions that would be expected by chance (i.e., the number of correctly ordered pairs plus the number of incorrectly ordered pairs divided by two). The observed and expected values were compared using within-subjects t tests (one tailed). As is apparent in Table II, at all ages, children's performance was reliably greater than chance for both the short and the long sequences. Thus, the children's immediate recall of the sequences was well organized, regardless of their age and the level of challenge of the sequence.

Finally, to illustrate the variability within the samples as well as to characterize the typical performance profiles of the children in each sample, for each age group and each sequence length, we created distributions of the frequencies with which the children produced each possible number of individual target actions and each possible number of pairs of actions in the target order, and determined the modal levels of production on each dependent variable. The values are provided in Table III; within the table, modal levels of performance are italicized. Although the number of

Table II

Experiment 1: Analyses Against Chance Levels of Ordered Recall Performance

Age Group	Sequence Length	Observed	Expected	(df)	t-Test Value	Probability
16 months	Two steps	1.00	.50	(6)	2.45	.05
	Three steps	1.57	.79	(6)	2.33	.05
20 month	Three steps	1.64	.82	(10)	3.04	.01
	Four steps	2.50	1.33	(5)	2.08	.05
24 months	Four steps	2.55	1.41	(10)	2.88	.01
	Five steps	2.70	1.80	(9)	2.13	.05
28 months	Five steps	3.25	1.83	(11)	3.14	.005
	Six steps	3.75	2.38	(11)	3.10	.01
32 months	Six steps	4.00	2.42	(11)	3.28	.005
	Seven steps	4.42	2.54	(11)	3.49	.005

Note: Degrees of freedom vary because trials on which children produced 0 or only 1 individual target action, and thus produced no pairs of actions (correctly or incorrectly ordered), were excluded from analyses.

Table III

Experiment 1: Frequencies (in %) and Modal Levels of Production of Individual Target Actions and Pairs of Actions in the Target Order (*n* = 12 Each Age Group)

Age Group	Sequence Length	Number Produced							
		0	1	2	3	4	5	6	7
Individual target actions									
16 months	Two steps	0	42	*58*					
	Three steps	25	17	25	*33*				
20 months	Three steps	8	0	33	*58*				
	Four steps	17	33	8	0	*42*			
24 months	Four steps	8	0	0	17	*75*			
	Five steps	8	8	0	33	*50*	0		
28 months	Five steps	0	0	0	0	33	*67*		
	Six steps	0	0	0	0	8	8	*83*	
32 months	Six steps	0	0	0	0	8	0	*92*	
	Seven steps	0	0	0	0	0	8	42	*50*
Pairs of actions in target order									
16 months	Two steps	42	*58*						
	Three steps	*42*	25	33					
20 months	Three steps	8	33	*58*					
	Four steps	*50*	8	8	33				
24 months	Four steps	8	8	25	*58*				
	Five steps	17	8	*33*	17	25			
28 months	Five steps	0	0	8	*58*	33			
	Six steps	0	0	0	33	*58*	8		
32 months	Six steps	0	0	8	17	*42*	33		
	Seven steps	0	0	0	7	42	*50*	0	

Note: Modal levels of performance are italicized.

children in each sample is small (*n* = 12), there were a number of suggestive patterns. First, for both dependent measures, there was greater variability among the younger children than among the older children; younger children were especially variable on long sequences. Second, for the variable of individual target actions, modal performance was to produce all possible actions. The only exception to this pattern was that the 24-month olds produced the same number of individual target actions on the four-step and five-step sequences (i.e., four target actions). Third, the pattern was not as orderly for the variable of pairs of actions in the target order as it was for the variable of individual target actions. At 16, 20, and 24 months of age, on the short sequences, modal performance was to produce all possible correctly ordered pairs of actions; modal performance on the long sequences was lower than modal performance on the short sequences. At 28 and 32 months of age, modal performance was higher on the long, relative to the short sequences. Even on the short sequences, however, the children did not tend to produce all possible pairs of actions in the target order.

C. DISCUSSION

The results of the present experiment indicate that the sequence lengths chosen for each of the age groups were reasonable and apparently developmentally appropriate. For both short and long sequences, the children recalled a high proportion of possible individual target actions. Within age groups, the proportion of individual target actions produced immediately after modeling on short and long sequences did not differ. Between age groups, older children tended to produce a larger proportion of the individual target actions of the sequences, relative to the younger children. However, the difference was significant only for the 20- compared with the 24-month olds. With one exception (i.e., 24-month olds on five-step sequences), for all age groups and sequence lengths, modal performance was to produce all possible target actions.

Consistent with the pattern observed on the variable of individual target actions produced, there were few statistically significant mean differences in the levels of immediate recall of the temporal order of the sequences, either within an age group (on short vs. long sequences), or between age groups (on sequences of the same length). In addition, in all age groups, on both sequence lengths, ordered reproduction of the sequences was reliably greater than chance. Nevertheless, there were suggestions that, within an age group, temporal organization of the long sequences presented a greater challenge than temporal organization of the short sequences. Moreover, between age groups, the older children seemed better able to deal with the demands of temporal organization of the sequences. These trends were apparent in larger differences between observed and expected levels of ordered reproduction (a) of short relative to long sequences at a given age; and (b) on sequences of a given length, among the older relative to the younger children. Modal levels of performance also suggested that the long sequences presented more of a challenge to the children, relative to the short sequences. Among the three younger age groups (i.e., 16-, 20-, and 24-month olds), on the short sequences, the modal level of performance was perfect ordered reproduction; this level was not matched on the long sequences. At the two older ages (i.e., 28 and 32 months), perfect reproduction was not the mode, even on the short sequences.

In Experiment 1, we found that after modeling, neither the proportion of individual target actions nor the proportion of pairs of actions in the target order produced by the children differed across short and long event sequences. In Experiment 1, we also found few age differences when children of adjacent ages were compared on only one event length. Additionally, the chance analyses indicated that children were able to produce well-organized recall for both the short and long sequences. In Experiment 2, we tested 16-, 20-, and 24-month-old children on the full range of the sequence lengths used in Experiment 1. In Experiment 2, by testing children on all event lengths, we sought to further document the levels of challenge for which age-related differences emerge, as well as to examine the upper-level of complexity which children of each age can recall and organize. We did not include 28- and 32-month-old children because their modal performance of the individual target actions on the two longest sequence lengths was equal to the maximum available performance, suggesting that they would also perform quite well on the shorter sequence lengths. Thus, we focused on the three younger age groups in order to examine their performance under the highest levels of challenge.

II. Experiment 2

A. METHOD

1. Participants

Thirty-six children participated in a cross-sectional study. Twelve of the children were 16 months of age ($M = 16$; 0, range $= 15$; 19–16; 10), 12 were 20 months of age ($M = 20$; 6, range $= 19$; 27–20; 18), and 12 were 24 months of age ($M = 24$; 3, range $= 23$; 20–24; 12). One additional child was tested, but the data are not included here due to problems with recording the session.

2. Materials

The children in each age group were tested for immediate recall of a six sequences that ranged from two to seven steps in lengths. One sequence of each length was selected from those used in Experiment 1.

3. Procedure

Children were tested following the identical protocol described in Experiment 1. The order of presentation of the six sequences was counterbalanced. The sessions were videotaped for later analysis and dependent measures were derived as in Experiment 1. To enable comparisons across sequence lengths, we used the proportion of target actions and correctly ordered pairs of actions in all analyses.

B. RESULTS AND DISCUSSION

To examine children's levels of performance as a function of age and sequence length, we conducted a 3 (age: 16 months, 20 months, 24 months) × 6 (length: two, three, four, five, six, seven steps) × 2 (phase: baseline, immediate) ANOVA on children's production of individual target actions and pairs of actions in target order. Results from both analyses indicated main effects of age [target actions: $F(2, 30) = 13.53$, $p < .001$; pairs: $F(2, 30) = 13.24$, $p < .001$], sequence length [target action: $F(5, 165) = 21.00$, $p < .001$; pairs: $F(5, 165) = 33.82$, $p < .001$], and phase [target actions: $F(1, 33) = 200.46$, $p < .001$; pairs: $F(1, 33) = 201.20$, $p < .001$, $p < .043$]. In addition, both measures demonstrated age × sequence length interactions [target actions: $F(10, 165) = 2.76$, $p < .01$; pairs: $F(10, 165) = 2.46$, $p < .01$] and age × phase interactions [target actions: $F(2, 33) = 3.48$, $p < .05$; pairs: $F(2, 33) = 8.75$, $p < .001$]. Critically, children of all ages evidenced recall of sequences across the entire range of difficulty presented (see Table IV). Because we established that children learned the events, we concentrate on children's immediate recall performance below.

Because our focus was on examining how children's immediate recall was impacted by changes in sequence length across age, we conducted 3 (age: 16 months, 20 months, 24 months) × 6 (sequence length: two-, three-, four-, five-, six-, seven steps) mixed ANOVAs on children's production of individual target actions and pairs of actions in target order immediately following modeling. For both measures of performance, we found main effects of age [target actions: $F(2, 33) = 12.25$, $p < .001$; pairs: $F(2, 33) = 13.11$, $p < .001$] and sequence length [target actions: $F(5, 165) = 24.86$, $p < .001$; pairs: $F(5, 165) = 28.60$, $p < .001$], and age × sequence length interactions [target actions: $F(10, 165) = 2.51$, $p < .01$; pairs: $F(10, 165) = 1.92$, $p < .05$]. For both dependent variables, the main effect of age indicated that 24-month-old children (actions: $M = .49$, $SD = .37$; pairs: $M = .33$; $SD = .40$) had higher immediate recall of the sequences than 20- and 16-month olds (actions: $Ms = .37$ and $.29$, $SDs = .34$ and $.31$; pairs: $Ms = .21$ and $.15$; $SDs = .34$ and $.30$, respectively), who did not differ from each other. For target actions, the main effect of sequence length resulted from children recalling a significantly higher proportion of actions for the two-step sequence ($M = .57$, $SD = .45$) than all other sequence lengths; and a significantly lower proportion of actions for the seven-step sequence ($M = .22$, $SD = .20$) than all other

Table IV

Experiment 2: Descriptive Statistics for Immediate Recall of the Individual Target Actions
and Temporal Order of Actions, in Proportions

		Phase of Testing			
		Baseline		Immediate Recall	
Age	Length	Mean	(SD)	Mean	(SD)
Proportion of individual target actions produced					
16 months	Two steps	.21	(.33)	.92	(.19)
	Three steps	.06	(.13)	.53	(.30)
	Four steps	.08	(.12)	.35	(.27)
	Five steps	.08	(.10)	.37	(.25)
	Six steps	.15	(.11)	.33	(.16)
	Seven steps	.10	(.09)	.30	(.17)
20 months	Two steps	.25	(.34)	.96	(.14)
	Three steps	.14	(.17)	.64	(.36)
	Four steps	.19	(.22)	.44	(.32)
	Five steps	.15	(.15)	.53	(.32)
	Six steps	.26	(.15)	.51	(.27)
	Seven steps	.11	(.11)	.25	(.21)
24 months	Two steps	.21	(.33)	.88	(.31)
	Three steps	.28	(.28)	.92	(.15)
	Four steps	.21	(.10)	.71	(.38)
	Five steps	.23	(.24)	.73	(.27)
	Six steps	.29	(.14)	.86	(.20)
	Seven steps	.15	(.13)	.44	(.25)
Proportion of pairs of actions produced in the target order					
16 months	Two steps	.08	(.29)	.83	(.39)
	Three steps	.00	(.00)	.33	(.33)
	Four steps	.00	(.00)	.14	(.26)
	Five steps	.00	(.00)	.21	(.26)
	Six steps	.00	(.00)	.08	(.10)
	Seven steps	.00	(.00)	.08	(.11)
20 months	Two steps	.08	(.29)	.92	(.29)
	Three steps	.00	(.00)	.50	(.43)
	Four steps	.03	(.10)	.14	(.22)
	Five steps	.04	(.10)	.40	(.34)
	Six steps	.07	(.13)	.28	(.22)
	Seven steps	.00	(.00)	.10	(.13)
24 months	Two steps	.08	(.29)	.83	(.39)
	Three steps	.13	(.23)	.83	(.33)
	Four steps	.00	(.00)	.53	(.48)
	Five steps	.08	(.16)	.56	(.40)
	Six steps	.08	(.10)	.60	(.24)
	Seven steps	.01	(.05)	.26	(.18)

lengths. In addition, performance on the three-step sequence ($M = .43$, $SD = .38$) was higher than that for the four-step sequence ($M = .33$, $SD = .32$), whereas performance on five- and six-step sequences ($Ms = .35$ and $.40$, $SDs = .32$ and $.29$, respectively) did not differ from that on three- and four-step sequences. For correctly ordered pairs of actions, children evidenced significantly greater recall for the two-step sequences ($M = .47$, $SD = .50$) than all other lengths, and greater recall for the three-step sequence ($M = .30$, $SD = .40$) than for four-, six-, and seven-step sequences ($Ms = .14$, $.19$, and $.08$, $SDs = .30$, $.25$, and $.14$, respectively) which did not differ from each other; performance on the five-step sequence ($M = .22$, $SD = .32$) was greater than that for the seven-step sequence.

These main effects were qualified by age × sequence length interactions, which revealed that the three age groups differed in their ability to recall and organize the target actions that they had observed being modeled. The descriptive statistics associated with this interaction are shown in Table IV. For individual target actions and pairs of actions, 16-month olds' performance was readily impacted by increasing levels of demand of the event sequences. They demonstrated better recall of individual actions for two-step sequences than all other sequence lengths, which did not differ from each other. Twenty-month olds showed more incremental effects of the level of challenge. They produced an equal proportion of target actions on the two- and three-step sequences, although their production of proportion of target actions on the two-step sequences exceeded all other lengths. Immediate recall of three-step sequences was significantly different from recall of the seven-step sequences. There were no other differences across event lengths. Thus, after an initial decline in performance as events were extended from two to four steps in length, there were few differences in recall of target actions of sequences of intermediate lengths and greater. In contrast, the performance of target actions by the 24-month olds was the least impacted by sequence length. There was no difference between their production of actions for two- through six-step event sequences. However, production of proportion of target actions was significantly lower for the seven-step sequences than for the two-, three-, five-, and six-step sequences. Performance on four-step sequences did not differ from any other length.

A similar pattern of performance was seen for children's ability to organize information during recall as indicated by correctly ordered pairs of target actions. Sixteen-month olds demonstrated significantly higher proportions of recall for correctly ordered pairs of actions on two-step events than all other sequence lengths. Thus, their performance was quickly degraded by increasing levels of challenge beyond the shortest sequence length. Performance of 20-month olds was also better on two-step sequences than all other sequence lengths. In addition, they produced a higher proportion of correctly ordered pairs on three-step sequences than on four- and seven-step sequences. There were no other differences in their proportion of ordered pairs of actions performed. Finally, 24-month olds produced higher proportions of correctly ordered pairs of actions on two- and three-step sequences than on seven-step sequences. Performance on four-, five-, and six-step sequences did not differ from that of other lengths.

To examine whether the effects on the organization of recall persisted after the amount was controlled, we conducted an ANCOVA on children's proportion of correctly ordered actions controlling for the proportion of target actions performed. After controlling for the number of target actions performed, the main effect of sequence length remained: $F(5, 164) = 5.75$, $p < .001$. However, there was no main effect of age nor was there an age $\times$ sequence length interaction. Thus, whereas the length of the events impacted children's ability to organize their recall, there were no differences in children's ability to organize their recall after the number of target actions was controlled. Thus, children demonstrate equally good organization of the elements of the sequence that they are able to produce regardless of age.

To further examine children's ability to order the actions that they recall, as in Experiment 1 we compared the number of correctly ordered pairs of actions that would be expected by chance to the number of correctly ordered pairs that were observed (see Table V). The observed and expected values were compared using within-subjects t tests (one tailed). Results from these analyses indicated age-related patterns in the ability of children to organize their recall. At all ages, children who performed both target actions on the two-step sequences produced them in the correct order. The 16-month olds also demonstrated reliable ordering of three-, four-, and five-step sequences. The 20-month olds reliably ordered three-, five-, and six-step sequences. The 24-month olds were above chance on the organization of their recall for all sequence lengths. Thus, with increasing age, children demonstrated ordered recall on increasingly complex sequences. The one exception to a smooth pattern of ordered recall was that 20-month-old children did not correctly order their performance of the four-step sequence. For this sequence ("popper"), children regularly attempted to perform the goal-state of the event, the final action, and this had a negative impact on their organization of children's recall because our scoring procedure focused on children's first performance of each target action. From results on this measure and the ANOVAs on individual target actions and correctly ordered pairs of actions, it is clear that older children were better able to respond to the challenge of the longer event sequences.

Table V
Experiment 2: Analyses Against Change Levels of Ordered Recall Performance
for Immediate Recall

Age	Length	Observed	Expected	(df)	*t*-Test Value	Probability≤
16 months	Two steps	1.0	.50	(9)		
	Three steps	1.0	.56	(7)	2.97	.02
	Four steps	1.67	1.00	(2)	4.00	.03
	Five steps	1.43	.86	(6)	2.25	.04
	Six steps	.71	.86	(6)	−.80	.23
	Seven steps	.75	.88	(7)	−1.00	.18
20 months	Two steps	1.0	.5	(10)		
	Three steps	1.33	.72	(8)	3.77	.01
	Four steps	1.0	1.0	(4)	.00	1.00
	Five steps	2.11	1.17	(8)	4.46	.01
	Six steps	1.89	1.39	(8)	3.00	.01
	Seven steps	1.0	.93	(6)	.35	.37
24 months	Two steps	1.0	.50	(9)		
	Three steps	1.67	.88	(10)	5.87	.001
	Four steps	2.11	1.28	(8)	2.89	.02
	Five steps	2.45	1.45	(10)	3.40	.01
	Six steps	3.00	2.08	(11)	3.74	.01
	Seven steps	1.73	1.18	(10)	3.83	.01

III. General Discussion

In the present research, we sought to identify developmentally appropriate levels of challenge for event sequences used during elicited imitation with typically developing children. In Experiment 1, we presented sequences of two lengths to children, using the existing literature as a guide for the complexity of events selected. Because of children's high level of success in performing the individual target actions for both short and long sequences in Experiment 1, in Experiment 2 we tested children in the three youngest age groups (16, 20, and 24 months) using all of the sequence lengths from the previous experiment. Together, results from these two studies document the effects of age and sequence length on children's immediate recall during elicited imitation.

Perhaps the most readily appreciable index of the lengths of sequences that are developmentally appropriate for children across the second and third years of life is the modal level of performance of the children in the present samples. Table III reflects the modal levels of production of the individual target actions of the sequences and of pairs of actions in the target order for Experiment 1. As is apparent in the table, across the 16–32-month period, modal performance was to produce all possible target actions. That is, in nine of the 10 cases, the most typical behavior of the children was to produce all of the target actions they saw modeled. The only exception was among the 24-month olds who, on the long sequences, typically produced only four of five possible target actions. Also reflected in Table III, is that, on the short sequences in Experiment 1, 50% or more of the children produced the modal number of individual target actions. Although on the long sequences used the most typical behavior was to produce all possible target actions, with the exception of 28-month olds this level of performance typically was achieved by half or fewer of the children. Thus, there was more variability in children's behavior on the long sequences, compared with the short sequences.

With respect to the second measure of performance, production of pairs of actions in the correct temporal order, there are four important aspects of the observed patterns. First, by 16 months of age, the children readily produced ordered pairs of actions on "easy" sequences. However, when they were challenged with more difficult (i.e., longer) sequences, their performance degraded substantially. Second, the performance of the children 20–32 months of age was quite orderly: On the short sequences in Experiment 1, the most typical behavior for 16- to 24-month-old children was to produce all possible ordered pairs of actions for the enabling sequences. The 28- and 32-month-old children who were tested on sequences containing both enabling and arbitrary connections demonstrated near perfect modal performance. Whereas younger children in Experiment 1 performed fewer pairs of actions on the long sequences relative to the short sequences, the 28- and 32-month-old children produced a greater modal number of pairs of actions on long relative to short sequences, although for neither length was modal performance indicative of perfect organization. This pattern may be attributable to the nature of the six- and seven-step sequences used with the oldest children. Whereas the shorter sequences were wholly constrained by enabling relations, the longer sequences were a mixture of enabling and arbitrary temporal relations. Although children's performance on mixed sequences such as these has been observed to be reliably greater than chance (Bauer, Dow et al., 1998; Bauer & Fivush, 1992), it does not match their performance on sequences that have a greater number of temporal constraints. Finally, additional evidence that the sequence lengths used in the present experiments were relatively well matched to the abilities of the children comes from fact that there were few indications of differences in the proportion of pairs of actions produced in the target order by the children of different ages. This indicates that the sequences were of roughly comparable levels of challenge, throughout the age range. That above-chance levels of performance were consistently observed is yet another indication that the sequence lengths were developmentally appropriate.

Additional support for the identification from modal levels of performance of developmentally appropriate sequence lengths comes from Experiment 2. For recall of both individual target actions and pairs of correctly ordered actions, 16-month-old children performed better on two-step sequences than on longer sequences, with the exception of individual actions recalled on three-step sequences. Despite the significant declines in recall as sequence lengths reached four steps and higher, as indicated by the chance analyses 16-month-old children were able to demonstrate ordered recall of sequences as long as five steps, although few children produced a sufficient number of target actions to enter into analyses for the four- and five-step sequences.

In contrast to the 16-month olds, the 20- and 24-month-old children were better able to respond to the level of challenge presented with greater length. For the 20-month olds, although they performed best on the two-step sequences, they were able to demonstrate ordered recall of sequences up to six steps in length. Twenty-four-month olds showed better than chance levels of recall for sequences up to seven steps in length. However, results of the ANOVAs indicated that 24-month-old children showed decrements in performance for seven-step sequences relative to the other sequence lengths.

Identification of such systematic patterns in children's immediate recall of the individual target actions and temporal order of actions of test sequences is very important to the effort to use elicited imitation of multi-step sequences to test children from special populations. During the first year of life, the developmental status of infants from special populations can be assessed with cognitive tasks that measure specific abilities, such as visual recognition memory and speed of processing (e.g., Rose & Feldman, 1996). However, in the second year of life, due to lack of appropriate measures, assessments often are restricted to rather global indices such as the Denver Developmental Scales and the Bayley Scales of Infant Development. Lower-than-normal scores on such measures are informative, yet they cannot help to establish the specific source or sources of cognitive deficit, due to their global nature.

The methodological significance of the present research for efforts to use elicited and deferred imitation with children from special populations is readily apparent. Because the task taps a particular cognitive function, namely, declarative memory (see Bauer, Chapter 1, this volume), it permits a more targeted assessment of cognition than that afforded by more global measures of intellectual development. Moreover, the apparent sensitivity of the elicited-imitation task to perhaps subtle deficits (e.g., de Haan *et al.*, 2000; see Chapters 4–7, this volume) implies that the task may be useful as an early diagnostic tool. In work with special populations in particular, it is important that children be tested with materials that present an appropriate level of challenge. In this regard, one of the attractive features of the elicited-imitation paradigm is that the level of challenge of to-be-recalled material can be adjusted upward and downward to make it more or less challenging. However, a difficulty that an "adjustable" task presents is how to "scale" it to children of different ages. The results of the present research can be used to guide researchers and perhaps eventually, clinicians, in selection of age-appropriate measures.

The results of the present research also can be expected to inform efforts to use elicited imitation of multistep sequences outside the domain of memory. For example, Kochanska *et al.* (1998) used elicited imitation to study young children's motivation to comply with maternal demands in a teaching context. In the study, mothers presented to their 13- to 15-month-old children three-step sequences. Kochanska *et al.* measured the children's physical orientation to the mother, their responsiveness to maternal demonstration, and their affective expression. They found relations between the theoretical construct of committed compliance and orientation to the mother during the task. In a related study, children who had more positive interactions with their mothers at 14 months of age were found to more willingly imitate their mothers at 22 months (Kochanska, Forman, & Coy, 1999; see also Forman & Kochanska, 2001). Bauer and Burch (2004) used elicited imitation to examine relations between maternal use of language to structure a task and 24-month-old children's own language abilities and temperament characteristics. They found different patterns of relations between the variables in the context of imitation of four-step, five-step, and six-step sequences. That different patterns were observed across different sequence lengths is readily interpretable in light of the results of the present research: different patterns were observed in the context of tasks presented at a developmentally appropriate level (i.e., four-step sequences) and tasks that were more challenging (i.e., five- and six-step sequences). Whereas the answer to the question of how to scale a task always will depend on the goals of the research, the present study informs the decision by providing information on sequence lengths that seem to present to children of different ages comparable levels of challenge.

In conclusion, identification of developmentally appropriate sequence lengths for children in the second and third years of life will further work on individual profiles of developmental change in healthy infants who appear to be developing normally. It also may bring with it theoretical advances in our understanding of plasticity in early memory development, as well as clinical advances. It also may inform research on social, as well as cognitive, development. In the present research, we provided direct empirical evidence regarding the lengths of multistep sequences that are developmentally appropriate for children throughout the second and third years of life. The goal of this aspect of the research was not to prescribe a sequence length, but to provide information that would aid researchers in selection of materials that they can expect to be more or less challenging to children of different ages. In addition to work with children who are healthy and developing normally, we expect the results to be informative to researchers working with children from special populations, and to researchers who are using the elicited-imitation paradigm to address questions outside the domain of memory.

Acknowledgment

The research reported in this chapter was supported by grants from the NICHD (HD28425, HD42483) to Patricia J. Bauer.

REFERENCES

Barr, R., Dowden, A., & Hayne, H. (1996). Developmental changes in deferred imitation by 6- to 24-month-old infants. *Infant Behavior & Development, 19*, 159–170.

Bauer, P. J. (1992). Holding it all together: How enabling relations facilitate young children's event recall. *Cognitive Development, 7*, 1–28.

Bauer, P. J., & Burch, M. M. (2004). Developments in early memory: Multiple mediators of foundational processes. In J. Lucariello, J. A. Hudson, R. Fivush, & P. J. Bauer (Eds.), *Development of the Mediated Mind: Culture and Cognitive Development. Essays in Honor of Katherine Nelson* (pp. 101–125). Mahwah, NJ: Lawrence Erlbaum Associates.

Bauer, P. J., Dow, G. A., Bittinger, K. A., & Wenner, J. A. (1998a). Accepting and exempting the unexpected: 30-month-olds' generalization of event knowledge. *Cognitive Development, 13*, 421–452.

Bauer, P. J., & Fivush, R. (1992). Constructing event representations: Building on a foundation of variation and enabling relations. *Cognitive Development, 7*, 381–401.

Bauer, P. J., & Hertsgaard, L. A. (1993). Increasing steps in recall of events: Factors facilitating immediate and long-term memory in 13.5- and 16.5-month-old children. *Child Development, 64*, 1204–1223.

Bauer, P. J., Hertsgaard, L. A., Dropik, P., & Daly, B. P. (1998b). When even arbitrary order becomes important: Developments in reliable temporal sequencing of arbitrarily ordered events. *Memory, 6*, 165–198.

Bauer, P. J., & Mandler, J. M. (1992). Putting the horse before the cart: The use of temporal order in recall of events by one-year-old children. *Developmental Psychology, 28*, 441–452.

Bauer, P. J., & Travis, L. L. (1993). The fabric of an event: Different sources of temporal invariance differentially affect 24-month-olds' recall. *Cognitive Development, 8*, 319–341.

Bauer, P. J., Wenner, J. A., Dropik, P. L., & Wewerka, S. S. (2000). Parameters of remembering and forgetting in the transition from infancy to early childhood. *Monographs of the Society for Research in Child Development, 65*, (4, Serial No. 263).

Bauer, P. J., Wiebe, S. A., Waters, J. M., & Bangston, S. K. (2001). Reexposure breeds recall: Effects of experience on 9-month-olds' ordered recall. *Journal of Experimental Child Psychology, 80,* 174–200.

Carver, L. J., & Bauer, P. J. (1999). When the event is more than the sum of its parts: Nine-month-olds' long-term ordered recall. *Memory, 7,* 147–174.

Carver, L. J., & Bauer, P. J. (2001). The dawning of a past: The emergence of long-term explicit memory in infancy. *Journal of Experimental Psychology: General, 130,* 726–745.

de Haan, M., Bauer, P. J., Georgieff, M. K., & Nelson, C. A. (2000). Explicit memory in low-risk toddlers born between 27–42 weeks of gestation. *Developmental Medicine and Child Neurology, 42,* 304–312.

Forman, D. R., & Kochanska, G. (2001). Viewing imitation as child responsiveness: A link between teaching and discipline domains of socialization. *Developmental Psychology, 37,* 198–206.

Kochanska, G., Forman, D. R., & Coy, K. C. (1999). Implications of the mother-child relationship in infancy socialization in the second year of life. *Infant Behavior & Development, 22,* 249–265.

Kochanska, G., Tjebkes, T. L., & Forman, D. R. (1998). Children's emerging regulation of conduct: Restraint, compliance, and internalization from infancy to the second year. *Child Development, 69,* 1378–1389.

Meltzoff, A. N. (1988). Infant imitation and memory: Nine-month-olds in immediate and deferred tests. *Child Development, 59,* 217–225.

Rose, S. A., & Feldman, J. F. (1996). Memory and processing speed in preterm children at eleven years: A comparison with full-terms. *Child Development, 67,* 2005–2021.

Wenner, J. A., & Bauer, P. J. (1999). Bringing order to the arbitrary: One- to two-year-olds' recall of event sequences. *Infant Behavior & Development, 22,* 585–590.

HEARING THE SIGNAL THROUGH THE NOISE: ASSESSING THE STABILITY OF INDIVIDUAL DIFFERENCES IN DECLARATIVE MEMORY IN THE SECOND AND THIRD YEARS OF LIFE

Patricia J. Bauer, Melissa M. Burch,[†] and Jennifer A. Schwade[‡]*

* DEPARTMENT OF PSYCHOLOGY, EMORY UNIVERSITY, ATLANTA, GEORGIA, USA
[†] SCHOOL OF COGNITIVE SCIENCE, HAMPSHIRE COLLEGE, AMHERST, MASSACHUSETTS, USA
[‡] DEPARTMENT OF PSYCHOLOGY, CORNELL UNIVERSITY, ITHACA, NEW YORK, USA

I. Introduction

As a field, we have made excellent progress in charting group or mean-level changes in declarative memory in the first years of life. However, we know little about individual profiles of typical development. One reason for the lack of data relevant to this issue is historical: Traditionally, cognitive developmental science has considered group trends to be "signal" and individual variability about the mean to be "noise." Additionally, whereas examination of individual profiles requires longitudinal data, most of the research in cognitive developmental science has been cross-sectional. In the field as a whole, these trends have begun to change, as exemplified by, for example, microgenetic examinations during periods

Advances in Child Development and Behavior
Patricia Bauer : Editor

of rapid development (e.g., Flynn, Pine, & Lewis, 2006; Siegler, 1996). However, likely due in no small part to the relative youth of the study of declarative memory in infancy and early childhood (see Bauer, 2002a, for discussion), how declarative memory abilities develop in individual children and at what point these abilities may indicate stable individual differences have not yet become a focus of research. Attention to variability in early declarative memory not only is important in its own right, but as argued later, it is also an essential component in examination of relations between individual differences in early memory and other individual characteristics, such as temperament and language.

In the present research, we took important steps in the study of individual profiles of developmental change in early declarative memory. Specifically, in two experiments, we examined immediate recall ability longitudinally during the second and third years of life. The major purpose of the studies was to inform the question of whether variability about the mean constitutes random noise, or whether (and when) it is indicative of stable individual differences in children's performance. This question was addressed by examining patterns of correlation throughout the period of each study. In one experiment, we also included measures of long-term recall performance, for the same purposes.

Although less attention has been paid to them, relative to the attention paid to mean or group level trends, there are also individual differences in early declarative memory. Early in development, when declarative memory is newly emergent, individual differences are apparent in whether or not children show evidence of memory. For example, roughly 50% of 9-month olds evidence ordered recall after 1 month whereas 50% do not (e.g., Bauer, Wiebe, Waters, & Bangston, 2001; Carver & Bauer, 1999). As declarative memory ability is more reliably observed in the population, individual differences take the form of variability in the *amount* remembered. For example, in Bauer, Wenner, Dropik, and Wewerka (2000), under "optimal" conditions (i.e., verbally cued memory for enabling sequences that children had experienced three times prior to imposition of a 1-month delay), even among children in whom declarative memory is reliable and robust (20 month olds), some children recalled all possible target actions whereas others recalled as few as one action. Similarly, some children evidenced perfect temporally ordered recall whereas others revealed no evidence of ordered recall. Moreover, individual differences in early memory performance have implications for later verbal accessibility of early memories: Levels of nonverbal recall at ages 22–32 months have been found to be related to levels of verbal accessibility of memories at age 3 years (Bauer, Kroupina, Schwade, Dropik, & Wewerka, 1998).

Now that it is apparent that there are not only normative, group or mean-level developmental changes in early declarative memory, but individual differences in children's performance as well, it is increasingly important to focus on the variability about the mean. An important question is whether there is systematicity in the variability: is the variability indicative of stable individual differences, or is it merely random noise? In contrast to group trends in development, which can effectively be investigated cross-sectionally, examination of possible individual profiles of change demands longitudinal data. It is only through repeated observation that we will be able to determine whether and when children exhibit stable individual patterns of memory performance. Examining patterns of performance on immediate and long-term declarative tasks longitudinally were major goals of the present research. One of the attractive features of the elicited-imitation paradigm is that it can be made more or less difficult or challenging. That is, sequences can be longer or shorter, thereby providing a range of values for performance and thus, superior predictive utility (see Chapter 2).

In two experiments, we used sequences of the lengths identified in Chapter 2 and tested children longitudinally. The major goal of the longitudinal investigations was to determine whether and when stable profiles of individual performance on immediate declarative memory tasks emerge. Just as throughout the second year of life there are changes in the reliability with which declarative memory is observed in the population (Bauer *et al.*, 2000), we may expect that during the same period, the behavior also will become stable within an individual. To examine this question, longitudinal data are necessary. There has been some research of this type on children's verbal memory during the third and fourth years of life. For example, Farrant and Reese (2000) found evidence of consistency from 25 to 40 months in children's independent autobiographical reports, and Haden, Ornstein, Eckerman, and Didow (2001) found evidence of stability from 30 to 42 months in children's verbal reports about specific test events. With the exception of Heimann and Meltzoff (1996), who reported stability in recall of single, object-specific actions from 9 to 14 months, we know of no longitudinal studies investigating consistency in children's nonverbal recall. Moreover, there are no studies examining individual variability in recall across the period of transition from infancy to early childhood. Thus, a goal of the present research was to examine performance on declarative memory tasks (elicited imitation) within the same children, at various time points throughout the second and third years of life. We pursued the goal in two longitudinal samples. In Experiment 1, children's immediate declarative memory abilities were tested at 16, 20, 24, 28, and 32 months of age. In Experiment 2, we extended the age range in both directions, and also increased the spacing between assessments: 13, 18, 24, 30, and 36 months of age. In Experiment 1, in addition to examining stability in children's declarative memory over time, we tested whether children's performance was consistent on events of two different lengths. In addition to tests of immediate recall, in Experiment 2 we obtained measures of long-term recall performance across the period of study. Experiments 1 and 2 were conducted concurrently, with different samples of children drawn from the same population. The ages at enrollment and spacing of observations were selected to permit dense sampling across a period of significant developmental change in the reliability and robustness of recall (see Bauer, 2002b, for discussion).

II. Experiment 1

Experiment 1 was a longitudinal study of immediate declarative memory performance across the second and into the third year of life. The longitudinal design permitted examination of individual profiles of change across the ages of 16, 20, 24, 28, and 32 months via patterns of correlation between levels of immediate recall at earlier and later ages. It also permitted examination of patterns of correlation between levels of immediate recall of short and long sequences at a given age.

A. METHOD

1. Participants
Twenty-three children participated (12 girls). Twelve of the 23 children (6 girls) composed the cross-sectional sample of 16-month olds included in Chapter 2; the other 11 children were added for the longitudinal examination, in order to increase the power of the design. Twenty-one of the children completed all five sessions, which took place at roughly 4-month intervals between the ages of 16 and 32 months; the other two children completed the first four sessions, but were unavailable for the fifth and final session. Descriptive information regarding the children's ages at each session, and the lengths of time between sessions, is provided in Table I, panel A.

2. Materials, Procedure, and Scoring
The materials were the same as those used in Chapter 2. At each age, the children were tested for immediate recall of one short sequence and

Table I

Experiments 1 and 2: Descriptive Statistics for Age at Test and Intersession Intervals

Experiment/ Observation	Sample Size	Variable			
		Mean Age at Test	Range of Age at Test	Mean Intersession Interval	Range of Intersession Interval
Panel A: Experiment 1					
16-Month	23	16;06	15;21–16;28	NA	NA
20-Month	23	20;12	19;28–21;04	4;06	3;07–4;24
24-Month	23	24;15	23;27–25;20	4;03	3;06–5;16
28-Month	23	28;13	27;26–29;14	3;29	2;15–5;07
32-Month	21	32;12	31;26–33;08	3;28	3;04–4;25
Panel B: Experiment 2					
13-Month	22	13;02	12;20–13;13	NA	NA
18-Month	22	18;04	17;20–18;29	5;03	4;24–6;00
24-Month	22	24;17	23;19–25;09	6;12	5;16–7;01
30-Month	22	31;03	29;04–32;21	6;16	5;15–8;03
36-Month	22	36;27	35;28–38;13	5;24	4;11–7;11

one long sequence. As in Burch *et al.*, sequence complexity increased with age: at 16 months, children were tested on 2- and 3-step sequences; at 20 months, children were tested on 3- and 4-step sequences; at 24 months, children were tested on 4- and 5-step sequences; at 28 months, children were tested on 5- and 6-step sequences; and at 32 months, children were tested on 6- and 7-step sequences. At adjacent ages, children were tested on different sequences (e.g., different 3-step sequences at 16 and 20 months).

The testing procedure was the same as that used in Chapter 2. That is, at each session, after presentation of two practice sequences, the children were tested for immediate recall of one short sequence followed by one long sequence. For each sequence, there was a baseline phase; then the sequence was modeled two times in succession, with narration; and then the children were permitted to imitate the sequence. The baseline and imitation phases were child controlled.

Presentation of the sequences of the same length was completely counterbalanced across age (e.g., half of the 16-month olds were tested on one of the 3-step sequences and the other half were tested on the other). The sessions were videotaped for later coding following the same procedures as outlined in Chapter 2. The same dependent measures were derived (number of individual target actions produced and number of pairs of actions produced in target order).

B. RESULTS

To facilitate comparisons across ages and test sequences of different lengths, all analyses were conducted on scores reflecting the proportion of the total possible individual target actions and the proportion of the total possible pairs of actions in the target order produced by each child. Descriptive statistics on mean levels of performance are provided in Table II, in proportions. In the present analyses, we focused analyses on postmodeling levels of performance because (a) in Chapter 2, we established that children in the target age range perform at higher levels after modeling of the test sequences, relative to prior to modeling; and (b) our main interest was the stability of children's immediate imitation performance across sequence lengths at one age point and on developmentally appropriate levels of challenge across development.

1. Within-Age-Group Comparisons of Performance on Sequences of Different Lengths

To determine whether levels of immediate recall at any time point differed as a function of sequence length, and whether there were effects of children's gender, we conducted 2 (gender: girls, boys) × 2 (sequence length: short, long) mixed analyses of variance, with repeated measures on sequence length, for each observation, for both dependent measures. There were neither main effects of nor interactions involving gender at

Table II

Experiment 1: Descriptive Statistics for Immediate Recall of the Individual
Target Actions and Temporal Order of Actions (as Measured by Pairs of Actions in the
Target Order), in Proportions

		Target Actions		Pairs of Actions	
Observation/Sequence Length		Mean	SD	Mean	SD
16-Month	2-Step	.80	.29	.61	.50
	3-Step	.51	.36	.37	.41
20-Month	3-Step	.87	.26	.74	.37
	4-Step	.77	.28	.59	.36
24-Month	4-Step	.90	.21	.70	.30
	5-Step	.81	.29	.67	.28
28-Month	5-Step	.90	.19	.80	.26
	6-Step	.91	.14	.78	.20
32-Month	6-Step	.98	.05	.80	.14
	7-Step	.85	.19	.74	.28

any time point, on either dependent measure. For this reason, gender was not considered further.

In terms of children's immediate recall of the individual target actions of the sequences, at both the 16- and 32-month observations, the effects of sequence length were significant: $F(1, 21) = 9.27$, $p < .007$, and $F(1, 19) = 10.97$, $p < .004$, respectively. At both observations, the children recalled larger proportions of the individual target actions of the short sequences relative to the long sequences (see Table II, for means). Similar, though nonsignificant, trends were observed at the 20- and 24-month observations ($ps < .11$ and .08, respectively). There was no suggestion of an effect of sequence length at the 28-month observation. At 16 months, the difference in the levels of recall of the individual target actions of the short and long sequences produced a parallel trend in the proportion of pairs of target actions produced: $F(1, 21) = 3.49$, $p < .08$. The trend disappeared when differential production of the target actions of the sequences was controlled via ANCOVA. When the variance associated with differential production of the individual target actions of the sequences was not controlled, there were no other effects of or trends for sequence length. However, the ANCOVAs yielded a main effect of sequence length at 32 months: $F(1, 18) = 22.18$, $p < .0002$. At the oldest age they were tested, children's ordered recall of the short sequences was greater than that of the long sequences even after the number of target actions was controlled.

2. Between-Age Comparisons of Performance on Sequences of the Same Length

To examine whether, on sequences of a given length, children performed at higher levels when they were older, relative to when they were younger (the children were tested on different sequences at each time point), we conducted one-way ANOVAs for each step length, for both dependent measures. The one-way ANOVAs were conducted on sequences 3, 4, 5, and 6 steps in length only (performance on 2- and 7-step sequences was not analyzed because these sequence lengths were tested at one age only, namely, 16 and 32 months, respectively). For the measure of the proportion of individual target actions produced, there were main effects of age for each sequence length. For the 3-step and 6-step sequences, the effects were statistically significant: $F(1, 22) = 13.59$, $p < .002$, and $F(1, 20) = 5.73$, $p < .03$, respectively. For the 4- and 5-step sequences, the effects fell just below the conventional level of statistical significance: $Fs(1, 22) = 4.08$, $p < .06$, and 3.65, $p < .07$, respectively. Thus, for each sequence length, the children tended to recall more of the individual target actions of the sequences when they were older than they had when they were younger.

Age-related effects and trends on immediate recall of the individual target actions of the sequences did not necessarily translate into effects of age on children's ordered recall. Main effects of age were significant on the 3- and 5-step sequences: $Fs(1, 22) = 9.72$, $p < .005$, and 6.34, $p < .02$. In both cases, the children produced more pairs of actions in target order when they were older than they had when they were younger. However, on the 4- and 6-step sequences, the effects of age on children's ordered recall did not even approach significance. Moreover, with the variance associated with differential production of the individual target actions of the sequences controlled, none of the effects of age on children's ordered recall was reliable.

3. Concurrent Correlations

To determine whether at a given point in time, children's levels of immediate recall of the short sequences was related to their immediate recall of the long sequences, we calculated Pearson product–moment correlations. The obtained values are provided in Table III. As is apparent from the table, there was continuity in the proportion of individual target actions that the children recalled on the short and long sequences at the 20-, 24-, and 28-month observations. There was continuity in levels of ordered recall of the short and long sequences only at the 24- and 28-month observations. One possible reason for the lack of correlation at the earliest time point is the restricted range of the variables: On 2-step sequences (the length of the short sequences at 16 months), children could produce 0, 1, or 2 individual target actions and 0 or 1 ordered pairs of

Table III

Experiment 1: Concurrent Correlations Between Levels of Performance on Short Sequences and Levels of Performance on Long Sequences at the 16-, 20-, 24-, 28-, and 32-Month Observations

	Observation				
Dependent Measure	16-Month	20-Month	24-Month	28-Month	32-Month
Individual target actions	−.10	.40[+]	.51[*]	.58[**]	.24
Pairs of actions	−.04	.19	.39[+]	.54[**]	.09

Note: [+]$p < .10$; [*]$p < .05$; [**]$p < .01$; for 16-, 20-, 24-, and 28-month observations, df $= 21$; for 32-month observation, df $= 19$.

actions. On the variable of pairs of actions in the target order, even at 20 months, the short sequences had a range of only 0–2. Whereas at 32 months, the possible range for both the short and long sequences was wide, restriction in the range actually observed could explain the lack of correlation between the number of individual target actions produced on the short and long sequences at the latest time point (90% of the children produced all possible target actions on the short sequences). It cannot, however, explain the lack of correlation on the variable of number of pairs of actions produced: The possible ranges were 0–5 and 0–6 on the short and long sequences, respectively; the observed ranges were 2–5 and 1–6 on the short and long sequences, respectively. In spite of the lack of correlation at the 32-month observation, overall, these analyses suggest that, throughout most of the second and into the third year of life, an individual child's competence at immediate recall generalizes across sequence lengths.

4. Cross-Lagged Correlations

To determine whether and when stable individual patterns of immediate recall performance emerge, we evaluated the degree of correlation between children's performance at earlier time points and their performance at later time points. The correlation coefficients are provided in Table IV. For both dependent measures, performance at 16 months of age was largely unpredictive of performance at the later time points. One exception is that performance on both short and long sequences at 16 months predicted the proportion of individual target actions produced on long sequences at 28 months, and the proportions of pairs of actions produced in the target order at 28 months and, to a weaker extent, 32 months. Whereas performance on the short sequences at 16 months was negatively related to performance at 28 and 32 months, performance on the long sequences at 16 months was positively related to performance on the long sequences at 28 months. We do not have a ready interpretation for this pattern. It is possible that the effect is specific to the 2-step sequence used at the 16-month time point.

At 20 months of age, children's immediate recall of the individual target actions of the short sequences emerged as a consistent predictor of immediate recall of the individual target actions of the short sequences at subsequent observations. That is, immediate recall of the individual target actions of the short sequences at 20 months predicted immediate recall of the individual target actions of the short sequences at 24, 28, and 32 months; performance on the short sequences at 24 months predicted performance on the short sequences at 28 and 32 months; and performance

Table IV

Experiment 1: Cross-Lagged Correlations Between Levels of Performance at the
16-, 20-, 24-, 28-, and 32-Month Observations

Measure/ Observation/ Sequence Length	Observation/sequence length							
	20-Month		24-Month		28-Month		32-Month	
	3-Step	4-Step	4-Step	5-Step	5-Step	6-Step	6-Step	7-Step
Individual target actions								
16-Month								
2-Step	.05	−.15	−.14	−.14	−.19	−.45*	−.21	−.34
3-Step	−.13	.14	.28	.16	.08	.36+	−.04	.16
20-Month								
3-Step			.45*	.38+	.47*	.07	.46*	.27
4-Step			.23	.17	.30	.05	.44*	.30
24-Month								
4-Step					.55*	.34	.41+	−.02
5-Step					.55*	.62*	.34	.38+
28-Month								
5-Step							.52*	.48*
6-Step							.35*	.45*
Pairs of actions in target order								
16-Month								
2-Step	.29	−.16	−.22	−.23	−.35+	−.44*	.14	−.40+
3-Step	−.09	.29	.10	.31	.07	.48*	−.10	.06
20-Month								
3-Step			.21	.19	.10	−.19	.19	.13
4-Step			.03	.28	.32	.27	.32	.40+
24-Month								
4-Step					.32	.21	.08	−.08
5-Step					.57*	.72**	.32	.47*
28-Month								
5-Step							.19	.57*
6-Step							.07	.45*

Note: $^+p < .10$; $^*p < .05$; $^{**}p < .01$; for 16-, 20-, 24-, and 28-month observations, df = 21; for 32-month observation, df = 19.

on the short sequences at 28 months predicted performance on the short sequences at 32 months. The emergence of immediate recall of the individual target actions of the long sequences as a consistent predictor of subsequent performance lagged behind: Immediate recall of the individual target actions of the long sequences at 24 months predicted the same at 28 and 32 months; immediate recall of the individual target actions of the long sequences at 28 months predicted the same at 32 months. Across time points, immediate recall of the individual target actions of the short sequences was largely unpredictive of production of the individual target actions of the long sequences (two exceptions being a marginal relation from 20 to 24 months and a significant relation from 28 to 32 months). In contrast, beginning at 24 months, immediate recall of the individual target actions of the long sequences was predictive of production of the individual target actions of the short sequences at the next observation.

Whereas on the variable of individual target actions produced performance on the short sequences emerged as a consistent predictor at 20 months of age, on the variable of pairs of actions produced in the target order, performance on the short sequences never emerged as a consistent predictor. Specifically, from 20 months on, the only significant cross-lagged correlation with short sequences was between performance at 28 months and ordered recall of long sequences at 32 months. Ordered recall of long sequences was a significant predictor of ordered recall of long sequences beginning at 24 months of age: The proportion of pairs of actions of the long sequences produced in the target order at 24 months predicted the same at 28 and 32 months; the proportion of pairs of actions of the long sequences produced in the target order at 28 months predicted the same at 32 months. Finally, immediate ordered recall performance on the long sequences was predictive of ordered recall on short sequences at the next observation only from 24 to 28 months.

In summary, performance at 16 months of age was largely unpredictive of performance at subsequent ages. Some of the lack of predictive utility of the first observation may be attributed to the restricted range of the variables, as noted earlier. However, restricted range cannot account for the odd pattern of negative and positive correlation observed between performance on short sequences versus long sequences (respectively) at 16 months and performance at the 28-month observation. In contrast to the unusual relations between performance at 16 and 28 months, the pattern of predictive relations between immediate recall of the individual target actions of the short sequences at 20 months and immediate recall of individual target actions at subsequent observations is readily interpretable: It appears that by 20 months of age, immediate recall of the individual target actions of short sequences is a stable individual trait. Beginning at 24 months, there is also stability in the levels of immediate recall of the individual target actions of long sequences. Consistent with suggestions of more protracted development of ordered recall ability, relative to the ability to recall individual target actions (e.g., Bauer *et al.*, 2000), it was not until 24 months of age that individual variation in immediate ordered recall performance stabilized and became reliably predictive.

C. DISCUSSION

In this longitudinal study, a sample of children was followed from 16 to 32 months, with observations spaced at 4-month intervals. As was observed in the cross-sectional samples in Chapter 2, in the present experiment, at a given age, children tended to produce a larger proportion of the individual target actions of the short sequences, relative to the long sequences. Across ages, on sequences of a given length, children tended to recall a larger proportion of the individual target actions of sequences when they were older than they had recalled when they were younger. This indicates that, at least when tested with sequences the lengths of which are developmentally appropriate, children are able to "rise to the occasion" of a larger number of individual actions available for recall.

Children's levels of immediate ordered recall were largely unaffected by sequence length. Instead, they varied as a function of children's ages. First, at a given age, children's levels of production of pairs of actions in the target order on short and long sequences were comparable. In fact, when the variance associated with differential levels of recall of the individual target actions of the sequences was controlled, the only significant effect of sequence length was at 32 months, at which time children recalled a larger proportion of pairs of actions in the target order on the 6-step relative to the 7-step sequences. Across ages, there were changes in the proportion of pairs of actions produced in the target order, and in modal levels of production of ordered pairs of actions. That is, the children recalled a larger proportion of pairs of actions in target order of the 3-step sequences at 20 months than they had at 16 months, and they recalled a larger proportion of pairs of actions in target order of the 5-step sequences at 28 months than they had at 24 months.

The observed patterns of concurrent and cross-lagged correlation revealed stable immediate recall performance profiles by 20–24 months of age; immediate recall of the individual target actions of sequences stabilized before immediate recall of the temporal order of sequences. Within a session, immediate recall of the individual target actions of the short and long sequences was related beginning at 20 months of age. Across sessions, immediate recall of the individual target actions of short sequences emerged as a consistent predictor at 20 months of age, and immediate recall of the individual actions of long sequences emerged as a consistent predictor at 24 months of age. Both within and across sessions, it was not until 24 months of age that ordered recall performance emerged as a reliable predictor of itself. It is conceivable that the lack of predictive utility of observations from the 16-month session was due to restricted range of the dependent measures. The data from Experiment 2, in which there were greater ranges of possible values for the dependent variables, afforded address of this possibility.

III. Experiment 2

Like Experiment 1, Experiment 2 was a longitudinal study of immediate recall performance. Relative to Experiment 1, it covered a wider age range, encompassing the period of 13–36 months. Observations were at 6-month intervals, as opposed to the 4-month intervals used in the previous experiment (i.e., observations were obtained at 13, 18, 24, 30, and 36 months of age). In addition, beginning at the 18-month observation, children were tested for long-term recall of sequences to which they had been exposed at the preceding session (i.e., at 18 months, children were tested for long-term recall of one sequence to which they had been exposed at 13 months). Experiment 2 thus permitted a test for replication of the findings of Experiment 1, with extension of the study to children both younger and older in age, and to assessments of long-term recall. Because the interval between testing sessions was a full 6 months, it permitted for stronger tests of the cross-lagged patterns observed in Experiment 1. In addition, rather than on one sequence of each of two lengths, for the immediate recall assessments, the children were tested on two sequences of a given length. By using the mean level of performance across two sequences of the same length, we were permitted both a more stable estimate of performance and a greater range for each dependent measure.

A. METHOD

1. Participants

Twenty-two children participated in the longitudinal sample. All of the children took part in five sessions, which took place when the children were roughly 13, 18, 24, 30, and 36 months of age. Two additional children were enrolled in the study but did not complete all five testing sessions. Descriptive information regarding the children's ages at each session, and the lengths of time between sessions, are provided in Table I, panel B. Children were recruited from the same source and represent the same population as in Experiment 1.

2. Materials, Procedure, and Scoring

At each session, the children were tested for immediate recall of two sequences. Beginning at the 18-month observation, they also were tested for long-term recall of one sequence from the immediately preceding session. Sequence complexity increased with age: at 13, 18, 24, 30, and 36 months, children were tested on 2-, 3-, 4-, 5-, and 6-step sequences, respectively. At 13, 18, and 24 months of age, the orders of the sequences were constrained by enabling relations. Because of the aforementioned difficulties inherent in designing longer sequences that were completely constrained by enabling relations, at 30 and 36 months, the 5- and 6-step sequences (respectively) that were used each contained a mixture of enabling and arbitrary relations.

The testing procedures were comparable to those used in Experiment 1. At all sessions, the order of presentation of the sequences used for immediate testing was counterbalanced across participants. The sequences selected for long-term recall testing (which began at the 18-month session), were counterbalanced across participants. In addition, the order of testing of the immediate recall (tested at all sessions) and long-term recall (tested beginning at 18 months) sequences was counterbalanced across participants. The sessions were videotaped for later coding following the same procedures as outlined in Chapter 2. The same dependent measures were derived (number of individual target actions produced and number of pairs of actions produced in target order).

B. RESULTS

To facilitate comparisons across age groups (and thus, test sequence length), all analyses were conducted on scores reflecting the proportion of the total possible individual target actions and the proportion of the total possible pairs of actions in the target order produced by each child. Descriptive statistics on children's mean levels of performance are provided in Table V, in proportions. At all ages, children were tested for immediate recall of two sequences. The mean of children's performance on the two sequences is reflected in the table and was used in all analyses. The values for long-term recall are based on one sequence only. As in Experiment 1, we focused analyses on postmodeling levels of performance.

1. Between-Age Comparisons of Performance

Children's levels of immediate and long-term recall were examined in separate sets of analyses. For immediate recall, for both the proportion of individual target actions produced and the proportion of pairs of

Table V

Experiment 2: Descriptive Statistics for Immediate and Long-Term Recall of the Individual Target Actions and Temporal Order of Actions (as Measured by Pairs of Actions in the Target Order), in Proportions

	Test of Recall and Dependent Measure							
	Immediate Recall				Long-Term Recall			
	Individual Actions		Pairs of Actions		Individual Actions		Pairs of Actions	
Observation	Mean	SD	Mean	SD	Mean	SD	Mean	SD
13-Month	.69	.31	.48	.42	NA	NA	NA	NA
18-Month	.85	.21	.75	.29	.56	.34	.25	.43
24-Month	.94	.14	.73	.20	.33	.23	.07	.18
30-Month	.92	.12	.76	.18	.40	.25	.15	.27
36-Month	.95	.08	.72	.14	.39	.31	.19	.23

actions produced in the target order, we conducted 2 (gender: girls, boys) $\times$ 5 (age: 13, 18, 24, 30, and 36 months) mixed ANOVAs, with repeated measures on age. There were no main effects of gender, for either dependent measure. For both measures, there were main effects of age: $Fs(4, 80) = 10.11, p < .0001$, and $5.23, p < .0009$, for individual target actions and pairs of actions in the target order, respectively. However, the main effects were qualified by interactions with gender: $Fs(4, 80) = 3.46$, $p < .02$, and $3.02, p < .03$, for individual target actions and pairs of actions in the target order, respectively. Analyses of the interactions revealed effects of age only for the girls in the sample: $Fs(4, 36) = 10.93, p < .0001$, and $8.47, p < .0001$, for individual target actions and pairs of actions in the target order, respectively. The girls recalled a lower proportion of the individual target actions and a lower proportion of pairs of actions in the target order at the 13-month observation relative to all subsequent observations, which did not differ from one another (Tukey, $p < .05$). Among the boys, there were no age effects on either dependent measure. When the variance associated with differential production of the individual target actions of the sequences was controlled via ANCOVA, the main effect of age, $F(4, 79) = 3.04, p < .03$, indicated that across gender groups, the children produced a smaller proportion of pairs of actions in the target order at the 13-month observation, relative to all subsequent observations, which did not differ from one another. These analyses suggest that at least across the 18–36-month age period, the sequence lengths selected for each age were roughly comparable in the level of challenge that they presented to the children.

Observations of children's long-term recall performance were available for the 18-, 24-, 30-, and 36-month observations. We conducted separate 2 (gender: girls, boys) × 3 (age: 18, 24, 30, and 36 months) mixed ANOVAs, with repeated measures on age, for each dependent measure. There was a main effect of age for children's long-term recall of the individual target actions of the sequences: $F(3, 56) = 2.95$, $p < .05$. However, none of the pairwise comparisons was significant (Tukey, $p < .05$). There was no effect of age on children's long-term recall of the temporal order of the sequences. For both dependent measures, girls tended to perform at lower levels, relative to boys (individual target actions: $Ms = .34$ and .48, $SDs = .25$ and .31; pairs of actions: $Ms = .09$ and .22, $SDs = .21$ and .33, respectively). In both cases, the effects fell below the conventional level of statistical significance, $Fs(1, 20) = 3.64$, $p < .08$, and 3.99, $p < .06$, for individual target actions and pairs of actions, respectively. Gender and age did not interact. When the variance associated with differential delayed recall of the individual target actions of the sequences was controlled in an ANCOVA, none of the effects reached significance.

2. Cross-Lagged Correlations: Immediate Recall

To address the question of whether children's immediate recall performance at earlier observation points was predictive of their immediate

Table VI

Experiment 2: Cross-Lagged Correlations between Immediate Recall Performance at the 13-, 18-, 24-, 30-, and 36-Month Observations

Measure/Observation	Observation			
	18-Month	24-Month	30-Month	36-Month
Individual target actions				
13-Month	.23	.42*	.47*	−.08
18-Month		.57**	.42*	−.14
24-Month			.74**	−.21
30-Month				−.03
Pairs of actions in target order				
13-Month	.10	−.03	.31	−.07
18-Month		.27	−.06	−.06
24-Month			.30	−.06
30-Month				.10

Note: $^*p \leq .05$; $^{**}p < .01$; for all observations df $= 20$.

recall performance at later observation points, we computed cross-lagged correlations. The correlation coefficients are provided in Table VI. For the variable of individual target actions produced, performance at 13 months was not related to performance at 18 months, but was related to performance at both 24 and 30 months. Performance at 18 months was related to performance at both 24 and 30 months, and performance at 24 months was related to performance at 30 months. Thus, as in Experiment 1, in the present experiment, immediate recall of the individual target actions of the sequences was a consistent predictor. In contrast to Experiment 1, in which predictive relations emerged at 20 months, in the present experiment, they were present, albeit not perfectly consistently, from the time of the first observation. It is likely that the difference between the two experiments is due to the wider possible range of the variable in the present experiment, relative to Experiment 1.

Whereas the wider possible range of the variable may have permitted earlier prediction of children's immediate recall of the individual target actions of the sequences, restriction of observed range may be responsible for the lack of cross-lagged prediction to the 36-month observation. Inspection of the data revealed that only one child produced 4 of the possible 6 target actions, and two children produced 5 of the possible 6 target actions. The remaining 19 children produced 5.5 or all 6 possible target actions. Thus, rather than to instability in performance, the lack of prediction to the 36-month observation likely should be attributed to children's consistently high levels of immediate recall of the actions of the sequences.

In contrast to the pattern observed in Experiment 1, in the present experiment, children's immediate recall of the temporal order of the sequences never emerged as a consistent predictor: None of the cross-lagged correlations were reliable. Given that there was ample variability in the data, the lack of correlation between earlier and later time points cannot be attributed to restriction of range. To further examine the possibility of stability in immediate ordered recall performance over time, for each time point, for each child, we determined whether the number of pairs of actions produced in the target order was at or above the median, or below the median. We then determined whether for each adjacent pair of observations (i.e., 13- and 18-month, 18- and 24-month, 24- and 30-month, and 30- and 36-month), children fell into the same cell (i.e., consistently below the median, or consistently at or above the median) or into different cells. The results of this procedure are provided in Table VII. For both the 13–18-month comparison and the 18–24-month comparison, children were more likely to perform consistently than inconsistently (binomial $ps = .067$ and $.026$, respectively). For the 24–30-month and 30–36-month comparisons, the children were equally likely to perform

Table VII

Experiment 2: Descriptive Statistics on the Frequency of Ordered Recall Performance at or Above the Median Versus Below the Median at Adjacent Observations

Observation	Level of Performance	Level of Performance/Observation	
		Below the Median	At or Above Median
		18-Month	
13-Month	Below the median	4	4
	At or above median	3	11
		24-Month	
18-Month	Below the median	5	2
	At or above median	4	11
		30-Month	
24-Month	Below the median	5	4
	At or above median	6	7
		36-Month	
30-Month	Below the median	4	7
	At or above median	3	8

Note: The children falling into the upper left and lower right quadrants of the table showed consistent performance at adjacent observations: consistently below the median and consistently at or above the median, respectively.

consistently and inconsistently in relation to the median. Thus, when evaluated in this rather global manner, there was evidence of cross-lagged consistency in immediate ordered recall performance across the second year of life. Neither analytic approach revealed consistency in immediate ordered recall performance across the third year of life as verbal recall is beginning to become more reliable.

3. Cross-Lagged Correlations: Long-Term Recall

To determine whether children's long-term recall performance at an earlier time was predictive of their long-term recall performance at a later time, we computed cross-lagged correlations. None of the correlations reached the conventional level of statistical significance. The correlation between long-term recall of the temporal order of the sequence over the interval from 18 to 24 months and long-term recall of the temporal order of the sequence over the interval from 30 to 36 months approached significance: $r(20) = .39, p < .10$. With that exception, over the 6-month intervals between sessions, we were not able to predict children's recall. One possible explanation for the lack of predictive utility of the earlier long-term recall scores of later long-term recall performance is that, within the age range tested, long-term recall ability is not a stable trait of individual children. However, there are a number of other reasons why we may have failed to observe predictive relations, including, but not limited to (a) the limited ranges of the predictor variables (at the earlier time points, in particular), (b) near-floor levels of long-term recall performance, and (c) the length of the retention interval. Because of the number of possible explanations, we suggest that it would be premature to conclude that the reason for lack of relation was instability in long-term recall over this age period.

C. DISCUSSION

In this longitudinal study, a sample of children was followed from 13 to 36 months, with observations spaced at 6-month intervals. Across the period of observation, the children were tested on sequences of increasing length, from 2-step sequences at 13 months to 6-step sequences at 36 months. Beginning at 18 months, they were tested for long-term recall of one of the sequences on which they had been tested at the prior session.

Among the girls in the sample, the level of immediate recall of the individual target actions of the sequences at the first observation at 13 months was lower than the levels of immediate recall at all subsequent observations; levels of immediate recall of the individual target actions of the sequences at the 18-, 24-, 30-, and 36-month observations did not differ from one another. Among the boys in the sample, there were no age effects in the proportion of individual target actions produced. These findings indicate that the sequence lengths presented to the children at the different ages presented roughly comparable levels of challenge, and that the sequence lengths were developmentally appropriate at each age. Beginning at 13 months of age, at each time point, the proportion of individual target actions recalled immediately after modeling was predictive of immediate recall at subsequent time points, up to and including the 30-month observation. The only exception was that the 13-month observation did not predict to the 18-month observation (but did predict to the 24- and 30-month observations). These findings complement and extend those of Experiment 1 in which predictive relations were observed beginning at 20 months. Notably, there were no cross-lagged relations to the 36-month observation. It is likely that in the present experiment, the lack of prediction of performance at 36 months was due to ceiling effects: only 1 of the 22 children in the sample produced fewer than 5 of the 6 possible target actions.

As a group, children's immediate ordered recall was lower at the 13-month observation, relative to all subsequent observations, which did not differ from one another. Unlike the finding for individual target actions, which was restricted to the girls in the sample, when measured in terms of children's ordered recall, with the variance associated with production of the individual target actions of the sequences controlled, the effect extended to both gender groups. This finding suggests that ordered recall of the simplest sequence (i.e., 2 steps) is more challenging for 13 month olds than is recall of longer sequences for children 18 months of age and older. Moreover, the suggestion that ordered recall presents a greater challenge for younger relative to older children is consistent with the findings of Bauer *et al.* (2000). In spite of the apparent challenge, immediate ordered recall performance was reliably greater than chance at all time points. In contrast to Experiment 1, in which parametric cross-lagged correlations to ordered recall performance were predictive beginning at 24 months of age, in the present experiment, across the 6-month intervals between sessions, ordered recall performance was not predictive. Nevertheless, across the second year of life, children were more likely to consistently perform at or above the median, or consistently below the median, than they were to perform inconsistently. This pattern was not observed from 24 to 30 months or from 30 to 36 months of age, however.

Finally, in the present research, we included observations of long-term recall as well as of immediate recall. That is, beginning at the 18-month observation, we tested children for recall of one of the sequences they had experienced at the immediately preceding session. Overall, children's levels of long-term recall were quite low. Although a significant main effect of age indicated that the children recalled a larger proportion of the individual target actions of the sequences when they were older, relative to when they were younger, none of the pairwise comparisons was statistically significant. There was no effect of age on children's ordered recall. Moreover, perhaps in part because of the near-floor levels of ordered recall observed, none of the cross-lagged correlations were reliable. Although it will be left to future research to determine the cause or causes of children's low levels of long-term recall, it is noteworthy that this is the first study in which long-term recall of multistep sequences experienced only once has been tested over such a long delay.

IV. General Discussion

The main goal of the present experiments was to begin to examine the variability about the group mean level of performance and determine whether it is indicative of stable individual differences, or merely of random noise. Recent longitudinal investigations have provided evidence of stability in verbal recall across the third and fourth years of life (Farrant & Reese, 2000; Haden *et al.*, 2001). In the present research, we tested for consistency in levels of nonverbal recall across the second and third years of life. We evaluated the stability of performance in two ways: we examined correlations within a session (Experiment 1 only) and correlations between sessions (Experiments 1 and 2). In Experiment 1, concurrent correlations between the number of individual target actions produced on short and long sequences were apparent at 20, 24, and 28 months (but not at 16 or 32 months); concurrent correlations between the number of pairs of actions produced in the target order on short and long sequences were apparent at 24 and 28 months (but not at 16, 20, or 32 months). We suggest that the lack of consistency is best attributed to restriction of range. Early in the observation period, the possible range of the variables was restricted (i.e., on short sequences, from 0 to 2 individual target actions at 16 months, and from 0 to 2 pairs of actions in the target order at 20 months); at 32 months of age, the observed range of the variables was restricted (i.e., on short sequences, 90% of the children produced all possible target actions). Whatever be the actual reason (or reasons) for apparent concurrent instability at the early and later observations, at the least, these analyses suggest that, throughout most of the second and into the third year of life, an individual child's competence at immediate declarative memory generalizes across sequence lengths. That stability on measures of ordered recall might lag behind stability on measures of recall of individual actions is not surprising, given that recall of temporal order imposes greater cognitive demands than recall of individual actions (Bauer *et al.*, 2000).

The second way in which we tested for consistency in levels of performance was to examine cross-lagged correlations. In Experiment 1, cross-lagged correlations between earlier and later measures of children's immediate recall of the individual target actions of the sequences were apparent beginning at 20 months. Children's performance on the short sequences at 20 months of age was predictive of their performance on the short sequences at 24, 28, and 32 months of age. Children's performance on the long sequences did not become predictive until 24 months of age. The findings of cross-lagged correlations are consistent with those of concurrent correlations. Together, they provide strong support for the conclusion that by 20–24 months of age, variability about the group mean level of immediate recall of the individual actions of event sequences is meaningful. This conclusion was supported and extended in Experiment 2, in which cross-lagged correlations between children's performance at earlier and later sessions were first observed at 13 months, and consistently observed by 18 months. It is likely that the earlier prediction afforded in Experiment 2 relative to Experiment 1 was due to the wider possible range of the variables in Experiment 2. The exception to the apparent rule of stability in the capacity for immediate recall of the individual target actions of sequences suggested in these samples was that in Experiment 2, predictive relations did not extend to the 36-month observation. Once again, we attribute the predictive failure to restriction of observed range: As noted earlier, only one of the twenty-two 36-month-old children in the sample produced fewer than 5 of the 6 possible target actions. Together, the results of the longitudinal studies suggest that variability about the mean levels of immediate recall of the actions of sequences is meaningful throughout the second and most of the third year of life.

Whereas there was strong evidence of consistency in children's immediate recall of the individual actions of sequences, the findings regarding systematicity in the variability of children's immediate ordered recall were mixed. In Experiment 1, cross-lagged correlations obtained between the 24-month and both 28- and 32-month observations, as well as between the 28- and 32-month observations. The most consistent predictor was children's ordered recall performance on the long sequences. In contrast, in Experiment 2, none of the cross-lagged correlations reached statistical significance. That ordered recall performance on long sequences in Experiment 1 proved to be most predictive may account for the lack of cross-lagged correlations observed in Experiment 2: In the latter study, the children were tested on the equivalent of "short" sequences. Because the two longitudinal studies were conducted concurrently, at the time of design of Experiment 2, we did not yet have the results of Experiment 1 and thus, were not aware of the apparent limitations on the predictive utility of performance on short sequences. In light of this feature of the design of Experiment 2, it is noteworthy that when examined as a function of whether the number of ordered pairs of action produced was at or above the median versus below the median, there was evidence of consistency in performance from 13 to 18 months and from 18 to 24 months. Even as measured by this more global metric, however, in Experiment 2, there was no consistency in children's ordered recall performance across the third year of life.

In Experiment 2, in addition to testing children's immediate recall, beginning with the 18-month observation, we included assessments of recall over 6-month delays. With regard to questions of stability in long-term recall performance, the results were largely uninformative, due to near-floor levels of performance. That is, after the 6-month delays, the children produced relatively few of the individual target actions of the sequences and even fewer of them in the target order. None of the cross-lagged correlations of children's performance at earlier and later observations reached statistical significance.

In light of the results of Bauer *et al.* (2000), the low levels of long-term recall performance observed in Experiment 2 seem incongruous: In Bauer *et al.*, 83% of the children who had been 20 months of age at the time of experience of events showed evidence of ordered recall of at least portions of them 6 months later. One possible reason for the different levels of performance in the two studies is that in Bauer *et al.*, the children were exposed to the test sequences a total of three times prior to imposition of the delay. In contrast, in Experiment 2 of the present research, children experienced the sequences only once before the delays were imposed. In fact, in most of the laboratory work on long-term recall of multistep sequences, either delays were short (e.g., Barr & Hayne, 1996; Bauer & Hertsgaard, 1993; Howe & Courage, 1997) or, as in Bauer *et al.* (2000), the children were exposed to test sequences multiple times prior to imposition of long delays (e.g., Bauer, Hertsgaard, & Dow, 1994). As a result of these features of the literature, we know little about young children's long-term recall of specific laboratory events based on a single experience. This leaves open the possibility that the differences in levels of performance may be due to the effects of multiple versus single experiences of the event in prior research and the present research, respectively. In this regard, it is perhaps telling that whereas prior to 30 months, the children remembered little about the sequences, from 30 to 36 months, they remembered a substantial number of individual target actions. The timing of this apparent increase in the ability to remember unique events over long delays corresponds relatively well with reports that by late in the third year of life, children provide evidence of memory for unique, naturally occurring events over long delays (see Fivush, 1997 for a review). More research on young children's abilities to remember unique, controlled, laboratory events over long delays, and whether variability in long-term recall performance is systematic, is necessary.

The present research informed the question of whether variability about the group mean level of recall is indicative of stable individual differences in declarative memory ability, or is better characterized as random variation. Across the second and into the third year of life, we observed stability in children's immediate declarative memory performance. The findings thus indicate that there is "signal" in the "noise." In so doing, they provide motivation for further research on relations ·between individual differences in early declarative memory and other characteristics that vary systematically across children. Such investigations can be expected to be mutually informative: We stand to learn about the factors that affect memory development, as well as how developments in memory affect performance in other domains.

Acknowledgment

The research reported in this chapter was supported by grants from the NICHD (HD28425, HD42483) to Patricia J. Bauer.

REFERENCES

Barr, R., & Hayne, H. (1996). The effect of event structure on imitation in infancy: Practice makes perfect? *Infant Behavior & Development, 19*, 253–257.

Bauer, P. J. (2002a). Long-term recall memory: Behavioral and neuro-developmental changes in the first 2 year of life. *Current Directions in Psychological Science, 11*, 137–141.

Bauer, P. J. (2002b). Building toward a past: Construction of a reliable long-term recall memory system. In N. L. Stein, P. J. Bauer & M. Rabinowitz (Eds.), *Representation, memory, and development: Essays in honor of Jean Mandler* (pp. 17–42). Mahwah, NJ: Erlbaum.

Bauer, P. J., & Hertsgaard, L. A. (1993). Increasing steps in recall of events: Factors facilitating immediate and long-term memory in 13.5- and 16.5-month-old children. *Child Development, 64*, 1204–1223.

Bauer, P. J., Hertsgaard, L. A., & Dow, G. A. (1994). After 8 months have passed: Long-term recall of events by 1- to 2-year-old children. *Memory, 2*, 353–382.

Bauer, P. J., Kroupina, M. G., Schwade, J. A., Dropik, P., & Wewerka, S. S. (1998). If memory serves, will language? Later verbal accessibility of early memories. *Development and Psychopathology, 10*, 655–679.

Bauer, P. J., Wenner, J. A., Dropik, P. L., & Wewerka, S. S. (2000). Parameters of remembering and forgetting in the transition from infancy to early childhood. *Monographs of the Society for Research in Child Development, 65*(4) (Serial no. 263).

Bauer, P. J., Wiebe, S. A., Waters, J. M., & Bangston, S. K. (2001). Reexposure breeds recall: Effects of experience on 9-month-olds' ordered recall. *Journal of Experimental Child Psychology, 80*, 174–200.

Carver, L. J., & Bauer, P. J. (1999). When the event is more than the sum of its parts: Nine-month-olds' long-term ordered recall. *Memory, 7*, 147–174.

Farrant, K., & Reese, E. (2000). Maternal style and children's participation in reminiscing: Stepping stones in children's autobiographical memory development. *Journal of Cognition and Development, 1*, 193–225.

Fivush, R. (1997). Event memory in early childhood. In N. Cowan (Ed.), *The development of memory in childhood* (pp. 139–161). Hove East Sussex, UK: Psychology Press.

Flynn, E., Pine, K., & Lewis, C. (2006). Using the microgenetic method to investigate cognitive development: An introduction. *Infant and Child Development, 16*, 1–6.

Haden, C. A., Ornstein, P. A., Eckerman, C. O., & Didow, S. M. (2001). Mother-child conversational interactions as events unfold: Linkages to subsequent remembering. *Child Development, 72*, 1016–1031.

Heimann, M., & Meltzoff, A. N. (1996). Deferred imitation in 9- and 14-month-old infants: A longitudinal study of a Swedish sample. *British Journal of Developmental Psychology, 14*, 55–64.

Howe, M. L., & Courage, M. L. (1997). Independent paths in the development of infant learning and forgetting. *Journal of Experimental Child Psychology, 67*, 131–163.

Siegler, R. S. (1996). *Emerging minds: The process of change in children's thinking.* New York: Oxford University Press.

DECLARATIVE MEMORY PERFORMANCE IN INFANTS OF DIABETIC MOTHERS

Tracy Riggins, Patricia J. Bauer,[†] Michael K. Georgieff,[‡] and Charles A. Nelson[§]*

* DEPARTMENT OF PSYCHOLOGY, UNIVERSITY OF MARYLAND, COLLEGE PARK, MARYLAND, USA
[†] DEPARTMENT OF PSYCHOLOGY, EMORY UNIVERSITY, ATLANTA, GEORGIA, USA
[‡] DEPARTMENT OF PEDIATRICS AND CENTER FOR NEUROBEHAVIORAL DEVELOPMENT, UNIVERSITY OF MINNESOTA, MINNEAPOLIS, MINNESOTA, USA
[§] HARVARD MEDICAL SCHOOL, CHILDREN'S HOSPITAL BOSTON, MASSACHUSETTS, USA

I. Introduction

Converging evidence from multiple lines of research has implicated medial temporal lobe (MTL) structures, including the hippocampus, in the conscious recollection of facts and events (i.e., declarative memory; Squire, 1992; see Chapter 1). Some of the most compelling support for this association comes from studies in adults showing that discrete lesions to the hippocampus and surrounding MTL regions result in profound deficits in memory performance (e.g., Mishkin & Appenzeller, 1987; Scoville & Milner, 1957). Fortunately, isolated lesions to these regions are not common in human infants. Nevertheless, the prolonged immaturity of these

73

structures during the perinatal period makes them vulnerable to abnormalities in the fetal environment (see Bachevalier, 2001 and Seress, 2001 for review of hippocampal development in nonhuman and human primates, respectively). Following this line of reasoning, it is hypothesized that infants whose brains develop in an abnormal prenatal milieu may experience perturbations in the development of these neural structures, which could ultimately result in impairments in memory ability later in life. One example of such an abnormal prenatal environment is the one that accompanies the diabetic pregnancy.

In the United States, approximately 3–10% of pregnancies are complicated by abnormal glycemic control (Nold & Georgieff, 2004; US Food & Drug Administration, 2004). Of these, 80% are caused by gestational (as opposed to pregestational) diabetes mellitus, a figure that is expected to rise significantly in coming years as the current overweight pediatric population enters into their child-bearing years (Nold & Georgieff, 2004). The prenatal environment that accompanies the diabetic pregnancy is characterized by several chronic metabolic insults that can affect fetal brain health, including hyperglycemia, iron deficiency, and hypoxemia (i.e., insufficient oxygenation of the blood). Clinical conditions resulting from multiple metabolic abnormalities are rarely pure events and in fact multiple pathways exist through which maternal diabetes results in alterations to the general fetal metabolic milieu. One such pathway is as follows: pregnancy increases insulin requirements due to the increased production of hormones. In up to 10% of women, this increased insulin need is not met, resulting in "gestational diabetes" characterized by maternal hyperglycemia (i.e., high levels of glucose in the expectant mother's blood). This excess glucose passes easily through the placenta and causes the fetus to become hyperglycemic as well. Hyperglycemia can cause the fetus to become chronically hypoxemic (or oxygen deficient in the blood), which can stimulate available fetal iron to be shunted away from the brain and into the red blood cells (to compensate for the low oxygen environment; Georgieff et al., 1990; Georgieff, Schmidt, Mills, Radmer, & Widness, 1992). In addition, hyperglycemia can result in the fetus releasing its own insulin, which in turn may drive the fetal blood sugar to abnormally low values, particularly if the mother's blood sugar is rapidly lowered. Thus, through this and other pathways, gestational diabetes may result in fetal hyperglycemia/hypoglycemia, chronic hypoxemia, and iron deficiency (see Nold & Georgieff, 2004, for a comprehensive review).

Each of these chronic metabolic abnormalities has been shown to be a risk factor for the developing brain (e.g., Beard, 2008; Hawdon, 1999; Lozoff & Georgieff, 2006; Malone, Hanna, & Saporta, 2006; Malone et al., 2008; Rao et al., in press; Volpe, 2001; Widness et al., 1981). Their combined and cascading effects during the diabetic pregnancy have been shown to alter fetal and postnatal physical development (as reflected by increased rates of macrosomia or large birth weight), motor development (as reflected by increased jitteriness, lethargy, and movement disorders), and cognitive development. For example, early reports on the cognitive outcome of infants of diabetic mothers (IDMs) by Rizzo and colleagues (Rizzo, Metzger, Burns, & Burns, 1991; Rizzo, Metzger, Dooley, & Cho, 1997) documented an inverse correlation between maternal lipid and glucose metabolism measures obtained late in the diabetic pregnancy and IQ scores as well as measures of cognitive functioning in middle to late childhood. Moreover, these findings suggested that the severity of diabetes during pregnancy was directly related to long-term cognitive risk: the more unregulated the diabetic condition the worse the cognitive outcomes. More recent data have also suggested that the diabetic pregnancy increases risk for major disorders of cognition, such as schizophrenia, up to sevenfold in children (Cannon, Jones, & Murray, 2002; Van Lieshout & Voruganti, 2008). These findings not only highlight the severity of outcomes that are associated with the diabetic pregnancy, but also their persistent effects throughout the lifespan.

Severity of diabetes during pregnancy is tightly linked with the severity of the metabolic risk factors described above (fetal iron deficiency, hypoxemia, and glucose abnormalities). Therefore, the specific effects of each factor on neurologic development are difficult to tease apart in human studies of maternal diabetes. Yet, because effects do differ, it is reasonable to suggest that certain cognitive deficits observed in IDMs (e.g., cognitive impairment) are due to alterations in specific brain regions (e.g., hippocampus) brought about by particular abnormalities in the fetal environment (e.g., iron deficiency). For example, Tamura *et al.* (2002) have shown that impairments in cognitive performance is driven by fetal iron deficiency, as newborn measures of reduced fetal iron stores are associated with diminished IQ scores at school age (cf. Lucas, Morley, & Cole, 1988; Stevens, Raz, & Sander, 1999). Similarly, in a recent large cohort study, maternal iron deficiency during gestation was associated with increased risk of schizophrenia in offspring in a dose-dependent manner (Insel, Schaefer, McKeague, Susser, & Brown, 2008).

Due to enhanced experimental control, data from rodent models have been more successful in linking individual risk factors with specific outcomes. As mentioned above, the hippocampus and surrounding regions exhibit protracted development during the prenatal period; thus, this region may be especially vulnerable to disruption during development. Data from rodents (Carlson *et al.*, 2009; de Ungria *et al.*, 2000; Jorgenson, Wobken, & Georgieff, 2003; Rao, Tkac, Townsend, Gruetter, &

Georgieff, 2003) support this argument and indicate that prenatal iron deficiency *selectively* damages the hippocampal structure (in the areas of the dentate gyrus, CA1 and CA3c) and alters cellular processes as well (e.g., long-term potentiation from CA1: see Jorgenson, Wobken, & Georgieff, 2004). It also suppresses the expression of brain-derived neurotrophic factor (BDNF) not only during the period of iron deficiency but also in adulthood, long after complete iron repletion (Tran, Carlson, Fretham, & Georgieff, 2008; Tran, Fretham, Carlson, & Georgieff, 2009). BDNF is critical for the neural proliferation, differentiation, and synaptic plasticity in the hippocampus. Iron deficiency also significantly alters gene expression, particularly of those genes involved in synaptogenesis and dendritic structure during the period of hippocampal differentiation and in adulthood (Carlson, Stead, Neal, Petryk, & Georgieff, 2007). Finally, the effects of prenatal iron deficiency have been observed at the behavioral level on tasks known to be mediated by the hippocampus (e.g., swim distance on the Morris water maze and radial arm maze behavior; Felt & Lozoff, 1996; Schmidt, Waldow, Salinas, & Georgieff, 2004, respectively).

These effects of iron deficiency are exacerbated if the animal is also hypoxemic (Rao *et al.*, 1999), which is the case in the intrauterine environment of IDMs. Hypoxic–ischemic events that arise early in development have been shown to independently alter metabolic activity in the hippocampus (using cytochrome oxidase; Nelson & Silverstein, 1994) and the distribution of iron-binding protein (ferritin), ultimately delaying the appearance of myelin in the brain (Cheepsunthorn, Palmer, Menzies, Roberts, & Connor, 2001; see also Nyakas, Buwalda, & Luiten, 1996). Hypoglycemia has been found to alter the hippocampus in the perinatal rat pup (e.g., Barks, Sun, Malinak, & Silverstein, 1995) with rapidly proliferating areas being particularly at risk (i.e., CA1, and LTP, in the perinate and the dentate gyrus in the adult, see Yamada *et al.*, 2004). Thus, the protracted and complex development of the hippocampus may make it a primary target for metabolically based disruption of structure and function in IDMs.

In summary, due to the fact that the hippocampus is (a) necessary for memory performance, and (b) may be selectively at risk for perturbations in development when exposed to the abnormal prenatal environment that characterizes the diabetic pregnancy, we hypothesized that IDMs would show deficits in performance on declarative memory tasks that cannot be accounted for by general cognitive impairments. To explore this hypothesis, in our investigation we utilized two measures of memory: (a) recall as measured by behavioral imitation in the elicited/deferred imitation paradigm, and (b) recognition as measured by electrophysiological responses recorded at the scalp to familiar and novel stimuli.

The data for this report are from an ongoing longitudinal investigation examining the long-term impact of the abnormal prenatal environment experienced by IDMs on the developing brain and memory performance (see DeBoer, Wewerka, Bauer, Georgieff, & Nelson, 2005; deRegnier, Nelson, Thomas, Wewerka, & Georgieff, 2000; Georgieff, Wewerka, Nelson, & deRegnier, 2002; Nelson *et al.*, 2000; Nelson, Wewerka, Borscheid, deRegnier, & Georgieff, 2003; Riggins, Miller, Bauer, Georgieff, & Nelson, 2009a for previous reports on this sample). We present data from infants at 12 and 24 months of age. At both assessments, the IDM and control groups participated in three imitation tasks measuring declarative memory via behavior (i.e., immediate recall, 10-min delayed recall, and interleaved presentation). After a 1-week delay, participants returned to the laboratory and measures of recognition memory for one familiar sequence and one novel sequence were recorded via infants' electrophysiological responses to pictures of these stimuli (i.e., event-related potentials or ERPs).

Previous research utilizing ERPs has defined two components in the electrophysiological response that reflect aspects of long-term visual recognition memory (Bauer *et al.*, 2006; Bauer, Wiebe, Carver, Waters, & Nelson, 2003; Carver, Bauer, & Nelson, 2000; Lukowski *et al.*, 2005). These components have been shown to correlate with behavioral recall in both younger infants and older children (Bauer *et al.*, 2003, 2006; Carver *et al.*, 2000; Riggins, Miller, Bauer, Georgieff, & Nelson, 2009b). The first component (referred to as the Nc) is a deflection in the waveform that occurs approximately 400–800 ms after stimulus onset (Courchesne, Ganz, & Norcia, 1981; Nelson, 1994). Typically, this deflection is maximally negative at frontal and central midline leads and thus has been termed the "negative central component" or "Nc" (Nelson, 1994). Reports suggest that when using an average reference this deflection appears positive at lateral-posterior sites, although it has not yet been established whether this activity originates in the same cortical areas as the anterior-based Nc (Bauer *et al.*, 2006; Lukowski *et al.*, 2005). The Nc is thought to reflect attentional processes that are modulated by memory (Carver *et al.*, 2000; Courchesne *et al.*, 1981; de Haan & Nelson, 1997; Nelson, 1994; Nelson, Henschel, & Collins, 1993; Richards, 2003) and originate in regions in the frontal cortex (e.g., the anterior cingulate; Reynolds & Richards, 2005), with larger deflections indicating greater allocation of attention (Nelson *et al.*, 1993). The Nc is typically followed by slow wave activity, which is the second component of interest. This component is represented by a diffuse deflection in the waveform following the presentation of an event or stimulus, and is thought to reflect continued cognitive processing of the stimulus (e.g., memory updating; de Haan & Nelson, 1997; see also de Haan, 2007; DeBoer et al., 2005 for further discussion).

The combined use of behavioral assessments of recall (via elicited or deferred imitation paradigms) and electrophysiological assessments of recognition memory (via ERPs) allows for a unique glimpse into the processes underlying memory performance in preverbal infants and children. Whereas the elicited imitation paradigm allows for an assessment of behavioral recall (Bauer & Mandler, 1992), ERPs allow for recording of the spatiotemporal distribution of neural events during stimulus processing (i.e., recognition memory; DeBoer et al., 2005; Nelson & Monk, 2001). Thus, the fusion of these two techniques begins to address the neurological underpinnings of memory development that are grounded in observable behavior. This methodological approach was utilized in the present report to explore whether, relative to a control group, IDMs' declarative memory abilities are impaired in the first and second years of life.

II. Method

A. PARTICIPANTS

Pregnant women were recruited at approximately 28 weeks gestation from hospitals in Minneapolis/St. Paul metropolitan region. Infants delivered at 32 weeks gestation or greater (as determined by maternal dates or by first trimester ultrasound) and who had a 5-min Apgar scores equal to or greater than 6 were included. At the time of delivery, infants were assessed for signs of iron deficiency via cord serum ferritin concentrations and exposure to hypoxemia and hyperinsulinemia via neonatal macrosomia.[1] Infants with ferritin levels less than 76 µg/L were considered iron deficient during the fetal period (Tamura et al., 2002), infants with levels less than 35 µg/L were considered deficient in brain iron stores during the fetal period (Siddappa et al., 2004), and infants whose birth weight z-scores were greater than 2 standard deviations above the population mean were considered at risk for chronic fetal hypoxemia and hyperinsulinemia.

---

[1]Since red blood cell counts are directly correlated with lack of maternal glycemic control and size for dates in both IDM and non-IDM infants, birth weight z-scores were used as a separate index of fetal risk exposure (see Akin et al., 2002; Green et al., 1992; Morris et al., 1985).

The sample reported on in this chapter consists of 70 infants (51 controls [26 female] and 19 IDMs [11 female]) of which 1% were Asian American, 4% were African American, 3% were Hispanic or Latino, and 91% were Caucasian. Due to the overlap between participants tested at both 12 and 24 months (i.e., 38 children, or 54%, contributed data at both sessions), group characteristics are presented for the entire sample, followed by empirical data from each age group (see summary in Table I).

1. Gestational Age

Each infant was delivered at 32 weeks gestation or more; however, there were differences between gestational ages in the final sample reported in this publication. On average, infants in the IDM group were born earlier ($M = 38$, $SD = 2$ weeks) than infants in the control group ($M = 39$, $SD = 1$ week), $F(1, 68) = 11.73$, $p < .01$. Given that optimal management of the diabetic pregnancy is to deliver between 37 and 38 weeks due to the increased risk of fetal death late in gestation (i.e., after 38 weeks; Lucas, 2001; Nold & Georgieff, 2004), this difference is not surprising. However, because performance on the elicited imitation task may vary as a function of premature birth (e.g., 27–34 weeks; see Chapter 5; de Haan, Bauer, Georgieff, & Nelson, 2000), gestational age was entered as a covariate in all analyses of elicited and deferred imitation performance in an attempt to statistically control for these effects.

2. Prenatal Iron Status

Immediately following delivery, cord blood serum was obtained, centrifuged, and frozen at $-80\,^{\circ}\text{C}$ until assayed for ferritin concentration. To determine if the two groups (control group $n = 40$, IDM group $n = 18$) were different in iron status at birth, a one-way analysis of variance (ANOVA) was computed on newborn serum ferritin levels with group (IDM, control) as the between-subjects factor. There were no differences between the control ($M = 140$, $SD = 82$) and IDM ($M = 104$, $SD = 114$) groups' newborn mean ferritin levels ($p = .18$). However, 50% (9/18) of the infants in the IDM group had newborn ferritin levels ≤ 76 µg/L compared to 20% (9/40) of infants in the control group; thus, significantly more infants in the IDM group were considered "iron deficient" than controls in the prenatal period, $\chi^2(1, N = 58) = 5.39$, $p < .05$. In addition, 44% (8/18) of the infants in the IDM group had newborn ferritin concentrations ≤ 35 µg/L compared to only 5% (2/40) of infants in the control group; thus, more infants in the IDM group experienced "brain iron deficiency" compared to controls, $\chi^2(1, N = 58) = 13.54$, $p < .001$.

Table I
Summary of Group Characteristics for the Control and IDM Groups

	Control			IDM			Statistics
	M	SD	n	M	SD	n	
Gestational age (weeks)	39	1	51	38	2	19	$F(1, 68) = 11.73, p < .01$
Birth weight (g)	3587.67	493.41	51	3757.67	863.84	19	ns
Birth weight z-score	.56	.97	51	1.85	2.07	19	$F(1, 68) = 12.76, p < .01$
Macrosomic	8% (4/51)			47% (9/19)			$\chi^2(1, N = 70) = 14.30, p < .001$
(bw z-score > 2)							
Newborn ferritin (µg/L)	140	82	40	104	114	18	ns
Iron deficient <76 µg/L	20% (8/40)			50% (9/18)			$\chi^2(1, N = 58) = 5.39, p < .05$
Brain iron deficient <35 µg/L	5% (2/40)			44% (8/18)			$\chi^2(1, N = 58) = 13.54, p < .001$
Postnatal ferritin (µg/L)	55	36.04	11	47.8	25.48	5	ns
12 Month MDI	103	9	49	96	8	17	$F(1, 64) = 6.37, p < .05$
12 Month PDI	100	15	49	95	18	16	ns
30 Month MDI	102	12	44	93	13	11	$F(1, 53) = 4.41, p < .05$
30 Month PDI	98	12	43	92	15	11	ns
Age at 12 month EI (days)	369	11	29	371	12	14	ns
Age at 24 month EI (days)	726	14	50	731	14	15	ns

ns = not significant, MDI = Bayley Scales of Infant Development, Mental Developmental Index, PDI = Bayley Scales of Infant Development, Physical Developmental Index, EI = Elicited Imitation assessment.

3. Postnatal Assessments

In order to determine whether the low iron status was pervasive across the first year of life, a follow-up measure of iron status was also obtained between 6- and 12-months of age by the infant's primary care provider. Eleven of the control participants ($M = 55$ μg/L, SD $= 36$ μg/L) and 5 of the IDM participants ($M = 48$ μg/L, SD $= 26$ μg/L) contributed data for this measure. At the postnatal follow-up assessment, iron status did not differ between the groups ($p = .70$). All infants, regardless of group status, had ferritin concentrations within the normal range (range 21–143 μg/L). Thus, if iron deficiency occurred prenatally, it was resolved by the end of the first year of life. This finding of postnatal iron sufficiency following prenatal iron deficiency due to experience of a diabetic fetal milieu is consistent with the follow-up of newborn iron deficiency reported for the larger longitudinal group from which this subsample was derived (Georgieff *et al.*, 2002), and suggests that any differences found in the current investigation related to iron status are not due to ongoing nutrient deficits during the postnatal period, but rather are residua of previous deficits.

4. Prenatal Hypoxemia, Hyperglycemia, and Reactive Hypoglycemia

To determine if the two groups differed in weight at birth, a one-way ANOVA with group (IDM, control) as the between-subjects factor was computed on birth weight z-scores. The IDM group's mean standardized birth weight score ($M = 1.85$, SD $= 2.07$) was significantly greater than that of the control group ($M = .56$, SD $= .97$, $F(1, 68) = 12.76$, $p < .01$). Whereas only 8% (4/51) of the control participants had a birth weight z-score greater than 2 standard deviations above the population mean, 47% (9/19) of the infants in the IDM group had birth weight z-scores greater than 2 standard deviations above the mean. Therefore infants in the IDM group were suspected to have experienced risk factors such as hypoxemia (Akin *et al.*, 2002; Georgieff *et al.*, 1990; Green, Khoury, & Mimouni, 1992; Morris, Grandis, & Litton, 1985) or hyperinsulinemia (Schwartz & Teramo, 2000) significantly more often than controls during the prenatal period, $\chi^2(1, N = 70) = 14.30$, $p < .001$.

5. Summary of Sample Characteristics

In sum, although the IDM group as a whole was exposed to greater risk prenatally than the control group (as indexed by neonatal serum ferritin concentrations and macrosomia), these risk factors did not always apply at the level of the individual. Diabetes during gestation is a highly variable condition and the sample included in the present report reflects the wide spectrum of disease severity commonly found in maternal–infant pairs. Therefore, estimates of group differences in our sample will be conservative due to the heterogeneous risk profile of the IDM group. Given that our sample accurately reflects variability in the population, the current report is well suited to address the impact of the average range of metabolic fetal milieu associated with the diabetic pregnancy and our findings can be generalized to the greater population.

B. ASSESSMENTS

1. Bayley Scales of Infant Development

The Bayley Scales of Infant Development, second edition (BSID-II), were administered at 12 months ($n = 66$; $M = 12$ months, 4 days, SD = 42 days) and/or 30 months of age ($n = 55$; $M = 30$ months, 10 days, SD = 17 days). There were no differences between the groups at the age of test ($ps > .25$).

To investigate possible group differences in general cognitive functioning, two separate univariate ANOVAs were conducted on the mental development index (MDI) and physical development index (PDI) scores for both the 12- and 30-month assessments. Although the PDI did not differ between the groups at 12 or 30 months of age ($p = .26$ and $.13$, respectively), the MDI score, which is thought to index general cognitive abilities, did differ between the two groups at both 12 and 30 months of age. At 12 months of age, although both the control and IDM group's mean score fell well within the bounds of the population standard norms (100 ± 15), the control group's score ($M = 103$, SD = 9) was significantly greater than that of the IDM group ($M = 96$, SD = 8), $F(1, 64) = 6.37$, $p < .05$. Similarly, at 30 months of age, both groups' mean MDI score was within the normal range, yet the control group's score ($M = 102$, SD = 12) was significantly greater than that of the IDMs ($M = 93$, SD = 13), $F(1, 53) = 4.41$, $p < .05$.

2. 12-Month-Old Imitation

A total of 43 infants (29 control, 14 IDM) participated at the 12-month assessment. For the declarative memory tasks: 41 infants (28 control, 13 IDM) contributed data to the immediate recall task, 39 infants (27 control, 12 IDM) contributed data to the 10-min delayed recall task, and 41 infants contributed data to the interleaved presentation task (27 controls, 14 IDMs). Missing data were attributable to video equipment failure ($n = 2$) and experimenter error ($n = 2$). Mean corrected age (i.e., based on due date) at the first testing session was approximately 12 months

(370 ± 11 days; range 350–398); there were no differences between the groups in age at time of test ($p = .64$).

After a 1-week delay ($M = 7$ days, SD $= 1$), infants returned to the laboratory for the electrophysiological recording. There were no differences between the groups in length of delay ($p = .71$). A total of 14 infants (7 control, 7 IDM) provided artifact-free data at the 12-month ERP session; reasons for missing data were refusal to wear the cap ($n = 4$), too few artifact-free trials ($n = 23$), or families missed the session ($n = 2$). Such attrition is consistent with previous reports of ERP research with infants (e.g., Nelson *et al.*, 1993, see also DeBoer *et al.*, 2005) and no differences were suspected between infants who provided artifact-free data and infants who did not (see Gunnar & Nelson, 1994).

3. 24-Month-Old Imitation

A total of 65 children (50 control, 15 IDM) participated at the 24-month assessment. For the declarative memory tasks: 59 children (44 controls, 15 IDMs) contributed data to the immediate and 10-min delayed recall tasks, and 58 children contributed data to the interleaved presentation task (43 controls, 15 IDMs). Missing data ($n = 6$) were again attributable to random factors unrelated to group characteristics. The mean corrected age at the first testing session was 24 months ($M = 24$ months, 7 days, SD $= 14$ days; range 23 months 11 days–25 months 15 days); there were no differences in age at test between the groups ($p = .30$).

After a 1-week delay ($M = 7$, SD $= 1$), children returned to the laboratory for the electrophysiological recording. There were no differences between the groups in length of delay ($p = .63$). A total of 17 children (9 control, 8 IDM) provided artifact-free data at the 24-month ERP session; reasons for missing data were refusal to wear the cap ($n = 9$), too few artifact-free trials ($n = 25$), unacceptable reference recording ($n = 4$), or artifact contaminated data due to excessive eye and/or muscle movement ($n = 10$).

4. Longitudinal Sample

A total of 38 participants (28 controls [16 female], 10 IDMs [6 female]) contributed data at both the 12- and 24-month sessions. Infants did not contribute data to the 12-month session due to the following circumstances: funding not being available at time of test ($n = 23$), families missed the session ($n = 2$), or data were yet not available for analysis at the time of this report ($n = 2$). Participants did not contribute data to the 24-month session because families missed the session ($n = 1$), dropped out of the study ($n = 3$), or the infants were too young for the assessment at the time of this report ($n = 1$).

C. MATERIALS

Each event sequence consisted of target actions (two actions for 12 month olds, four actions for 24 month olds) that produced an interesting and desirable end state (e.g., turning on a light; see Appendix and Bauer, Wenner, Dropik, & Wewerka, 2000; Carver & Bauer, 1999, 2001 for examples). Event sequences for each participant were randomly selected from an existing pool containing 11 different two-step event sequences and eight different four-step event sequences (see Appendix). All events were constrained by enabling relations. The event sequences were counterbalanced across tasks and participants; thus, in the final sample each sequence occurred with equal probability in each task.

Stimuli used during ERP testing were digitized pictures of each target action of the old/familiar event (i.e., one event sequence from the elicited imitation observed at the first laboratory session 1-week prior) and a new event (i.e., one sequence the infant had not seen previously). In addition, pictures of the end state of the correctly completed actions were also shown for the two-step events. The sequences were counterbalanced across participants; thus, each sequence had equal probability of being seen as the familiar and novel stimuli across the participants.

D. DESIGN AND PROCEDURE

At both the 12- and 24-month sessions, participants visited the laboratory for three testing sessions that lasted approximately 1 h each. The first session consisted of a warm-up period followed by the imitation paradigm during which measures of immediate recall, 10-min delayed recall, and interleaved presentation performance were obtained. In the immediate and 10-min delayed recall tasks a baseline phase was completed, then the target actions (accompanied by verbal labels) for a given event sequence were modeled two times in immediate succession and infants are allowed to imitate (either immediately or after a delay[2]). Alternatively, in the interleaved presentation version of the task, the target actions (and verbal labels) of one event sequence were presented

[2]The delay period of the deferred imitation task was "filled;" that is, during the delay infants participated in the baseline and imitation phases of the immediate imitation task. A filled delay was used for two reasons: first, it mimics real world experience where intervening events between encoding and retrieval are quite common and second, previous research has suggested performance on tasks with filled and unfilled delays does not differ significantly (Bauer, Van Abbema, & de Haan, 1999).

interspersed with steps from another event sequence. After this inter-leaved demonstration of both sequences, the infants were given the props for each sequence for imitation in turn (see Bauer, 2004; Bauer & Starr, 2003 for further elaboration). Performance on two different sequences was recorded for each of the three tasks and averaged together in order to obtain the dependent measure of recall.

As in previous research, the baseline phase served as a control for gen-eral problem solving skills or fortuitous production of the event sequences (e.g., Bauer *et al.*, 2000). No baseline measure was used in the interleaved task due to the fact it is an analog to a working memory task and the cog-nitive processes of interest were the binding and integration of the infor-mation over time (Bauer, 2004). If the elements of the sequence had been presented in advance of modeling, one could not have been certain that the processes were carried out during modeling. Therefore, baseline measures from the immediate and 10-min delayed recall tasks were used in lieu of an actual baseline measure with the interleaved sequences. (Specific event sequences for each task were similar in difficulty and counterbalanced across participants; thus, each sequence occurred with equal probability in each task, again validating the use of the baseline measures from four sequences as representative of overall baseline performance.)

After a 1-week delay, infants returned to the laboratory for the electro-physiological recording during which they viewed randomly presented pictures of one familiar and one novel event sequence from the immediate imitation task. Infants wore nylon Electrocaps$^{X\copyright}$ that were held in place via Velcro straps tucked under their chins (Figure 1) and were tested while seated on their caregivers' laps approximately 75 cm from a com-puter screen in a dimly lit room. The screen was set within a black barrier so that infants could only view a portion of the room during testing. A maximum of 100 trials were presented to the 12-month-old infants and a maximum of 120 trials were presented to the 24 month olds in a fixed random order with each picture occurring an equal number of times during an individual session.

Data were recorded from multiple scalp electrodes (at both ages: Fz, Cz, Pz, F3, F4, F7, F8, FC5, FC6, C3, C4, CP1, CP2, CP5, CP6, P3, P4, T3, T4, T5, T6, O1, and O2; at 12 months only: AF3, AF4; at 24-months only: PO3, PO4, PO7, PO8) placed according to the modified interna-tional 10–20 system (Jasper, 1958), two electro-ocular electrodes placed in a transverse position above and below the eye, and two mastoid electrodes affixed via foam adhesive pads. Electrodes were filled with a conductive gel and a mildly abrasive cleanser was used to ensure that impedances were generally below 10 kΩ. EEG signals were recorded

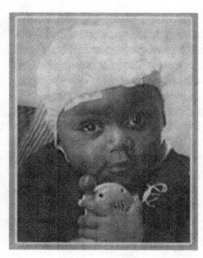

Fig. 1. Example of the EEG recording cap on a 12-month-old infant.

using a Grass Neurodata Acquisition System with Model 12A5 amplifiers. EEG gain was set at 20,000 and EOG gain was set at 5000. Bandpass filters were set between .1 and 30 Hz and a notch filter was set at 60 Hz. Each trial consisted of a 100 ms baseline followed by stimulus presentation for 500 ms and data were recorded for 1200 ms after the end of the stimulus presentation. Throughout the recording epoch, EEG was sampled every 10 ms (100 Hz) referenced to Cz. The intertrial interval varied randomly between 500 and 1000 ms, including the 100 ms baseline of the following stimulus.

On the third visit to the laboratory (at 12 and/or 30 months of age), participants were administered BSID-II.

One of three experienced researchers conducted each imitation session and one of two researchers with clinical experience conducted each Bayley Scales assessment. Imitation sessions were recorded via videotape and coded offline by experienced coders who were unaware of the hypothesis of the investigation; reliability was established.

E. SCORING

1. Imitation Task Data

The imitation tasks were scored as described in Chapter 2. Two different dependent measures were derived: (a) the number of individual target actions produced, and (b) the number of pairs of actions produced in the target order (referred to as ordered recall). For a two-step sequence, the maximum number of target actions was two and maximum number of pairs of target actions in the correct order was one. For a four-step sequence, the maximum number of target actions was four and maximum number of pairs of target actions in the correct order was three. Data were derived by taking the average performance of target actions and pairs of target actions in the correct order on the two different sequences for each task (immediate, 10-min delayed, and interleaved). To facilitate comparisons across age groups proportions are reported.

2. ERP Data

The ERP data were rereferenced offline using an average reference technique for the 12-month-old data (following the procedures outlined in Bauer *et al.*, 2006) and a mathematically linked mastoid reference for the 24-month data (as outlined in Carver *et al.*, 2000).[3] Averages for each condition (familiar/novel) were obtained for each participant, with the constraint that an equal number of trials were included for each condition. Trials were excluded if the EEG signal exceeded analog to digital values ($\pm 150 \, \mu V$) in any 100 ms window, or if the EOG signal changed more than 250 μV in any 100 ms window. Consistent with previous research, zero bad electrode channels were allowed during the cross-averaging of the 12-month-old data due to use of the average reference (Bauer *et al.*, 2006); data were accepted in the 24-month-old group if fewer than 10% of the channels were missing due to artifacts. The averaged waveforms were then visually inspected to exclude data contaminated by EOG or movement artifact. Grand means were created from the uncontaminated data for each group of infants (i.e., control and IDM) for each event type (i.e., familiar and novel). There were no group differences in the number of trials for either the 12-month (control: $M = 18$, SD $= 6$; IDM: $M = 14$, SD $= 8$, $p = .34$) or 24-month groups (control: $M = 38$, SD $= 13$; IDM: $M = 30$, SD $= 15$, $p = .29$).

---

[3]Due to an amplifier problem, data were lost that precluded us from using a mastoid reference in the 12-month-old sample. The focus of the present report is on differences between groups within each age group and no between age group comparisons will be made. We are aware of no data that indicate the influence of different reference configurations on Nc and slow wave components examined in this report.

III. Results

A. IMITATION

1. Baseline Measures at 12 and 24 Months of Age

To rule out possible influences of general problem solving skills on recall, univariate analyses of covariance (ANCOVAs) were calculated for target actions and pairs of actions in target order at the baseline assessment for both the immediate and 10-min delayed recall tasks with gestational age as the covariate for each age group (see Tables II and III, Panel A for descriptive statistics). No group differences were expected on the baseline measures since baseline measures are thought to index problem solving abilities and not memory processes *per se*. None of the analyses yielded significant main effects, indicating that there were no differences between the groups' performance on target actions or pairs of actions during the baseline phase at either 12 or 24 months of age. Consequently, variation in recall abilities between the groups cannot be solely accounted for by differences in problem solving skills or willingness and ability to interact with the props.

2. 12-Month Imitation Data[4]

Univariate ANCOVAs were calculated for target actions and ordered pairs of actions for the immediate, 10-min delayed, and interleaved presentation tasks with gestational age as a covariate (see Table II for descriptive statistics). Although there were no differences in performance on the immediate or interleaved presentation tasks, there were differences between the two groups' performance on the 10-min delayed recall task. Specifically, there were differences between the groups' recall of individual target actions, $F(1, 36) = 3.26$, $p = .079$, and recall of pairs of target actions in the correct order, $F(1, 36) = 6.59$, $p < .05$. Thus, when a 10-min delay was imposed, the IDM group produced fewer actions and these actions were less well organized compared to the control group.

To address the question as to whether these observed impairments were specific to memory performance or whether they could be accounted for by deficits in general cognitive abilities, we analyzed the data using both gestational age and MDI scores as covariates. When these scores were used to statistically control for differences in general cognitive abilities

---

[4]Findings for a subset of the sample presented in this chapter can be found in DeBoer, Wewerka, *et al.*, 2005; however, both reports indicate similar results regarding imitation performance.

Table II

Descriptive Statistics of Proportions of Target Actions and Pairs of Actions at Baseline
(A) and Recall (B) for Control and IDM Groups at 12 Months of Age

| | | Measure | | | |
| | | Target Actions | | Pairs of Actions Ordered Recall | |
Condition/Group		Mean	SD	Mean	SD
Panel A: baseline					
Immediate	Control	.27	.18	.04	.13
	IDM	.31	.25	.04	.14
10-min Delayed	Control	.31	.22	.06	.16
	IDM	.25	.27	.04	.14
Panel B: recall					
Immediate	Control	.68	.27	.45	.34
	IDM	.52	.33	.27	.39
10-min Delayed	Control	.53[†]	.29	.28*	.32
	IDM	.40[†]	.25	.08*	.19
Interleaved	Control	.56	.26	.24	.29
	IDM	.48	.23	.11	.21

[†] Denotes $p \le .10$; * denotes $p \le .05$.

and gestational age, performance of target actions was no longer different between the two groups ($p = .26$). However, group differences in ordered recall remained marginally lower in the IDM group, $F(1, 34) = 3.86$, $p = .06$. This suggests that impaired recall in the IDM group relative to the control group when a 10-min delay was imposed is not solely attributable to differences in general cognitive abilities or gestational age, but represents a specific deficit in memory (see DeBoer, Wewerka, *et al.*, 2005 for a similar finding).

To explore associations between characteristics of the prenatal environment and differences in behavioral recall, a series of correlational analyses were conducted between perinatal measures (i.e., ferritin, birth weight z-scores, gestational age) and the number of pairs of actions recalled after the 10-min delay. Only newborn ferritin levels were related to memory performance: lower iron stores predicted recall of fewer pairs of actions, $r(37) = .27, p = .08$.

3. 12-Month ERP Data and Relations with Imitation Data

In this section, results are organized by ERP components of interest (Nc amplitude and latency, followed by slow wave) and discussion of the midline leads precedes that of the lateral leads. To examine the effect of group on electrophysiological measures of recognition memory at the mid-line leads, we conducted 2 (group: control, IDM) × 2 (event type: familiar, novel) × 3 (lead: Fz, Cz, Pz) mixed ANOVAs with repeated measures on event type and lead, for each of the three dependent variables: peak amplitude of the Nc, latency to the peak amplitude of the Nc, and area under the curve for slow wave activity. To examine the effects on recognition indices at the lateral leads, we conducted a 2 (group: control, IDM) × 2 (event type: familiar, novel) × 2 (hemisphere: left, right) × 3 (coronal plane: temporal: T5/6, parietal: P3/4, occipital: O1/2) mixed ANOVAs with repeated measures on event type, hemisphere, and coronal plane, for each of the three dependent variables: peak amplitude of the Nc, latency to peak, and area under the curve for the slow wave activity.[5] Greenhouse-Geisser and Bonferroni corrections were used when necessary. Finally, to ground findings from the electrophysiological measures in behavior and relate data from these two different assessment modalities, correlations were conducted between the imitation data (recall of target actions[6]) and the ERP data (i.e., Nc amplitude, latency, and slow wave activity for midline and lateral leads). Significant relations are reported following the discussion of each component.

4. Nc

As illustrated in Figures 2 and 3, peak amplitude of the Nc component changed polarity from negative at the anterior and central leads (Fz: $M = -9.29\,\mu V$, Cz: $M = -7.86\,\mu V$) to positive at the posterior lead (Pz: $M = 9.04\,\mu V$), as indicated by a main effect of lead, $F(2, 24) = 31.55, p < .001$.

Due to an *a priori* prediction for an effect of condition for the Nc (negative component) at frontal and central midline leads (Carver *et al.*, 2000; Bauer *et al.*, 2003), a separate 2 (group: control, IDM) × 2 (event type: familiar, novel) × 2 (lead: Fz, Cz) repeated measures ANOVAs was conducted. Amplitude to the novel stimulus ($M = -9.96\,\mu V$, SD = 1.37) was slightly greater than to the familiar stimulus ($M = -7.18\,\mu V$, SD = 1.67), $F(1, 12) = 3.10, p = .10$. Follow-up analyses using paired samples *t*-tests for both the control and IDM groups indicated that in

[5]Previous research (Stolarova *et al.*, 2003) has shown that brain responses, specifically the topography and the latency of the Nc component, of preterm infants at the age of 6 months are more similar to those of their corrected age peers than to those of the chronological age controls. However, due to the fact that all infants were tested based on their corrected age of 12 or 24 months, gestational age was not covaried in the ERP analyses.

[6]Although ordered recall of target actions (i.e., pairs of actions) was also correlated with the electrophysiological measures, these findings were largely redundant and are not reported due to space limitations.

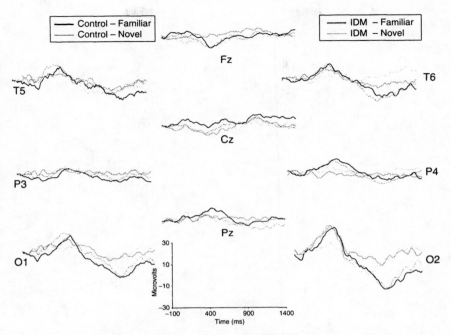

Fig. 2. Grand averaged ERPs to familiar and novel stimuli for 12-month-old control and IDM groups.

control group, Nc amplitude was significantly larger to the novel ($M = -9.29 \, \mu V$, SD = 4.15) compared to the familiar stimulus ($M = -3.14 \, \mu V$, SD = 7.34) at Cz, $t(6) = 2.76$, $p < .05$. However, for the IDM group, Nc amplitude was significantly larger to the novel ($M = -10.86 \, \mu V$, SD = 9.84) compared to the familiar stimulus ($M = -4.57 \, \mu V$, SD = 5.41) at Fz, $t(6) = 2.46$, $p < .05$; see Figure 3. These results reflect what is observed in the grand means (Figure 2) and suggest that although both groups are discriminating the novel from familiar stimuli, different patterns of activation underlie this ability in the two groups.

Interestingly, only difference scores between Nc amplitude to familiar and novel stimuli at Cz approached significance in predicting performance of target actions at immediate imitation ($r = .52$, $p = .07$); difference scores at Fz did not ($p = .72$). Greater differentiation (or a greater difference score) at Cz was positively related to performance of target actions during the immediate recall task 1-week prior (cf. Bauer *et al.*, 2003).

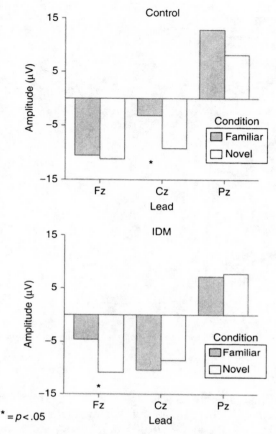

Fig. 3. *Nc amplitude to familiar and novel stimuli for 12-month-old control and IDM groups at midline leads (Fz, Cz, Pz).*

There were no significant effects for latency to peak of the Nc at the midline leads (all $ps > .16$) and no relations were found with behavioral recall.

Amplitude of the Nc component at lateral leads differed as a function of location on the scalp, as indicated by a main effect of coronal plane, $F(2, 24) = 9.57$, $p < .01$. Pairwise comparisons suggested that Nc amplitude at temporal ($M = 13.59 \mu V$, $SD = 5.47$) and occipital ($M = 17.52 \mu V$, $SD = 9.63$) electrodes was greater than the Nc amplitude at the parietal electrodes ($M = 8.34 \mu V$, $SD = 6.19$, $ps < .05$). Of particular interest, however, was the marginal 3-way group × condition × coronal plane interaction, $F(2, 24) = 3.63$, $p = .06$. Follow-up analyses indicated this interaction was driven by a group × condition interaction at the occipital leads $F(1, 12) = 5.84$, $p < .05$. As illustrated in Figure 4, when follow-up analyses were conducted by group, there was no difference between responses to the familiar and novel stimulus in the control group; however, in the IDM group, the amplitude of the Nc at occipital leads was significantly greater to the familiar stimulus ($M = 18.71$, SD $= 8.07$) than the novel stimulus ($M = 10.43$, SD $= 9.85$), $t(6) = 2.72$, $p < .05$. When the

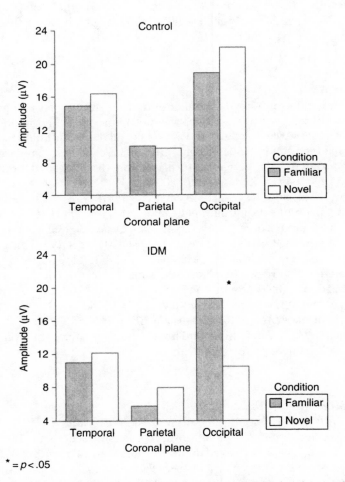

$^* = p < .05$

Fig. 4. Nc amplitude to familiar and novel stimuli in temporal, parietal, and occipital coronal planes for the control and IDM groups at 12 months of age.

follow-up analyses were conducted by event type, amplitudes to the familiar stimulus did not appear different between the IDM and control groups at the occipital leads; however, peak amplitude to the novel stimulus was significantly greater for the control group ($M = 22.0\,\mu V$, SD $= 11.0\,\mu V$) compared with that of the IDM group ($M = 10.4\,\mu V$, SD $= 9.9\,\mu V$).

Latency to peak for the Nc component at the lateral leads was marginally different as a function of coronal plane, $F(2, 24) = 3.17$, $p = .06$. Pairwise comparisons indicated that regardless of group or event type, latency to peak in the occipital leads ($M = 478.86$ ms, SD $= 68.01$) was significantly faster than latency to peak in the temporal leads ($M = 530.82$ ms, SD $= 66.35$, $p < .05$), and marginally faster than latency to peak in the parietal leads ($M = 523.68$ ms, SD $= 60.70$, $p = .06$).

5. Slow Wave

Differential processing of familiar and novel stimuli between groups, as measured by slow wave activity, was not apparent at the midline leads. However, slow wave activity at Cz was correlated with immediate imitation of target actions. Specifically, greater PSW to the familiar stimulus was associated with better performance on the immediate recall task, $r = .58$, $p = .04$ (cf. Riggins *et al.*, 2009b).

Analysis of slow wave activity at the lateral leads suggested a trend toward a main effect of group, $F(1, 12) = 3.65$, $p = .08$. The control group had greater area scores ($M = -5939.6$ ms μV, SD $= 3852.9$ ms μV) than the IDM group ($M = -1924.7$ ms μV, SD $= 4004.2$ ms μV). This group difference was significant at the occipital leads, $F(1, 12) = 5.18$, $p < .05$, as illustrated in Figure 5. There was also a main effect of coronal plane, $F(2, 24) = 5.56$, $p < .05$. Pairwise comparisons revealed that area scores at the occipital leads ($M = -6870.55$ ms μV, SD $= 6958.55$) was greater than at the parietal leads ($M = -1068.50$ ms μV, SD $= 4422.88$). Differences in slow wave activity between familiar and novel stimuli at lateral leads did not correlate with immediate recall performance ($ps > .38$).

6. 24-Month Recall Data

As with the 12-month imitation data, univariate ANCOVAs were conducted for target actions and ordered pairs of actions for the immediate, delayed, and interleaved imitation tasks at 24 months of age with gestational age as the covariate (see Table III for descriptive statistics). There were no effects of group on behavioral recall performance (all $ps > .19$).

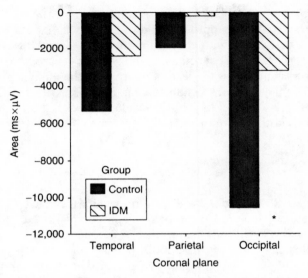

Fig. 5. *Area under the curve in temporal, parietal, and occipital coronal planes for the control and IDM groups at 12 months of age (controls > IDM, p < .05). * = p < .05.*

Table III

Descriptive Statistics of Proportions of Target Actions and Pairs of Actions at Baseline (A) and Recall (B) for Control and IDM Groups at 24 Months of Age

| | | Measure | | | |
| | | Target Actions | | Pairs of Actions Ordered Recall | |
Condition/Group		Mean	SD	Mean	SD
Panel A: baseline					
Immediate	Control	.32	.14	.08	.10
	IDM	.36	.16	.14	.17
10-min Delayed	Control	.26	.15	.07	.12
	IDM	.32	.10	.10	.08
Panel B: recall					
Immediate	Control	.86	.20	.71	.26
	IDM	.85	.19	.67	.24
10-min Delayed	Control	.83	.18	.61	.28
	IDM	.72	.27	.53	.32
Interleaved	Control	.84	.19	.64	.26
	IDM	.80	.22	.56	.29

7. 24-Month ERP Data and Relations with Imitation Data

The overall statistical approach followed for the 24-month ERP data is identical to that taken with the 12-month ERP data. However, due to slight differences in data collection for the two age groups, the vertex electrode (Cz) was entered as the lead of interest for the midline analyses and lateral lead analyses were conducted on frontal, parietal, and occipital leads (F7/8, P3/4, O1/2). As before, results involving the Nc component and relations with imitation data are presented followed by results for slow wave activity.

8. Nc

At the vertex electrode, there were no significant effects of Nc amplitude or latency. Analyses of the peak amplitude of the Nc at the lateral leads revealed a significant main effect of coronal plane, as a result of a shift in the polarity of the amplitude in this time window, $F(2, 30) = 135.81, p < .001$ (see Figures 6 and 7). Pairwise comparisons indicated that amplitude to the Nc at the frontal leads ($M = -17.92\ \mu V$, SD = 8.99) was

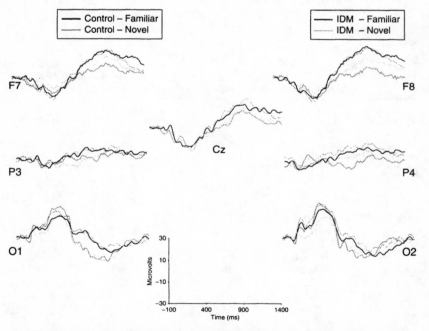

Fig. 6. Grand averaged ERPs to familiar and novel stimuli for 24-month-old control and IDM groups.

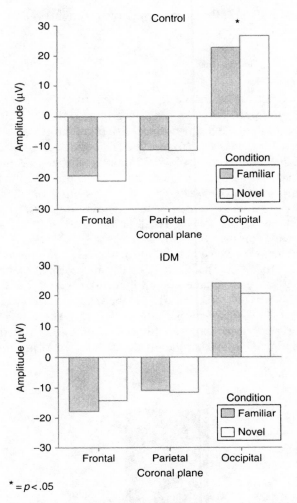

Fig. 7. *Nc amplitude to familiar and novel stimuli in temporal, parietal, and occipital coronal planes for the control and IDM groups at 24 months of age.*

different from that at the parietal leads ($M = -11.08$ µV, SD $= 8.19$; $p < .05$) and amplitude at both the frontal and parietal leads was different from that at the occipital leads ($M = 23.48$ µV, SD $= 12.04$; $ps < .001$). Of greater interest, however, was the three-way interaction between group, condition, and coronal plane, $F(2, 30) = 4.04$, $p < .05$. As illustrated in Figure 7, although the IDM group's Nc amplitude was similar for the familiar and novel stimuli over occipital leads ($p = 41$), the control group had a significantly greater peak to the novel stimulus ($M = 26.72 \, \mu V$, SD $= 7.19$) than the familiar stimulus ($M = 22.89 \, \mu V$, SD $= 7.35$), $t(8) = 3.13$, $p < .05$.

9. Slow Wave

Slow wave activity at the vertex (Cz), regardless of stimulus type, was significantly different between the two groups, $F(1, 15) = 9.34$, $p < .01$. As illustrated in Figure 8, the control group had larger area scores ($M = 9811.83 \, ms \, \mu V$, SD $= 3568.20$) than the IDM group ($M = 4632.13 \, ms \, \mu V$, SD $= 3392.70$). Similar to results at 12 months of age, at 24 months of age, slow wave activity at Cz to the familiar stimulus predicted immediate imitation of target actions ($r = .49$, $p = .05$; cf. Riggins *et al.*, 2009b). Interestingly, slow wave activity to the familiar stimulus at Cz *also* predicted recall of target actions for the delayed recall task ($r = .51$, $p < .05$) and the interleaved presentation task ($r = .61$, $p < .05$).

Finally, when slow wave activity at the lateral leads was analyzed, main effects of group, $F(1, 15) = 7.00$, $p < .05$, and coronal plane, $F(2, 30) = 37.72$, $p < .001$ were obtained (see Figure 9). Overall, the control group ($M = 4592.17 \, ms \, \mu V$, SD $= 3614.43$) had larger area scores than the IDM group ($M = -86.51 \, ms \, \mu V$, SD $= 3667.55$). There was also a reversal in polarity of slow wave in this time window: at the frontal ($M = 8398.67 \, ms \, \mu V$, SD $= 5909.56$) leads there was greater positive slow wave

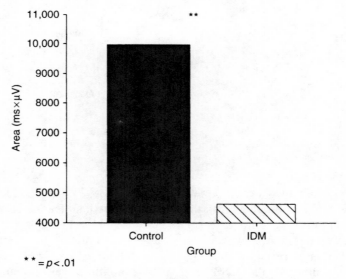

Fig. 8. *Slow wave activity at Cz for the control and IDM groups at 24 months of age.*

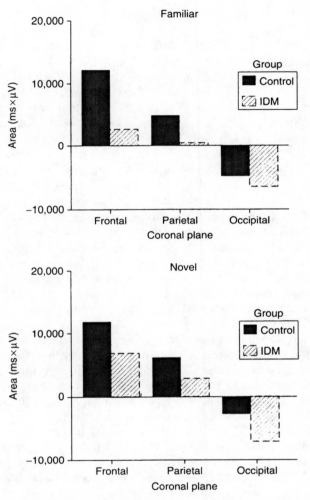

Fig. 9. Slow wave activity to the familiar and novel stimuli at frontal, parietal, and occipital lateral leads for the 24-month-old control and IDM groups (controls > IDM and frontal > parietal > occipital, p < .05).

than at the parietal ($M = 3610.44$ ms μV, SD = 5558.74) leads, and both of these were greater than the negative slow wave activity at the occipital leads ($M = -5250.63$ ms μV, SD = 5645.31; all ps < .05).

Slow wave activity to the novel stimulus for the lateral leads predicted recall of target actions at the immediate recall task, $r = .62, p < .05$ and recall of target actions for the interleaved presentation task, $r = .60, p < .05$.

IV. Discussion

At 12 months of age, IDMs differed from the control group on both measures of behavioral recall and electrophysiological indices of recognition memory. Specifically, group differences in behavioral memory measures arose when a 10-min delay was imposed before recall. Group differences in electrophysiological indices of memory arose in measures of Nc amplitude (at midline and lateral occipital leads) and measures of slow wave activity (at lateral leads). Consistent with other reports (e.g., Carver *et al.*, 2000; Lukowski *et al.*, 2005; Riggins *et al.*, 2009b), behavioral recall was related to amplitude of the Nc and slow wave activity to the familiar stimulus. Specifically, the difference in amplitude of the Nc component to the familiar and novel stimuli and slow wave activity to familiar stimuli at Cz was positively related to performance of target actions in the immediate recall task. These findings suggest that associations exist between immediate recall for target actions at Time 1 and (a) allocation of attention to the familiar and novel stimuli 1 week later (i.e., better memory performance at Time 1 was related to greater Nc amplitude differences at Time 2), and (b) memory updating to familiar stimuli (i.e., better memory performance at Time 1 was related to increased slow wave activity at Time 2).

To investigate whether these group differences persist over the first few years of life, we turn to the results from the 24-month age group. At this assessment, group differences in behavioral recall were no longer apparent on the imitation tasks. However, differences in electrophysiological measures of recognition memory remained in Nc amplitude at lateral occipital leads and slow wave activity at both midline and lateral leads. As was the case at 12 months, the number of target actions recalled in the immediate recall task at Time 1 was related to slow wave activity to the familiar stimulus at Cz at Time 2 (i.e., better memory performance at Time 1 predicted increased slow wave activity at Time 2). Thus, although there were no differences in behavioral recall of the event sequences, there were differences in electrophysiological measures of recognition memory.

These findings suggest that when paired with the imitation paradigm, ERPs may provide a sensitive measure that allows for the elucidation of differences in neural correlates of memory processes related to behavioral performance on the task. For example, this methodological combination may begin to reveal details regarding the nature of neural processes contributing to performance on this memory task. At 24 months of age, slow wave activity was not only correlated with measures of immediate recall, but was also correlated with measures of recall on the delayed recall and interleaved presentation tasks, a finding that may reflect (a) general development of the memory network, (b) changes in task demands that are not observable in behavior, or (c) a combination of the two. Although this is a question that deserves more research, there is some evidence to suggest that brain development is responsible for changes in relations between behavioral recall and electrophysiological responses (Bauer, 2006).

It is possible that variations in developmental trajectories may account for some of the observed differences between the IDM and control groups. At 12 months of age, the control group did not show evidence of differentiation between the novel and familiar stimuli at the occipital leads; however, at 24 months, the control group did show evidence of differentiation between the two classes of stimuli. Conversely, at 12 months, the IDM group did show evidence of differentiation between the familiar and novel stimuli at the occipital leads; however, the effect was in the *opposite* direction: amplitude was greater to the familiar as opposed to the novel stimulus. At the 24-month assessment, this difference disappeared and the ERP responses for the IDM group were similar to the familiar and novel stimuli. One possible interpretation: if we assume data from the control group at 12 and 24 months represent the typical developmental profile, the IDM group is following a delayed developmental trajectory (i.e., if there is a normative developmental shift from greater amplitude to familiar stimuli to greater amplitude to novel stimuli at occipital leads, the IDM group appears delayed in this transition in comparison with the control group). This developmental delay hypothesis is supported by the iron-deficient rodent data. For example, between postnatal day 15 (approximately a 2-month-old human) and at postnatal day 30 (approximately a >2-year-old human) where on certain hippocampal CA1 metrics (dendritic arborization, Jorgenson *et al.*, 2003; NR2B receptor appearance, Jorgenson *et al.*, 2003; and LTP, Jorgenson *et al.*, 2004), the iron-deficient animals show characteristics of a younger aged animal. Although early indicators suggest that they do catch up eventually, the developmental delay hypothesis is one we have been working on in the basic model, and although it remains speculative, the data generally support the concept.

One way to determine if the "developmental delay" hypothesis is correct in this case is to continue to follow the cohort over time. We recently published findings from the larger longitudinal sample when the children were approximately 42 months of age (Riggins *et al.*, 2009a, see Table IV for summary). Electrophysiological responses at occipital leads were not examined in that report, so we analyzed group differences in peak amplitude measures from that dataset (which contained 20 control

Table IV
Summary of Group Difference Findings at 12, 24, and 42 Months

	12-Month Assessment	24-Month Assessment	42-Month Assessment (Riggins *et al.*, 2009a)
Behavioral measures			
Immediate recall	None	None	IDM < control only on difficult task
Delayed recall	IDM < control	None	IDM < control only on moderate task
Interleaved presentation	None	None	n/a
Electrophysiological measures			
Nc amplitude (midline leads)	*Control:* novel > familiar at Cz *IDM:* novel > familiar at Fz	None	None
Nc amplitude (occipital leads)	*Control:* novel = familiar *IDM:* novel < familiar	*Control:* novel > familiar *IDM:* novel = familiar	None
Slow wave activity	Controls > IDMs	Controls > IDMs	Controls > IDMs

and 13 IDM participants) to familiar and novel stimuli at occipital leads (O1 and O2). There were no differences between the groups in their ERP responses to familiar and novel stimuli. Thus, perhaps by early childhood, the differential responses observed over occipital leads (possibly reflecting allocation of attentional resources) have resolved and are comparable between IDMs and controls.

Unfortunately, the same conclusion cannot be made regarding memory deficits, as group differences in memory performance were still apparent at the 42-month assessment when task demands were increased (Riggins *et al.*, 2009a). In short, using a modification of the elicited imitation paradigm, we examined the influence of task difficulty on memory performance. Difficulty was manipulated by altering the number of enabling relations between target actions; fewer enabling relations resulted in a more difficult memory task. When all relations were enabling (the easiest condition, as there was the most external "support" for successful memory performance), there were no group differences in behavioral recall (a finding similar to that at 24 months). However, when task difficulty increased, differences in behavior emerged in both immediate and delayed recall. Interestingly, as was the case at 12 months, these differences in behavioral performance were related to measures of iron stores (ferritin) assessed at birth (see Riggins *et al.*, 2009a for elaboration).

The finding of equivalent performance for sequences with the highest number of enabling relations is similar to results from the assessment at 24 months of age and suggests that with external support, memory abilities in IDMs can be brought to levels typical for the age group. However, as at both 12 and 24 months, differences in electrophysiological responses revealed that, regardless of whether behavioral performance was different or equivalent between groups, ERP indices of neural processing underlying the memory performance differed between the groups. As in the 12- and 24-month samples, slow wave activity at Cz was greater in the control compared to the IDM group (Riggins *et al.*, 2009a), and was related to behavioral performance. Thus, although imitation paradigms may provide a useful tool to examine memory performance, they may not detect subtle differences or differences in underlying processes, which may ultimately be revealed as task demands increase.

In conclusion, results from this investigation suggest that, on average, IDMs are at greater risk for memory impairment as a result of the abnormal prenatal environment in which they develop. As a group, they performed more poorly than controls on measures of behavioral recall and generated different electrophysiological response patterns to familiar and novel stimuli. Relations between these two measures support the hypothesis that the observed behavioral differences likely arise from the neural processes underlying cognitive performance and not some other noncognitive factors (e.g., temperament, willingness to imitate, etc.). However, it should be noted that considerable overlap exists between the two groups: not all IDMs performed poorly and not all controls preformed well on the behavioral and electrophysiological memory assessments. This overlap is likely the result of individual differences in the amount of risk experienced for each participant. Unfortunately, identifying damage or dysfunction in *individual* neurologically asymptomatic newborns remains challenging because the sequelae of fetal risk factors such as those that characterize the diabetic pregnancy (e.g., iron deficiency) are generally not severe enough for classic neuroimaging techniques to detect. Although the combination of behavioral and electrophysiological techniques, such as those used in the present report, may allow for some indication of early adversity, at this time outcome predictions for individual infants remain difficult. Fortunately, variations in risk do not have to be left solely to chance as preventative measures can be taken. Although differences exist between IDMs and controls in declarative memory performance, these effects appear to be titrated to the degree of metabolic regulation during the prenatal period. Thus, outcomes can be improved with proper medical care. Pregnant mothers with gestational diabetes can greatly reduce the potential risk if they are educated about their disease and take the necessary steps to better control their blood glucose levels, blood pressure, and cholesterol levels. Screening pregnant women for diabetes and iron deficiency during the last trimester and monitoring their glycemic control may greatly reduce the risk to developing memory systems.

Acknowledgments

The research reported in this chapter was supported by grants from the National Institute of Health to Charles A. Nelson (NS34458), Michael K. Georgieff (HD29421), and Patricia J. Bauer (HD28425, HD 4243); and by a grant from the NIH National Center for Research Resources (RR00400). We are grateful to the members of the Center for Neurobehavioral Development, Developmental Cognitive Neuroscience Laboratory and Cognition in the Transition Laboratory. In particular, we thank Neely Miller for comments on the chapter; Sandi Wewerka and Jennifer Haight for their assistance with data collection and coding; and the families who participated in this research. Portions of these data were presented at the biennial meeting for Society for Research in Child Development in Tampa Bay, FL, April 2003.

Appendix

Two-step sequences used at the 12-month assessment

1. "Make a Glowball"
   "Open the lid"
   "Pull out the drawer"
2. "Make a Gong"
   "Hang up the bell"
   "Ring it"
3. "Turn on the light"
   "Put in the car"
   "Push the stick"
4. "Find Bubbles"
   "Put in the block"
   "Push it in"
5. "Make a Happy Face"
   "Open the door"
   "Push in the block"

6. "Find the Bear"
   "Slide the bar"
   "Open the door"
7. "Make a Balloon"
   "Put in the balloon"
   "Press it"
8. "Make an Airplane"
   "Unfold it"
   "Fly it"
9. "Make a Rattle"
   "Cover it"
   "Shake it"
10. "Make a Jumper"
    "Push in the ball"
    "Pop it"
11. "Go for a Duck Walk"
    "Put down the ramp"
    "Go for a walk"

Four-step sequences used at the 24-month assessment

1. "Make a Rattle"
   "Put on the bottom"
   "Put in the ball"
   "Cover it up"
   "Shake it"
2. "Make a Drum"
   "Put it together"
   "Put on the bottom"
   "Put on the drum"
   "Spin it"
3. "Make a Gong"
   "Lift it up"
   "Put on the bar"
   "Hang up the bell"
   "Ring it"
4. "Make the Worms Dance"
   "Open it up"
   "Pull it out"
   "Put it in"
   "Turn it"

5. "Make a Glow Ball"
   "Put it together"
   "Put on the ring"
   "Put in the ball"
   "Go for a ride"
6. "Make a Jumper"
   "Put on the bottom"
   "Put on the top"
   "Push in the ball"
   "Make it jump"
7. "Go for a Car Ride"
   "Put on the top"
   "Stick it on"
   "Put it in"
   "Go for a ride"
8. "Go for a bug ride"
   "Open it up"
   "Put on the ramp"
   "Push it in"
   "Go for a ride"

REFERENCES

Akin, M., Ceran, O., Atay, E., Atay, Z., Akin, F., & Akturk, Z. (2002). Postpartum maternal levels of hemoglobin A1c and cord C-peptide in macrosomic infants of non-diabetic mothers. *The Journal of Maternal-Fetal & Neonatal Medicine, 12*, 274–276.

Bachevalier, J. (2001). Neural bases of memory development: Insights from neuropsychological studies in primates. In C. A. Nelson & M. Luciana (Eds.), *Handbook of developmental cognitive neuroscience* (pp. 365–379). Cambridge, MA: The MIT Press.

Barks, J. D., Sun, R., Malinak, C., & Silverstein, F. S. (1995). gp120, an HIV-1 protein, increases susceptibility to hypoglycemic and ischemic brain injury in perinatal rats. *Experimental Neurology, 132*, 123–133.

Bauer, P. J. (2004). New developments in the study of infant memory. In D. M. Teti (Ed.), *Handbook of research methods in developmental psychology* (pp. 467–488). Oxford, UK: Blackwell Publishers.

Bauer, P. J. (2006). Constructing a past in infancy: A neuro-developmental account. *Trends in Cognitive Sciences, 10*, 175–181.

Bauer, P. J., & Mandler, J. M. (1992). Putting the horse before the cart: The use of temporal order in recall of events by one-year-old children. *Developmental Psychology, 28*(3), 441–452.

Bauer, P. J., & Starr, R. M. (2003). Development of memory. In J. W. Guthrie (Ed.), *The encyclopedia of education, Vol. 5.* (2nd ed., pp. 1591–1593). New York, NY: Macmillan Reference Press.

Bauer, P. J., Van Abbema, D. L., & de Haan, M. (1999). In for the short haul: Immediate and short-term remembering and forgetting by 20-month-old children. *Infant Behavior & Development, 22*, 321–343.

Bauer, P. J., Wenner, J. A., Dropik, P., & Wewerka, S. S. (2000). Parameters of remembering and forgetting in the transition from infancy to early childhood. *Monographs for the Society for Research in Child Development, 65*(4) Serial No. 263.

Bauer, P. J., Wiebe, S. A., Carver, L. J., Lukowski, A. F., Haight, J. C., Waters, J. M., *et al.* (2006). Electrophysiological indices of encoding and behavioral indices of recall: Examining relations and developmental change late in the first year of life. *Developmental Neuropsychology, 29*, 293–380.

Bauer, P. J., Wiebe, S. A., Carver, L. J., Waters, J. M., & Nelson, C. A. (2003). Developments in long-term explicit memory late in the first year of life: Behavioral and electrophysiological indices. *Psychological Science, 14*, 629–635.

Beard, J. L. (2008). Why iron deficiency is important in infant development. *The Journal of Nutrition, 138*(12), 2534–2536.

Cannon, M., Jones, P. B., & Murray, R. M. (2002). Obstetric complications and schizophrenia: Historical and meta-analytic review. *The American Journal of Psychiatry, 159*, 1080–1092.

Carlson, E. S., Stead, J. D. H., Neal, C. R., Petryk, A., & Georgieff, M. K. (2007). Perinatal iron deficiency results in altered developmental expression of genes mediating energy metabolism and neuronal morphogenesis in hippocampus. *Hippocampus, 17*, 679–691.

Carlson, E. S., Tkac, I., Magid, R., O'Connor, M. B., Andrews, N. C., Schallert, T., *et al.* (2009). Iron is essential for neuron development and memory function in mouse hippocampus. *The Journal of Nutrition, 139*(4), 672–679.

Carver, L. J., & Bauer, P. J. (1999). When the event is more than the sum of its parts: 9-Month-olds' long-term ordered recall. *Memory, 7*(2), 147–174.

Carver, L. J., & Bauer, P. J. (2001). The dawning of a past: The emergence of long-term explicit memory in infancy. *Journal of Experimental Psychology: General, 130*, 726–745.

Carver, L. J., Bauer, P. J., & Nelson, C. A. (2000). Associations between infant brain activity and recall memory. *Developmental Science, 3*, 234–246.

Cheepsunthorn, P., Palmer, C., Menzies, S., Roberts, R. L., & Connor, J. R. (2001). Hypoxic/ischemic insult alters ferritin expression and myelination in neonatal rat brains. *The Journal of Comparative Neurology, 431*, 382–396.

Courchesne, E., Ganz, L., & Norcia, A. (1981). Event-related brain potentials to human faces in infants. *Child Development, 52*, 804–811.

DeBoer, T., Scott, L. S., & Nelson, C. A. (2005). Event-related potentials in developmental populations. In T. Handy (Ed.), *Methodological handbook for research using event-related potentials* (pp. 263–297). Cambridge, MA: The MIT Press.

DeBoer, T., Wewerka, S., Bauer, P. J., Georgieff, M. K., & Nelson, C. A. (2005). Explicit memory performance in infants of diabetic mothers at 1 year of age. *Developmental Medicine and Child Neurology, 47*, 525–531.

de Haan, M. (2007). Visual attention and recognition memory in infancy. In M. de Haan (Ed.), *Infant EEG and event-related potentials* (pp. 101–144). East Sussex: Psychology Press.

de Haan, M., Bauer, P. J., Georgieff, M. K., & Nelson, C. A. (2000). Explicit memory in low-risk infants aged 19 months born between 27–42 weeks of gestation. *Developmental Medicine and Child Neurology, 42*, 304–312.

de Haan, M., & Nelson, C. A. (1997). Recognition of the mother's face by six-month-old infants: A neurobehavioral study. *Child Development, 68*(2), 187–210.

deRegnier, R.-A., Nelson, C. A., Thomas, K., Wewerka, S., & Georgieff, M. K. (2000). Neurophysiologic evaluation of auditory recognition memory in healthy newborn infants and infants of diabetic mothers. *The Journal of Pediatrics, 137*, 777–784.

de Ungria, M., Rao, R., Wobken, J. D., Luciana, M., Nelson, C. A., & Georgieff, M. K. (2000). Perinatal iron deficiency decreases cytochrome c oxidase (CytOx) activity in selective regions of neonatal rat brain. *Pediatric Research, 48*, 169–176.

Felt, B. T., & Lozoff, B. (1996). Brain iron and behavior of rats are not normalized by treatment of iron deficiency anemia during early development. *The Journal of Nutrition, 126* (3), 693–701.

Georgieff, M. K., Landon, M. B., Mills, M. M., Hedlund, B. E., Faassen, A. E., Schmidt, R. L., et al. (1990). Abnormal iron distribution in infants of diabetic mothers: Spectrum and maternal antecedents. *The Journal of Pediatrics, 117*, 455–461.

Georgieff, M. K., Schmidt, R. L., Mills, M. M., Radmer, W. J., & Widness, J. A. (1992). Fetal iron and cytochrome c status after intrauterine hypoxemia and erythropoietin administration. *The American Journal of Physiology, 262*, R485–R491.

Georgieff, M. K., Wewerka, S. W., Nelson, C. A., & deRegnier, R.-A. (2002). Iron status of infants with low iron stores at birth. *The Journal of Pediatrics, 141*, 405–409.

Green, D. W., Khoury, J., & Mimouni, F. (1992). Neonatal hematocrit and maternal glycemic control in insulin-dependent diabetes. *The Journal of Pediatrics, 120*, 302–305.

Gunnar, M. R., & Nelson, C. A. (1994). Event-related potentials in year-old infants: Relations with emotionality and cortisol. *Child Development, 65*, 80–94.

Hawdon, J. M. (1999). Hypoglycaemia and the neonatal brain. *European Journal of Pediatrics, 158*(Suppl. 1), S9–S12.

Insel, B. J., Schaefer, C. A., McKeague, I. W., Susser, E. S., & Brown, A. S. (2008). Maternal iron deficiency and the risk of schizophrenia in offspring. *Archives of General Psychiatry, 65*, 1136–1144.

Jasper, H. H. (1958). The ten-twenty electrode system of the International Federation. *Electroencephalography and Clinical Neurophysiology, 10*, 371–375.

Jorgenson, L. A., Wobken, J. D., & Georgieff, M. K. (2003). Perinatal iron deficiency alters apical dendritic growth in hippocampal CA1 pyramidal neurons. *Developmental Neuroscience, 25*, 412–420.

Jorgenson, L., Wobken, J., & Georgieff, M. K. (2004). Fetal/neonatal iron deficiency decreases synaptic efficacy and the expression and localization of α alpha-CaMKII in the developing hippocampus. *Pediatric Research, 55*, 179A Presented at the Pediatric Academic Societies' Annual Meeting.

Lozoff, B., & Georgieff, M. K. (2006). Iron deficiency and brain development. *Seminars in Pediatric Neurology, 13*(3), 158–165.

Lucas, M. J. (2001). Medical complications of pregnancy: Diabetes complicating pregnancy. *Obstetrics and Gynecology Clinics of North America, 28*, 513–536.

Lucas, A., Morley, R., & Cole, T. J. (1988). Randomised trial of early diet in preterm babies and later intelligence quotient. *British Medical Journal, 317*(7171), 1481–1487.

Lukowski, A. F., Wiebe, S. A., Haight, J. C., DeBoer, T., Nelson, C. A., & Bauer, P. J. (2005). Forming a stable memory representation in the first year of life: Why imitation is more than child's play. *Developmental Science, 8*(3), 279–298.

Malone, J. I., Hanna, S. K., & Saporta, S. (2006). Hyperglycemic brain injury in the rat. *Brain Research, 1076*(1), 9–15.

Malone, J. I., Hanna, S., Saporta, S., Mervis, R. F., Park, C. R., Chong, L., et al. (2008). Hyperglycemia not hypoglycemia alters neuronal dendrites and impairs spatial memory. *Pediatric Diabetes, 9*(6), 531–539.

Mishkin, M., & Appenzeller, T. (1987). The anatomy of memory. *Scientific American, 256*, 2–11.

Morris, M. A., Grandis, A. S., & Litton, J. C. (1985). Glycosylated hemoglobin concentration in early gestation associated with neonatal outcome. *American Journal of Obstetrics and Gynecology, 153,* 651–654.

Nelson, C. A. (1994). Neural correlates of recognition memory in the first postnatal year. In G. Dawson & K. W. Fischer (Eds.), *Human behavior and the developing brain* (pp. 269–313). New York, NY: Guilford Press.

Nelson, C. A., Henschel, M., & Collins, P. F. (1993). Neural and behavioral correlates of cross-modal recognition memory by 8-month-old infants. *Developmental Psychology, 29,* 411–420.

Nelson, C. A., & Monk, C. (2001). The use of event-related potentials in the study of cognitive development. In C. A. Nelson & M. Luciana (Eds.), *Handbook of developmental cognitive neuroscience* (pp. 125–136). Cambridge, MA: MIT Press.

Nelson, C., & Silverstein, F. S. (1994). Acute disruption of cytochrome oxidase activity in brain in a perinatal rat stroke model. *Pediatric Research, 36,* 12–19.

Nelson, C. A., Wewerka, S. S., Borscheid, A. J., deRegnier, R.-A., & Georgieff, M. K. (2003). Electrophysiologic evidence of impaired cross-modal recognition memory in 8-month-old infants of diabetic mothers. *The Journal of Pediatrics, 142,* 575–582.

Nelson, C. A., Wewerka, S., Thomas, K. M., Tribby-Walbridge, S., deRegnier, R.-A., & Georgieff, M. (2000). Neurocognitive sequelae of infants of diabetic mothers. *Behavioral Neuroscience, 114,* 950–956.

Nold, J. L., & Georgieff, M. K. (2004). Infants of diabetic mothers. *Pediatric Clinics of North America, 51*(3), 619–637.

Nyakas, C., Buwalda, B., & Luiten, P. G. M. (1996). Hypoxia and brain development. *Progress in Neurobiology, 49,* 1–51.

Rao, R., de Ungria, M., Sullivan, D., Wu, P., Wobken, J. D., Nelson, C. A., *et al.* (1999). Perinatal iron deficiency increases the vulnerability of rat hippocampus to hypoxic ischemic insult. *The Journal of Nutrition, 129,* 199–206.

Rao, R., Ennis, K., Long, J. D., Ugurbil, K., Gruetter, R., & Tkac, I. (2010). Neurochemical changes in the developing rat hippocampus during prolonged hypoglycemia. *Journal of Neurochemistry, 114*(3), 728–738.

Rao, R., Tkac, I., Townsend, E. L., Gruetter, R., & Georgieff, M. K. (2003). Perinatal iron deficiency alters the neurochemical profile of the developing rat hippocampus. *The Journal of Nutrition, 133,* 3215–3221.

Reynolds, G., & Richards, J. (2005). Familiarization, attention, and recognition memory in infancy: An event-related potential and cortical source localization study. *Developmental Psychology, 41,* 598–615.

Richards, J. E. (2003). Attention affects the recognition of briefly presented visual stimuli in infants: An ERP study. *Developmental Science, 6*(3), 312–328.

Riggins, T., Miller, N. C., Bauer, P. J., Georgieff, M. K., & Nelson, C. A. (2009a). Consequences of maternal diabetes mellitus and neonatal iron status on children's explicit memory performance. *Developmental Neuropsychology, 34*(6), 762–779.

Riggins, T., Miller, N. C., Bauer, P. J., Georgieff, M. K., & Nelson, C. A. (2009b). Electrophysiological indices of memory for temporal order in early childhood: Implications for the development of recollection. *Developmental Science, 12*(2), 209–219.

Rizzo, T., Metzger, B. E., Burns, W. J., & Burns, K. (1991). Correlations between antepartum maternal metabolism and child intelligence. *The New England Journal of Medicine, 325* (13), 911–916.

Rizzo, T. A., Metzger, B. E., Dooley, S. L., & Cho, N. H. (1997). Early malnutrition and child, neurobehavioral development: Insights from the study of children of diabetic mothers. *Child Development, 68,* 26–38.

Schmidt, A. T., Waldow, K. J., Salinas, J. A., & Georgieff, M. K. (2004). The long-term behavioral effects of fetal/neonatal iron deficiency on a hippocampally dependent learning task in the rat. *Pediatric Research, 55,* 279A.

Schwartz, R., & Teramo, K. A. (2000). Effects of diabetic pregnancy on the fetus and newborn. *Seminars in Perinatology, 24,* 120–135.

Scoville, W. B., & Milner, B. (1957). Loss of recent memory after bilateral hippocampal lesions. *Journal of Neurology, Neurosurgery and Psychiatry, 20,* 11–21.

Seress, L. (2001). Morphological changes of the human hippocampal formation from midgestation to early childhood. In C. A. Nelson & M. Luciana (Eds.), *Handbook of developmental cognitive neuroscience* (pp. 45–58). Cambridge, MA: The MIT Press.

Siddappa, A. M., Georgieff, M. K., Wewerka, S., Worwa, C., Nelson, C. A., & deRegnier, R.-A. (2004). Iron deficiency alters auditory recognition memory in newborn infants of diabetic mothers. *Pediatric Research, 55,* 1034–1041.

Squire, L. R. (1992). Declarative and non-declarative memory: Multiple brain systems supporting learning and memory. *Journal of Cognitive Neuroscience, 4,* 232–243.

Stevens, C. P., Raz, S., & Sander, C. J. (1999). Peripartum hypoxic risk and cognitive outcome: A study of term and preterm birth children at early school age. *Neuropsychology, 13*(4), 598–608.

Stolarova, M., Whitney, H., Webb, S. J., deRegnier, R. A., Georgieff, M. K., & Nelson, C. A. (2003). Electrophysiological brain responses of six-month-old low risk premature infants. *Infancy, 4*(3), 437–450.

Tamura, T., Goldenberg, R. L., Hou, J., Johnston, K. E., Cliver, S. P., Ramey, S. L., *et al.* (2002). Cord serum ferritin concentrations and mental and psychomotor development of children at five years of age. *The Journal of Pediatrics, 140,* 165–170.

Tran, P. V., Carlson, E. S., Fretham, S. J. B., & Georgieff, M. K. (2008). Early-life iron deficiency anemia alters neurotrophic factor expression and hippocampal neuron differentiation in male rats. *The Journal of Nutrition, 138,* 2495–2501.

Tran, P. V., Fretham, S. J. B., Carlson, E. S., & Georgieff, M. K. (2009). Long-term reduction of hippocampal BDNF activity following fetal-neonatal iron deficiency in adult rats. *Pediatric Research, 65*(5), 493–498.

US Food and Drug Administration Website, Diabetes Facts (August, 2004). http://www.fda.gov/womens/taketimetocare/diabetes/fswomen.html.

Van Lieshout, R. J., & Voruganti, L. P. (2008). Diabetes mellitus during pregnancy and increased risk of schizophrenia in offspring: A review of the evidence and putative mechanisms. *Journal of Psychiatry & Neuroscience, 33,* 395–404.

Volpe, J. J. (2001). *Neurology of the newborn.* Philadelphia: W.B. Saunders (pp. 217–396).

Widness, J. A., Susa, J. B., Garcia, J. F., Singer, O. B., Sehgal, P., Oh, W., *et al.* (1981). Increased erythropoiesis and elevated erythropoietin in infants born to diabetic mothers and in hyperinsulinemic rhesus fetuses. *The Journal of Clinical Investigation, 67,* 637–642.

Yamada, K. A., Rensing, N., Izumi, Y., de Erausquin, G. A., Gazit, V., Dorsey, D. A., *et al.* (2004). Repetitive hypoglycemia in young rats impairs hippocampal long-term potentiation. *Pediatric Research, 55,* 372–379.

THE DEVELOPMENT OF DECLARATIVE MEMORY IN INFANTS BORN PRETERM

Carol L. Cheatham,[*,†] *Heather Whitney Sesma,*[‡] *Patricia J. Bauer,*[§] *and Michael K. Georgieff*[¶]

[*] DEPARTMENT OF PSYCHOLOGY, UNIVERSITY OF NORTH CAROLINA AT CHAPEL HILL, CHAPEL HILL, NORTH CAROLINA, USA
[†] NUTRITION RESEARCH INSTITUTE, UNIVERSITY OF NORTH CAROLINA AT CHAPEL HILL, KANNAPOLIS, NORTH CAROLINA, USA
[‡] INSTITUTE OF CHILD DEVELOPMENT, UNIVERSITY OF MINNESOTA, MINNEAPOLIS, MINNESOTA, USA
[§] DEPARTMENT OF PSYCHOLOGY, EMORY UNIVERSITY, ATLANTA, GEORGIA, USA
[¶] DEPARTMENT OF PEDIATRICS, CENTER FOR NEUROBEHAVIORAL DEVELOPMENT, UNIVERSITY OF MINNESOTA, MINNEAPOLIS, MINNESOTA, USA

I. BRAIN DEVELOPMENT IN THE PRESENCE OF RISK
   A. ERRORS OF OMISSION
   B. ERRORS OF COMMISSION
   C. ERRORS OF OMISSION AND COMMISSION

II. MEMORY RELATIONS WITH POSTNATAL AGE AND CORRECTED AGE

III. METHOD
   A. PARTICIPANTS
   B. MATERIALS, PROCEDURE, AND SCORING

IV. RESULTS AND DISCUSSION

V. SUMMARY, CONCLUSIONS, AND IMPLICATIONS

ACKNOWLEDGMENTS

REFERENCES

During the 40-week gestation period of the human, the brain develops from an unrecognizable mass of cells into the remarkable organ that takes in sensory information and translates it into actions. The rate of development is based on genetic programming that is modified by expectant intra- and extrauterine (postnatal) environments. The brain is most rapidly growing during fetal life (12–40 weeks postconception) and early neonatal life (first few weeks of life); any tissue that is rapidly growing is highly vulnerable to insults (e.g., lack of oxygen, lack of nutrients, trauma). Theoretically, due to this rapid change, it is also more malleable, and this plasticity allows recovery from insults given the proper support. What happens to the brain when the intrauterine life is interrupted, and the

Advances in Child Development and Behavior
Patricia Bauer : Editor

neonate is exposed to the postnatal environment sooner than expected? In this chapter, we detail the concepts that govern brain development during the prenatal and postnatal periods. This is followed by a discussion of two basic pathways through which pre- and postnatal events affect early brain development. Next, we present research from our laboratory in which we explored the brain–behavior relations in those born preterm. Finally, we discuss the implications of this research.

I. Brain Development in the Presence of Risk

Developmental outcome can be affected at any time in the life cycle by genetic events, environmental pressures, or as is most often the case, an interaction of genetics and environment. Firstly, it is important to understand that most genetic potentials show incomplete penetration. That is, they are only expressed under certain conditions. Whereas some genetic determinants alter physiology so significantly that environment has very little effect (e.g., Trisomy 18), other genes *require* environmental pressure before they are expressed (e.g., genetic predisposition to become diabetic). Nevertheless, the ungrounded concept of genes versus environment is misleading. Our existence depends on both genes *and* environment. As scientists, we are left to elucidate the interaction between the two and the relative contributions of each to health and behavior.

Secondly, the genetic and environmental effects on the developing brain, be they positive or negative, are based on timing, dose, and duration. Different stages of fetal and neonatal growth are associated with particular aspects of brain development. There are defined, genetically programmed periods during which certain brain development processes predominately occur (e.g., differentiation, myelination, synapse formation), and coincident pressures from the environment may or may not exact an effect on a particular process depending on the timing and severity of the stimulus. This concept is broadly applicable to events in the fetal and neonatal periods. For example, iron deficiency during the fetal and neonatal periods is related to changes in the hippocampal area (Siddappa *et al.*, 2003, 2004; see also Chapter 4, this volume) and consequently, recognition memory deficits at birth. However, iron deficiency acquired postnatally between 6 and 24 months of age is related to deficits in myelination (Algarin, Peirano, Garrido, Pizarro, & Lozoff, 2003; Roncagliolo, Garrido, Walter, Peirano, & Lozoff, 1998) and therefore, reduced speed of processing as well as dopamine-based processing deficits (Angulo-Kinzler *et al.*, 2002; Lozoff, Jimenez, Hagen, Mollen, & Wolf, 2000). Thus, the neural systems most susceptible to iron deficiency vary based on the timing of the insult and the systems' precise stage and rapidity of development at that moment.

Moreover, the timing, dose, and duration of stimuli can determine the long-term continuity of effects. To continue with the nutrient example, deficits related to iron deficiency in the fetal, neonatal, and infancy periods persist after iron repletion (Algarin *et al.*, 2003; Lozoff *et al.*, 2000) suggesting permanent changes to neuroanatomy or neurotransmitter activity. In contrast, iron deficiency in adolescents is related to memory deficits that are rapidly reversible with iron supplementation, suggestive of no structural effects and nonpermanent perturbations of dopaminergic neurotransmitter systems (for review, see Beard & Connor, 2003). Therefore, the same nutrient deficit leads to very different effects depending on the timing of the deficiency. The differential effects of dose are exemplified in lead levels: children who have suffered acute lead poisoning (high dose) exhibit persistent IQ deficits, encephalopathy, and even convulsions, whereas children with low levels of lead (e.g., measured in shed teeth) exhibit subtle impairments in cognitive functioning (for review, see Mendola, Selevan, Gutter, & Rice, 2002).

Lead levels also illustrate the effects of duration of exposure to an environmental agent: the acute poisoning is most often the result of high doses over a short period (such as is seen in ingestion of paint chips), whereas the low levels of lead measured in teeth and bone are the result of a slow accumulation of lead from various environmental sources. Another example of the effect of duration of exposure on outcomes can be found in hypoxia. Children with a history of preterm birth and birth hypoxia of short duration have been shown to earn lower scores on global intelligence measures relative to children born preterm with no hypoxia risk (Hokins-Golightly, Raz, & Sander, 2003). In contrast, infants who experience chronic hypoxia *in utero* have underdeveloped sympathetic and cardiovascular systems, which have been related to heart disease and adverse stress reactions in adulthood (Peyronnet *et al.*, 2002). Clearly, duration of an insult has profound effects on the developing infant.

Lastly, the regional vulnerability of the brain results in specific behavioral effects: the function associated with the vulnerable structure is also vulnerable to change from environmental pressures. Relevant to this discussion is the vulnerability of the hippocampus, a structure central to memory processing. In a study of hippocampal volume in children with preterm histories, Isaacs and her colleagues demonstrated that 13-year-olds who were born at less than 30 weeks gestation, relative to age-matched full-term controls, had reduced hippocampal volumes that were related to deficits in episodic memory (Isaacs *et al.*, 2000). Preterm birth frequently is accompanied by insults that exact change in the factors that support metabolic processes (e.g., hypoxia–ischemia, hypoglycemia, glucocorticoid exposure). These are changes to which the hippocampus is particularly vulnerable.

Although most of the models are in term animals, because humans are one of the few species to produce viable preterm offspring, damage to the hippocampus from the risk factors common to infants born preterm has been documented. Specifically, hypoxic-ischemia (loss of oxygen and blood flow to the brain) increases hippocampal cell loss and cell death (e.g., Jiang, Ding, & Tang, 2001; Nunez, Alt, & McCarthy, 2003); results in a dys-regulation of enzymatic activity necessary for the proper functioning of hip-pocampal cells (e.g., Hee Han, Choi, & Holtzman, 2002); and increases glutamate release, which can cause excitotoxic injury to the hippocampus (e.g., Yager, Armstrong, Miyashita, & Wirrell, 2002). Effects on the hippo-campus are intensified if the infant suffers nutrient deficiencies (e.g., Rao *et al.*, 1999), as they often do. Another source of cell loss is hypoglycemia: Hippocampal cells starved for glucose are damaged and possibly lost. Animal models of hypoglycemia show marked hippocampal injury relative to controls (e.g., Barks, Sun, Malinak, & Silverstein, 1995). The hippocam-pus is also selectively and permanently damaged by prolonged exposure to glucocorticoids (Neal, VanderBeek, Vazquez, & Watson, 2003). Dexa-methasone, a synthetic form of glucocorticoid, is routinely used to treat severe respiratory distress in infants born very preterm. Thus, several hippo-campal risk factors are implicated in the sequelae of infants born preterm, and hippocampal dependent memory processes of the infant born preterm are of particular interest to those working to improve outcomes of those born preterm.

The facts that the brain's development is affected by both genetic and environmental pressures; that the effects of experience are determined by timing, dose, and duration of stimuli; and that damage to vulnerable structures is manifest in deficiencies in related functions should be kept in mind throughout this chapter. We now turn to a discussion of the two basic pathways through which brain development in the infant born pre-term is "derailed," namely, *errors of omission* and *errors of commission*.

A. ERRORS OF OMISSION

One pathway through which the expected course of brain development may be interrupted is by errors of omission. Omission is said to have occurred when a factor important for brain development does not occur as expected. Errors of omission can occur at any point in the developmental trajectory. Periconceptional risk factors have been identified predominately epidemiologically, although each has a biologic mediator. Factors such as insufficient time between pregnancies, low prepregnancy weight, and poor maternal nutrition are omissions that can result in maldevelopment of the fetus, prematurity, or intrauterine growth restriction. After conception, the embryo still can be adversely affected by maternal nutritional deficiencies. The most well-known of these is maternal folate deficiency which can result in neural tube defects in the embryo (for review, see Stover, 2004). In addition, factors such as protein or iron deficiencies can result in decreased cell replication and thus, limited brain size and complexity (Cordero, Valenzuela, Rodriguez & Aboitiz, 2003; King *et al.*, 2004). Maternal zinc deficiency during the periconceptional and early embryonic periods results in lower rates of implantation in the uterus, decreased growth of the conceptus, and a higher rate of cardiac anomalies (Caulfield, Zavaleta, Shankar, & Merialdi, 1998).

The fetal brain is also vulnerable to omission factors. During the fetal period, the placenta provides oxygen and nutrients to the fetus while removing carbon dioxide and toxins. Placental insufficiency resulting from factors such as maternal malnutrition subsequently is related to fetal malnutrition or maternal hypertension (high blood pressure), which is a prime cause of intrauterine growth restriction. Intrauterine growth restriction is the second most common adverse event in the fetal and neonatal time period (prematurity being the first). The proper levels of nutrients (e.g., oxygen, protein, iron, zinc, carbohydrates) are necessary for both neuroanatomic processes (functions of cells and their supporting structures) and neurochemical processes (neurotransmitter and receptor synthesis) in the brain. Thus, the lack of proper placental support to the fetus can result in a profound disruption of brain development.

The concept of omission is particularly applicable to the infant who is born preterm. Premature delivery deprives the fetus of support from the placenta and therefore, of expected intrauterine nutrients important for brain development. Due to advancements of the late twentieth century in care of the neonate, the lower limit of viability (survival) is 22–23 weeks gestational age. Neonates born this early experience a full 17–18 weeks of a nonoptimal environment. Certain nutrients critical for brain development such as oxygen, glucose, proteins, myelin-supporting fats, iron, and growth factors are no longer being supplied by the placenta. Whereas the medical field has made great strides in support (e.g., nutritional, respiratory) of the infant in the weeks that follow preterm birth, the longer the fetus is *in utero*, the better the prognosis. As will be described later, certain aspects of poor memory outcome may be directly related to the degree of prematurity and independent of degree of illness (Curtis, Lindeke, Georgieff, & Nelson, 2002; de Haan, Bauer, Georgieff, & Nelson, 2000). Thus, neonatal events of omission are detrimental. However, omission is not the only brain development dysfunction pathway.

B. ERRORS OF COMMISSION

The second pathway in which brain development may be disrupted is through errors of commission. These are defined as adverse biological conditions to which the brain would not normally have been exposed and which have a noxious effect on brain development. Commission errors occur when an insult is "committed" to the young, developing brain. One basic example is found in disorders of genetics in that tri-somies, which result in a constellation of neurologic abnormalities, are the addition of a chromosome into the genetic material: some factor is present in the infant that would not normally be there. Environmental embryonic commission events include insults from toxins. Maternal alcohol abuse (for review, see West, Chen, & Pantazis, 1994), intrauterine infections (e.g., Mallard, Welin, Peebles, Hagberg, & Kjellmer, 2003), and environmental toxins (e.g., mercury, lead, ionizing radiation; e.g., Palomo, Beninger, Kostrzewa, & Archer, 2003), can result in restricted brain growth by decreasing cell replication, thereby reducing cell numbers and synaptic connections. These stressors can also affect brain development by altering the metabolism and thus, the function of the cells. The psychopathology associated with these factors includes mental retardation, hyperkinetic disorders, and significant emotional disturbance (for review, see Trask & Kosofsky, 2000). Although these factors have their most profound effect early in gestation, the older fetus is still vulnerable to maternally-transmitted infections and toxins.

The commission events most often associated with those born prematurely occur during birth and the neonatal period. Birth asphyxia, in which the supply of oxygen and blood to the brain is interrupted, is associated with placental insufficiency and umbilical cord blood flow restriction. Although some of the damage is likely due to "omission" of oxygen (discussed above), it is now becoming evident that much of the damage is actually caused by excess iron and reactive oxygen species after blood flow is restored (Dorrepaal et al., 1996). The antioxidant systems of the preterm brain are too immature to handle the excess and thus, the process can be considered damage that is "committed" to the brain. The pathological sequelae are directly related to the length of time required for the neonate to attain a normal Apgar score (assessed in the first few minutes after birth from factors such as color, tone, and responsiveness; Nelson & Ellenberg, 1981). In addition, a neonate who was born at less than 34 weeks gestation has an increased risk of intracranial hemorrhage (Thorp, Jones, Clark, Knox, & Peabody, 2001), the sequelae of which include cerebral palsy and mental retardation (Shevell, Majnemer, & Morin, 2003). Clearly large amounts of free blood are not normally found in the brain, and the neurons that are present in areas of the brain where the blood clots form are destroyed. Outcomes of infants who suffered an intraventricular hemorrhage are dependent on the severity of the infarction, that is, the more severe the bleed, the more severe the deficits (Levy, Masri, & McComb, 1997), and the lower the gestational age, the higher the incidence of more severe intraventricular hemorrhage (Thorp *et al.*, 2001).

C. ERRORS OF OMISSION AND COMMISSION

Most often, outcomes are a function of both omitted and committed events. For example, placental insufficiency leads to prenatal malnutrition, which is considered an omission event, but it also predisposes the neonate to hypoxia–ischemia at birth, an event of commission. The effects are, at times, difficult to examine independently. In the case of the infant who is born prematurely, birth itself is an omission of the intrauterine environment, and the early birth increases the chances of the commission of an intracranial hemorrhage due to the instability of the immature germinal matrix vasculature. In some cases, outcomes can be attributed solely to events of omission. Such is the case with infants born preterm who experience no complications or put simply, are born "healthy" with the exception of the omission of the last few weeks of gestation.

II. Memory Relations with Postnatal Age and Corrected Age

Infants born preterm offer an opportunity to explore the differential contributions of maturation and experience; those born preterm and "healthy" allow us to also elucidate the effect of pure "omission" of the expected intrauterine environment. An infant born preterm has weeks of experience beyond what would be expected developmentally. Until the children with preterm histories reach preschool age, researchers "correct" their ages from their expected due date. Thus, an infant born at 32 weeks who is postnatally 14 months old would be tested on and compared to 12-month norms (corrected age). No provision is made for the extra 8 weeks during which the infant born preterm had an opportunity to experience the environment. Does this experience matter? Does the infant born preterm exhibit precocious or accelerated development as a result of this extra opportunity? In what follows, we outline the research from our laboratory that explores these questions.

Recognition memory in the newborn infant exhibits differential effects of maturation (corrected age) and postnatal experience. deRegnier,

Wewerka, Georgieff, Mattia, and Nelson (2002) tested three groups: infants born premature and healthy tested at 35–38 weeks postconception when they were less than a week old, infants born full-term tested at 39–42 weeks postconception when they were less than a week old, and infants born full-term tested at 39–42 weeks postconception when they were 8–30 days old (experienced group). Recognition memory for mother's voice (familiar stimulus) and stranger's voice (novel stimulus) was assessed by measuring event-related potentials (ERPs). The group of infants born moderately preterm did not discriminate between their mothers' voices and strangers' voices, whereas both full-term groups did regardless of their level of experience. This finding would indicate that the development of auditory recognition pathways is primarily related to postconceptional development rather than postnatal experience with the sound. However, ERPs generated by the experienced group of infants born full-term were qualitatively different from the inexperienced newborn groups: the inexperienced groups showed longer latencies to mother's voice relative to the experienced group. This could be interpreted as a difference due to changes in synaptic connections and myelination: latencies decrease as synaptogenesis and myelination increase (Eggermont, 1988). However, there were no differences in latencies to the stranger's voice between the groups regardless of the level of experience, which one would expect if brain maturation independent of experience were a factor. Therefore, deRegnier *et al.* concluded that auditory recognition memory is primarily related to maturation, whereas experience exacts qualitative improvements in auditory recognition memory.

In infants born 8 weeks prematurely and healthy tested at 6 months postnatal age (4 months corrected age), researchers from our laboratory explored the development of infants' abilities to discriminate between novel and primed stimuli as measured by ERPs (Stolarova *et al.*, 2003). Neonatal health status was assessed by computing the Neurobiological Risk Score (NBRS) from medical records (Brazy, Eckerman, Oehler, Goldstein, & O'Rand, 1991). Conservatively, infants were included only if their NBRS was less than 3 (standard for low risk: NBRS < 4). Infants born 8 weeks prematurely and healthy were compared to two control groups: a postnatal-age control group of infants born full-term who were 6 months of age at the time of testing and a corrected-age control group of infants born full-term who were 4 months of age at the time of testing. Infants were presented with video images of female faces, some of which they saw only once (novel), some of which they saw twice in succession (immediate priming), and some of which they saw twice, but with four pictures intervening (delayed priming). In the infants born preterm, the ERP component indicative of attention (Nc) seen in response to the delayed primed stimuli was more similar to the same component seen in the ERP waveform of the infants born full-term and matched in corrected age (full-term 4-month-olds) than to that of the postnatally age-matched group (full-term 6-month-olds). Further, evidence of priming was seen only in the infants born full-term and tested at 6 months of age; there was no evidence of priming in either of the groups who were developmentally 4 months of age at the time of testing (infants born preterm and their corrected-age-matches). Therefore, Stolarova *et al.* concluded that the 2 months extra experience available to the infants born preterm relative to their maturationally matched counterparts (4-month-old infants born full-term) did not effectively enhance the development of the neural substrates underlying the ERP responses. Again, the behavior tested (primed recall) was found to be related more to the natural maturational course of the brain rather than to experience in the environment.

However, the same sample was also tested for recognition memory in a protocol that compared the waveform in response to pictures of mother's face versus pictures of a stranger's face (Sesma & Georgieff, 2003). Results for the latency of the Nc were similar: the infants born preterm were more like the corrected-age-matched full-term group in their time to reach peak amplitude than either group was like the postnatal-age-matched full-term group, suggesting that increased experience does not affect the maturation of processing speed for visual stimuli. However, as in the deRegnier *et al.* (2002) results, there were qualitative differences in the waveform: the amplitude of the overall Nc was attenuated in the infants born full-term and tested at 6 months of age relative to the infants born full-term and tested at 4 months of age. The amplitude of the Nc recorded from the infants born preterm was intermediate between the other two groups and did not statistically differ from either one (Sesma & Georgieff, 2003). The reduction in amplitude could be indicative of an experiential-based increase in processing efficiency for the older group of full-term infants (Karrer, Karrer, Bloom, Chaney, & Davis, 1998). The extra experience of the infants born preterm may have accelerated the development of the negative component (Nc) of the ERP waveform. Again, we see that the early development of the underlying substrates related to memory function proceeds on a maturational time course with experience contributing to qualitative improvements.

Thus far, we have discussed studies in which the investigators explored questions relative to unitary degrees of prematurity. It has been shown that degree of prematurity has a gradient effect on memory abilities: the more prematurely one is born, the greater the reduction in memory abilities. Rose and her colleagues have reported that infants born moderately premature do not exhibit any dysfunction of recognition memory, whereas those born very preterm do (Rose, Feldman, McCarton, & Wolfson, 1988). Studies of declarative memory in infants born preterm are few. However, research from our laboratory has shown that the differential effects of degree of prematurity can be found in declarative abilities as well (Cheatham, 2004; Cheatham, Bauer, & Georgieff, 2006; de Haan *et al.*, 2000).

As has been discussed extensively in this volume, elicited imitation has emerged as the paradigm of choice for research on declarative memory in typically developing children. We extended the task to premature infants. In this task, props are used to produce a sequence of actions that the infant, either immediately, after some delay, or both, is permitted to imitate. Two variables are of interest: production of individual target actions and production of pairs of actions in target order. de Haan *et al.* (2000) used elicited and deferred imitation to test the mnemonic abilities of infants born preterm and assessed at corrected age 16–22 months, who were healthy for their gestational ages and birthweights, and had no known temporal lobe damage at birth. It was hypothesized that they would show atypical patterns of declarative memory development. Three groups participated: infants born at 38–42 weeks (full-term), infants born at 35–37 weeks (moderately preterm), and infants born at 27–34 weeks (very preterm). After an initial test for any apparent gross or fine motor impairments, they were exposed to six novel three-step event sequences. They were not allowed to imitate the first three events (10-min delayed-recall condition); they were allowed to imitate the next three (immediate-recall condition). After administration of the immediate-recall condition, or a minimum of 10 min had passed, the children were given the props for the sequences in the delayed-recall condition and encouraged to produce the events.

There were no group differences in children's production of the individual target actions of the event sequences, in either condition (immediate recall, 10-min delayed recall), indicating that the children did not differ in their abilities to participate in the task. Nevertheless, on the more cognitively demanding aspect of the task, namely, ordered recall (i.e., producing the individual actions in the modeled order), there were deficits in the performance of the infants born very preterm relative to those born full-term. The performance of the infants born moderately preterm was intermediate, but did not differ significantly from that of the other groups. Additionally, there was a main effect of condition (immediate, 10-min delay) on both target actions and order. These data indicate that after a delay of only 10 min, temporally ordered information that healthy preterm infants have been prevented from acting upon immediately is not evidenced in memory.

In addition, the de Haan *et al.* (2000) data showed that children's performance in the immediate-recall condition was related to corrected age, whereas performance in the delayed-recall condition (delay of approximately

10 min) was correlated with gestational age and birthweight. It may follow from this finding that the systems that subserve delayed recall are compromised by the omission of the last few weeks of intrauterine support, whereas the neurological functions required for immediate recall improve as the infant acquires more experience in the environment. If experience results in improved performance on immediate recall, infants born preterm, having had more postnatal experience, should perform better relative to a group of infants born full-term and matched to the corrected age of the infants born preterm. Additionally, we addressed the question of risk: what are the differential effects on memory evident in infants with additional neurobiological risk factors? We addressed these questions in new data reported in this chapter.

III. Method

A. PARTICIPANTS

As reported in Cheatham (2004), we enrolled infants aged 12–14 months of age. In total, five groups participated: infants born moderately preterm (gestational ages 35–37 weeks, $M = 36.4$ weeks; corrected age $M = 12.2$ months, postnatal age $M = 13.0$ months), infants born very preterm (gestational ages 28–34 weeks, $M = 31.2$ weeks; corrected age $M = 12.3$ months, postnatal age $M = 14.4$ months), infants born full-term and matched to the corrected ages of the infants born preterm (12-month-olds with gestational ages 38–41 weeks, $M = 40.0$ weeks; age $M = 12.3$ months), infants born full-term and matched to the postnatal ages of those born moderately preterm (13-month-olds with gestational ages 38–42 weeks, $M = 40.0$ weeks; age $M = 13.2$ months), and infants born full-term and matched to the postnatal ages of those born very preterm (14-month-olds with gestational ages 38–42 weeks, $M = 39.8$ weeks; age $M = 14.2$ months). To be considered lower risk, infants born moderately preterm had to have been released from the special care nursery within 24 h and did not return to the hospital (parent report). Infants born very preterm were considered lower risk only if they had a NBRS of 2 or less (computed from medical records; Brazy *et al.*, 1991).

B. MATERIALS, PROCEDURE, AND SCORING

The infants were tested on four 2-step event sequences in an imitation paradigm: two on which they were tested for recall immediately after modeling (immediate recall) and two on which they were tested for delayed recall after a delay of 10 min (delayed recall). Task administration was videotaped and the infants' performance was scored as described in Chapter 2, this volume. The same dependent measures were derived, namely, production of individual target actions and production of pairs of actions in target order.

In addition to the imitation tasks, the Bayley Scales of Infant Development-II (BSID-II; Bayley, 1993) were administered. Only the Mental Developmental Index (MDI) scores were considered because at this age, the Psychomotor Developmental Index (PDI) scores are unstable due to their heavy reliance on the ability of the infant to walk. Many children with preterm histories score within the normal range (85–115) on global measures of intellectual development such as the Bayley Scales (Caputo, Goldstein, & Taub, 1979; Crowe, Deitz, Bennett, & TeKolste, 1988; Kalmar, 1996). The infants in this sample were no exception ($M = 99.85$, sd $= 9.57$). Normative scores were achieved by all but two infants. Interestingly, the lowest score (MDI $= 77$) was earned by an infant born full-term, and the highest score (MDI $= 123$) was earned by an infant born very preterm.

IV. Results and Discussion

For illustration purposes, the data for the number of individual target actions produced and levels of ordered reproduction of target actions are shown in Figure 1 (moderately preterm) and Figure 2 (very preterm) divided by degree of risk and delay condition.

The lower risk infants born moderately preterm and their two control groups (postnatal and corrected age) evidenced memory for the events (target actions: $F(1, 53) = 94.29$, $p < .0001$; ordered pairs: $F(1, 53) = 38.16$, $p < .0001$). That is, production of both individual target actions and pairs of actions in target order immediately and after the 10-min delay was higher after modeling than it was before modeling. Analysis of the production of target actions showed a group effect, $F(2, 53) = 5.05$, $p < .001$. *Post hoc* analyses revealed that the corrected-age controls differed statistically from the postnatal-age controls, $t(53) = -3.07$, $p < .05$. The performance of the infants born moderately preterm, who were maturationally 12 months of age, did not statistically differ from the experientially matched 13-month olds (postnatal-age control group; $t(53) = -2.17$, $p < .10$) or the maturationally matched 12-month-olds (corrected-age control group; $t(53) = -.73$, *ns*). This indicates that the infants born moderately preterm may have gains in certain aspects of memory as a result of a few weeks extra experience. For these infants in this specific aspect of

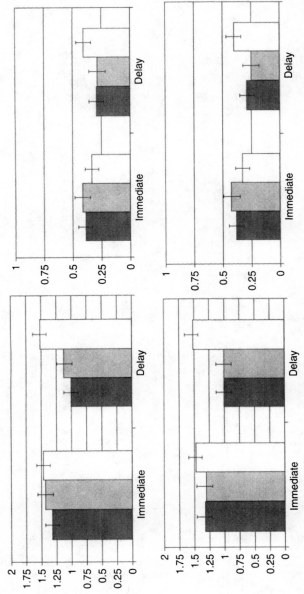

Fig. 1. Elicited imitation performance of the moderately preterm group (gray bars) and their postnatal-age controls (white bars). Top: lower risk moderately preterm group on target actions and ordered pairs (left and right, respectively). Bottom: higher risk moderately preterm group on target actions and ordered pairs (left and right, respectively).

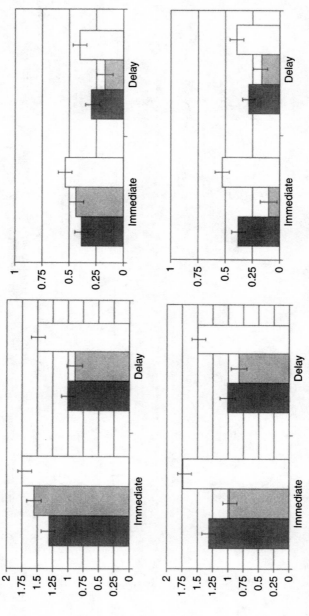

Fig. 2. Elicited imitation performance of the very preterm group (gray bars) and their postnatal-age controls (white bars). Top: lower risk very preterm group on target actions and ordered pairs (left and right, respectively). Bottom: higher risk very preterm group on target actions and ordered pairs (left and right, respectively).

the imitation task, the omission of the last few weeks of gestation appears to have been overcome. However, a closer inspection of the means revealed that their production of target actions was intermediate between the corrected- and postnatal-age controls. Although the performance of the infants born moderately preterm was not statistically different from the postnatal-age controls, they did not perform at the same level (LSMs = .88, .97, and 1.22 for corrected-age controls, moderately preterm, and postnatal controls, respectively; total possible = 2.0). The delay effect only approached significance, $F(1, 53) = 3.62$, $p < .10$. Furthermore, when the analyses were repeated controlling for MDI scores, the significance of the difference between the groups was no longer evidenced, $F(2, 50) = 1.99$, ns, although the patterns of performance remained the same (LSMs = .95, 1.01, and 1.13 for corrected-age controls, moderately preterm, and postnatal controls, respectively). Therefore, even though experience may have enhanced the performance of the infants born moderately preterm on the production of target actions, it was not sufficient to completely overcome the potential errors of omission in brain development introduced by their preterm birth.

For the production of pairs of actions in the target order, there was no difference between the groups. Performance of those born moderately preterm and their postnatal-age-matched and corrected-age-matched counterparts was nearly equal (LSMs = .24, .23, and .25 for corrected-age controls, moderately preterm, and postnatal controls, respectively; total possible = 1.0). Thus, the temporal ordering of to-be-remembered information was equally challenging for 12- and 13-month olds regardless of birth status and length of experience. Least square means indicated the performance of the postnatal-age controls dropped below the other two groups after controlling for MDI scores (LSMs = .26, .24, and .22 for corrected-age controls, moderately preterm, and postnatal controls, respectively). These findings preclude any conclusion about the effects of maturation and experience with regard to the production of actions in target order in those born moderately preterm. Nevertheless, in consideration of the full-term control groups (12-month-old corrected-age controls and 13-month-old postnatal-age controls), it is clear that even 4 weeks of extra experience did not improve performance on ordered target actions.

Included in the Cheatham (2004) sample were infants born moderately preterm who had experienced complications after birth and therefore, were not included in the above analyses of "healthy" infants born moderately preterm. Insults to these infants, by parent report, included nutritional deficiencies ($n = 8$), oxygen deprivation ($n = 4$), infection ($n = 1$), hematoma ($n = 1$), and failure to thrive resulting in readmission on postnatal day 7 ($n = 1$). Their average stay in the NICU/Special Care

Nursery was 10.3 days (range = 2–16 days). To assess the contribution of health status to the abilities of the infants born moderately preterm, analyses were conducted on the imitation performance of these 15 higher risk infants born moderately preterm. The pattern of results was the same as for the lower risk, "healthy" infants born moderately preterm with there being memory for the target actions, $F(1, 50) = 61.35$, $p < .001$, and for ordered pairs, $F(1, 50) = 39.10$, $p < .001$, and a group difference for target actions, $F(2, 50) = 5.58$, $p < .05$. Moreover, analyses conducted comparing the lower- and higher risk infants born moderately preterm revealed no differences between the groups (target actions: $F(1, 27) = .00$, *ns*; ordered pairs: $F(1, 27) = .00$, *ns*). It is important to note, however, that the effects of insults such as neonatal respiratory problems and nutritional deficiencies may not be seen until the child encounters increasing demands to learn ever greater amounts of new information during the school years (Luciana, Lindeke, Georgieff, Mills, & Nelson, 1999). Even infants who experience only the omission of the intrauterine environment may exhibit problems with higher order cognition in the school years (Curtis *et al.*, 2002).

The infants born very preterm in this sample and included in the "healthy," lower risk group had NBRS scores of 2 or less (standard for low risk: NBRS < 4; Brazy *et al.*, 1991). Their risk factors included being on mechanical ventilation (range 1–4 days; $n = 10$), hypoglycemia that was resolved in less than 6 h ($n = 2$), infection that was easily resolved ($n = 1$), Grade 1 hemorrhage in the germinal matrix that quickly resolved ($n = 2$), and no risk factors ($n = 2$). Two of the participants ($n = 15$) had two risk factors and therefore, had NBRS scores of 2. All participants remained in the NICU to feed and grow (average length of stay = 36 days; range = 10–57 days).

The lower risk infants born very preterm and their corrected-age and postnatal-age control groups also evidenced memory for the events: scores on performance of target actions, $F(1, 52) = 102.08$, $p < .0001$ and actions in target order, $F(1, 52) = 58.91$, $p < .0001$, were higher after modeling than before modeling for both immediate imitation and imitation after the delay (10 min). There was also a group effect in the analyses of target actions, $F(2,52) = 7.73$, $p = .001$. *Post hoc* analyses revealed the performance of the infants born very preterm on the production of target actions was more like that of the corrected-age controls, $t(52) = -.71$, *ns*, than that of the postnatal-age-matched controls, $t(52) = -2.77$, $p < .01$. In addition, across groups the infants produced more target actions during immediate recall than they did during 10-min delayed recall, $F(1, 52) = 15.21$, $p < .0001$. This was due to a significant drop in the performance of the infants born very preterm on target actions after the delay relative to their performance on target actions imitated immediately, even though the interaction only approached significance, $F(2, 52) = 2.62$, $p < .10$ (LSMs $= 1.32$, 1.57, and 1.72 for the corrected-age-matched, very preterm, and postnatal-age-matched immediate imitation, respectively; LSMs $= 1.01$, .90, and 1.50 for the corrected-age-matched, very preterm, and postnatal-age-matched delayed imitation, respectively). These patterns of significance held even after controlling for MDI scores, $F(2, 49) = 3.82$, $p < .05$. For immediate imitation of target actions, the performance of the lower risk infants born very preterm was again intermediate between the two control groups; on delayed target actions, this was no longer true (see top left panel, Figure 2). The 10-min delay was a significant factor in the ability of the lower risk infants born very preterm to evidence recall for the steps of the sequence.

All three groups performed equally well on the temporal ordering of actions, $F(2, 52) = 1.40$, *ns*. However, in this analysis, it was evident that the infants experienced more difficulty with the production of target actions in order after the delay, $F(1, 52) = 58.91$, $p < .0001$. Again, this was due to a drop in the performance after the delay of the infants born very preterm relative to their performance when allowed to imitate immediately, even though the interaction was not significant, $F(2, 52) = 2.78$, $p < .10$ (LSMs $= .37$, .43, and .52 for the corrected-age-matched, very preterm, and postnatal-age-matched immediate imitation, respectively; $Ms = .29$, .16, and .40 for the corrected-age-matched, very preterm, and postnatal-age-matched delayed imitation, respectively). After controlling for MDI scores, it was also evident that after modeling, the performance of the infants born very preterm (LSM $= .30$) was more like that of their corrected-age-matched counterparts (LSM $= .34$) than their postnatal-age-matched counterparts (LSM $= .47$), whereas the performance before modeling (a measure of initial encoding) was equal across groups (LSMs $= .15$, .11, and .11 for the corrected-age-matched, very preterm, and postnatal-age-matched, respectively), $F(1, 50) = 67.80$, $p < .0001$. These data suggest that experience enhances the ability of those born very preterm to immediately produce the target actions of the sequences (intermediate performance), but does not have the same effect on the ability of these infants to produce the target actions after the delay. Delayed recall or the ability to hold onto information for a period of time was decreased relative to immediate recall in the infants born very preterm, even when they do not have significant risk factors beyond the omission of several weeks of intrauterine support (see top right panel, Figure 2).

Included in the Cheatham (2004) sample were higher risk infants born very preterm. These infants were hospitalized an average of 61 days and had NBRS scores of 3–10 with multiple risk factors. Risk factors that distinguished this group from the lower risk infants born very preterm included mechanical ventilation for longer than 7 days ($n=5$), higher grade intraventricular hemorrhages ($n=4$), ongoing infections ($n=5$), and slow-to-resolve hypoglycemia ($n=1$). When the data for the production of target actions by the higher risk infants born very preterm were analyzed, one important difference from the performance of the lower risk infants emerged: the higher risk very preterm group did not exhibit intermediate performance.

The infants evidenced memory for the event sequences: in production of target actions, $F(1, 48)=67.54$, $p<.0001$, and in production of pairs of actions in target order, $F(1, 48)=47.73, p<.0001$. In the production of target actions, there was no statistical difference between the higher risk infants born very preterm and their corrected-age counterparts (LSMs $=.75$ and .88, respectively), whereas the postnatal-age-matched group (LSM $=1.24$) outperformed both the corrected-age-matched group and the very preterm group, $F(2, 48)=11.49, p<.0001$. Across groups, the infants trended toward production of more target actions when allowed to imitate immediately than when they had to wait until after the delay, $F(2, 48)=2.91, p<.10$. In addition, there was evidence that the higher risk infants born very preterm did not do as well on production of target actions after modeling as did the other two groups, (LSMs $=1.17$, .91, and 1.61 for the corrected-age-matched, higher risk very preterm, and postnatal-age-matched, respectively), $F(2, 48)=3.29, p<.05$. In terms of ordered recall, the higher risk infants born very preterm produced significantly fewer actions in the target order than did either of the two full-term groups (LSMs $=.24$, .07, and .29 for the corrected-age-matched, very preterm, and postnatal-age-matched, respectively), $F(2, 48)=8.92, p<.001$. No differences were seen when the analyses were repeated controlling for MDI, $F(2, 45)=7.20, p<.01$. Thus, whereas the performance of the lower risk infants born very preterm was intermediate between the two control groups, the performance of the higher risk infants born very preterm was lower, significantly at times, than the performance of both groups even on immediate production of target actions, which is a measure of initial learning abilities (see Figure 2). Clearly, the combination of omission and commission errors experienced by the higher risk infants born very preterm was detrimental to their abilities to learn and recall information.

V. Summary, Conclusions, and Implications

In summary, additional postnatal experience alone is not sufficient to counteract the deficits resulting from the loss of a few weeks of intrauterine life. However, the ability to recall modeled actions can be enhanced by extra experience when risk factors are at a minimum; the greater the number of risk factors in an infant's history, the smaller the positive effect of the additional experience. It was also evident that experience did more to enhance the ability to recall modeled actions immediately relative to after a short delay. Moreover, with shorter gestational periods, the ability to tolerate a delay of minutes decreases. This can be seen in a comparison of the results of the higher risk moderately preterm group and the lower risk very preterm group. Although precise risk assessment was not possible due to only having access to complete medical records for the very preterm group, the risk factors for these two groups are similar: both groups had minor respiratory problems, minor infections, and nonmajor neurological events. If we assume that the *major* difference between the higher risk moderately preterm group and the lower risk very preterm group is a difference in gestation length, the data imply that an absence of intrauterine support for longer than 5 weeks has a differential effect on the neural substrates that support the ability to recall events across a delay (see Figure 3).

Thus, development of the neural circuits that support recognition and recall memory proceeds on an orderly timecourse, and the earlier the expected environment is disrupted, the greater is the deficit in memory processing. An increase in postnatal experience does not seem to hasten the maturational time course of development of the substrate related to memory processing, but it does appear to have an enhancing effect on certain aspects of memory once they emerge, providing risk is low or the task is not too demanding (as in immediate recall). These results are indicative of the plasticity exhibited by the brain: when development of the brain does not proceed at an optimal level, resulting deficits may be partially ameliorated by experience in the environment.

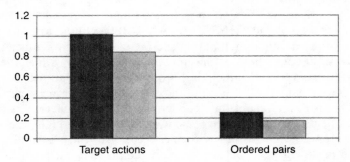

Fig. 3. Comparison of elicited imitation performance of the higher risk moderately preterm group (black bars) and the lower risk very preterm group (gray bars).

Evidence of this plasticity as well as the differential effects of neurobiological risk was reported in a study of 11-year olds with preterm histories assessed in our laboratory (Curtis *et al.*, 2002). This study included a follow-up of part of a sample previously tested (Luciana *et al.*, 1999) with the Cambridge Neuropsychological Testing Automated Battery (CANTAB; Fray, Robbins, & Sahakian, 1996; Sahakian & Owen, 1992), which was developed for use with neurologically impaired adults. The CANTAB is a computerized battery of nonverbal tests of memory and executive function. At initial assessment (ages 7–9 years; Luciana *et al.*, 1999), the children with NICU experience exhibited substantial deficits in spatial working memory, fine motor accuracy, spatial memory span, and pattern recognition memory. The children with preterm histories performed as well as full-term controls on the more basic levels of the tasks. Deficits only became evident when task difficulty increased: errors increased with task difficulty. Moreover, the NBRS scores computed from the NICU medical records on these children were predictive of the poor memory span and poor spatial working-memory performance exhibited at school age.

Interestingly, when a subset of these children returned to the laboratory 3 years later for repeat testing, fewer deficits and smaller effect sizes for the deficits were found (Curtis *et al.*, 2002) relative to the initial testing (Luciana *et al.*, 1999). The improvement in function can be interpreted as the result of compensatory processes in the brain. Curtis *et al.* (2002) suggest that the experience of preterm birth in some way slows the development of the prefrontal cortex on which the deficient behaviors rely. Eventually, with quality environmental support, the developmental lag appears to resolve. The children in this study were for the most part from middle- to upper-middle class rural homes and therefore, were from low-risk environments. Nevertheless, deficits in spatial memory and memory span were still evident. To further elucidate the deficits, Curtis *et al.* assessed the relative contributions of gestational age and risk factors. Spatial memory span was related to gestational age, independent of level of risk as measured by the NBRS. The CANTAB tasks used to measure spatial memory span require temporal ordering of information, much like the ordered recall component of the imitation paradigm on which we found deficits in the 16–22-month olds born preterm without risk (de Haan *et al.*, 2000). Again, the omission of the expected intrauterine environment during brain development, independent of other risk factors, had detrimental effects on the cognitive abilities of the individual. The deficits become more evident as task difficulty increases, which is similar to the increase in difficulty in the imitation paradigms that imposing the delay conferred in the Cheatham (2004) sample.

Collectively, these studies spanning ages from newborn to school age illustrate that being born early is detrimental to an infant's neurodevelopmental outcome, irrespective of risk factors. Moreover, it was shown that the trajectory of brain development has a post-conceptional age driven maturational course that includes expected environmental elements. When this expected intrauterine environment is absent as it is in preterm birth, experience in the extrauterine world does not accelerate the emergence of abilities reliant on continued brain development, but once an ability emerges, the additional experience acquired by the infant born preterm does seem to have enhanced the ability when risk factors and task demands are minimal. In normative development, the neural system matures to a certain point, the infant is born, and expected environmental inputs are then present to increase and refine the complexities of the brain. In the infant born preterm, the brain maturation and experiential inputs occur in concert. This phenomenon could explain the enhancements noted in the research described here. Simultaneous maturation and refinement in a neural system that has not been exposed to significant insults could result in slightly higher functioning, albeit in a differently developing brain. With regard to the infant born preterm who experiences a higher level of risk, the brain maturation could be "derailed" by events of both omission and commission to the extent that the atypical timing of the environmental inputs serves as an added risk factor, rather than an enhancing mechanism.

In the research reviewed, we reported deficits in auditory recognition memory, visual recognition memory, declarative memory, spatial working memory, spatial memory span, and pattern recognition memory. These abilities have in common a reliance, in part, on the medial temporal lobe and prefrontal lobe structures. The hippocampus and prefrontal connections important for declarative memory and executive functions are especially vulnerable to the types of neurobiological risk factors present in those born preterm (e.g., hypoxia–ischemia, hypoglycemia, nutritional deficiencies). Therefore, it is not surprising that we would find deficits in these same cognitive abilities in the infant born preterm. It is noteworthy that these deficits are evident independent of neurobiological risk and after controlling for general levels of abilities as measured by the MDI scale of the BSID-II.

Moreover, in ages ranging from newborn to 11 years, we reported potential evidence that quality experience helps to set the brain back on a more optimal trajectory. For infants born very early, the best predictors of outcome are most likely biological factors. For the moderately preterm, the influence of biological factors declines after the first year of life, and environmental factors, such as socio-economic status and quality of caregiver interactions, become more predictive of outcomes. The dynamic interaction between the preprogrammed maturation of the neural systems and the quality of the experiential inputs provides the basis for the optimal development of the human. Alterations in either the programming or the experience will result in a differently developing organism, and subsequent outcomes may be more positive or more negative from those expected in normative development as a result of these alterations.

Acknowledgments

Support for this research was provided by grants to the General Clinical Research Center, University of Minnesota (M01-RR00400), to Patricia J. Bauer (HD28425, HD 42483); and to the Center for Neurobehavioral Development (A09011007); an Institute of Child Development, University of Minnesota Small Grant to Carol L. Cheatham; and the National Science Foundation (graduate student fellowship to Carol L. Cheatham).

REFERENCES

Algarin, C., Peirano, P., Garrido, M., Pizarro, F., & Lozoff, B. (2003). Iron deficiency anemia in infancy: Long-lasting effects on auditory and visual system functioning. *Pediatric Research, 53*, 217–223.

Angulo-Kinzler, R. M., Peirano, P., Lin, E., Algarin, C., Garrido, M., & Lozoff, B. (2002). Twenty-four-hour motor activity in human infants with and without iron deficiency anemia. *Early Human Development, 70*, 85–101.

Barks, J. D., Sun, R., Malinak, C., & Silverstein, F. S. (1995). gp120 an HIV-1 protein, increases susceptibility to hypoglycemic and ischemic brain injury in perinatal rats. *Experimental Neurology, 132*, 123–133.

Bayley, N. (1993). *Bayley scales of infant development-II.* New York: Psychological Testing Corporation.

Beard, J. L., & Connor, J. R. (2003). Iron status and neural functioning. *Annual Review of Nutrition, 23*, 41–58.

Brazy, J. E., Eckerman, C. O., Oehler, J. M., Goldstein, R. F., & O'Rand, A. M. (1991). Nursery neurobiologic risk score: Important factor in predicting outcome in very low birth weight infants. *The Journal of Pediatrics, 118*, 783–792.

Caputo, D. V., Goldstein, K. M., & Taub, H. B. (1979). The development of prematurely born children through middle school. In T. M. Field, A. M. Sostek, S. Goldberg & H. H. Shuman (Eds.), *Infants born at risk* (pp. 219–248). New York: SP Medical and Scientific.

Caulfield, L. E., Zavaleta, N., Shankar, A. H., & Merialdi, M. (1998). Potential contribution of maternal zinc supplementation during pregnancy to maternal and child survival. *The American Journal of Clinical Nutrition, 68*, 499–508.

Cheatham, C. L. (2004). *Recall deficits in infants born preterm: Sources of individual differences.* Unpublished doctoral dissertation, University of Minnesota, Twin Cities.

Cheatham, C. L., Bauer, P. J., & Georgieff, M. K. (2006). Predicting individual differences in recall by infants born preterm and fullterm. *Infancy, 10,* 17–42.

Cordero, M. E., Valenzuela, C. Y., Rodriguez, A., & Aboitiz, F. (2003). Dendritic morphology and orientation of pyramidal cells of the neocortex in two groups of early postnatal undernourished–rehabilitated rats. *Brain Research. Developmental Brain Research, 142,* 37–45.

Crowe, T. K., Deitz, J. C., Bennett, F. C., & TeKolste, K. (1988). Preschool motor skills of children born prematurely and not diagnosed as having cerebral palsy. *Developmental and Behavioral Pediatrics, 9,* 189–193.

Curtis, W. J., Lindeke, L., Georgieff, M. K., & Nelson, C. A. (2002). Neurobehavioral functioning in neonatal intensive care unit graduates in late childhood and early adolescence. *Brain, 125,* 1646–1659.

de Haan, M., Bauer, P. J., Georgieff, M. K., & Nelson, C. A. (2000). Explicit memory in low-risk infants aged 19 months born between 27 and 42 weeks of gestation. *Developmental Medicine and Child Neurology, 42,* 304–312.

DeRegnier, R. A., Wewerka, S., Georgieff, M. K., Mattia, F., & Nelson, C. A. (2002). Influences of postconceptional age and postnatal experience on the development of auditory recognition memory in the newborn infant. *Developmental Psychobiology, 41,* 216–225.

Dorrepaal, C. A., Berger, H. M., Benders, M. J., van Zoeren-Grobben, D., Van de Bor, M., & Van Bel, F. (1996). Nonprotein-bound iron in postasphyxial reperfusion injury of the newborn. *Pediatrics, 98,* 883–889.

Eggermont, J. J. (1988). On the rate of maturation of sensory evoked potentials. *Electroencephalography and Clinical Neurophysiology, 70,* 293–305.

Fray, P. J., Robbins, T. W., & Sahakian, B. J. (1996). Neuropsychiatric applications of CANTAB. *International Journal of Geriatric Psychiatry, 11,* 329–336.

Hee Han, B., Choi, J., & Holtzman, D. M. (2002). Evidence that p38 mitogen-activated protein kinase contributes to neonatal hypoxic–ischemic brain injury. *Developmental Neuroscience, 24,* 405–410.

Hokins-Golightly, T., Raz, S., & Sander, C. J. (2003). Influence of slight to moderate risk for birth hypoxia on acquisition of cognitive and language function in the preterm infant: A cross-sectional comparison with preterm-birth controls. *Neuropsychology, 17,* 3–13.

Isaacs, E. B., Lucas, A., Chong, W. K., Wood, S. J., Johnson, C. L., Marshall, C., *et al.* (2000). Hippocampal volume and everyday memory in children of very low birth weight. *Pediatric Research, 47,* 713–720.

Jiang, L., Ding, Y., & Tang, Y. (2001). Relationship between c-fos gene expression and delayed neuronal death in rat neonatal hippocampus following hypoxic–ischemic insult. *Chinese Medical Journal, 114,* 520–530.

Kalmar, M. (1996). The course of intellectual development in preterm and fullterm children: An 8-year longitudinal study. *International Journal of Behavioral Development, 19,* 491–516.

Karrer, J. H., Karrer, R., Bloom, D., Chaney, L., & Davis, R. (1998). Event-related brain potentials during an extended visual recognition memory task depict delayed development of cerebral inhibitory processes among 6-month-old infants with Down syndrome. *International Journal of Psychophysiology, 29,* 167–200.

King, R. S., DeBassio, W. A., Kemper, T. L., Rosene, D. L., Tonkiss, J., Galler, J. R., *et al.* (2004). Effects of prenatal protein malnutrition and acute postnatal stress on granule cell genesis in the fascia dentata of neonatal and juvenile rats. *Brain Research. Developmental Brain Research, 150,* 9–15.

Levy, M. L., Masri, L. S., & McComb, J. G. (1997). Outcome for preterm infants with germinal matrix hemorrhage and progressive hydrocephalus. *Neurosurgery, 41*, 1111–1118.

Lozoff, B., Jimenez, E., Hagen, J., Mollen, E., & Wolf, A. W. (2000). Poorer behavioral and developmental outcome more than 10 years after treatment for iron deficiency in infancy. *Pediatrics, 105*, E51–E61.

Luciana, M., Lindeke, L., Georgieff, M., Mills, M., & Nelson, C. A. (1999). Neurobehavioral evidence for working-memory deficits in school-aged children with histories of prematurity. *Developmental Medicine and Child Neurology, 41*, 521–533.

Mallard, C., Welin, A. K., Peebles, D., Hagberg, J., & Kjellmer, I. (2003). White matter injury following systemic endotoxemia or asphyxia in the fetal sheep. *Neurochemical Research, 28*, 215–223.

Mendola, P., Selevan, S. G., Gutter, S., & Rice, D. (2002). Environmental factors associated with a spectrum of neurodevelopmental deficits. *Mental Retardation and Developmental Disabilities Research Reviews, 8*, 188–197.

Neal, C. R., Jr., VanderBeek, B. L., Vazquez, D. M., & Watson Jr., S. J. (2003). Dexamethasone exposure during the neonatal period alters ORL1 mRNA expression in the hypothalamic paraventricular nucleus and hippocampus of the adult rat. *Developmental Brain Research, 146*, 15–24.

Nelson, K. B., & Ellenberg, J. H. (1981). Apgar scores as predictors of chronic neurologic disability. *Pediatrics, 68*, 36–44.

Nunez, J. L., Alt, J. J., & McCarthy, M. M. (2003). A novel model for prenatal brain damage II: Long-term deficits in hippocampal cell number and hippocampal-dependent behavior following neonatal GABA receptor activation. *Experimental Neurology, 181*, 270–280.

Palomo, T., Beninger, R. J., Kostrzewa, R. M., & Archer, T. (2003). Brain sites of movement disorder: Genetic and environmental agents in neurodevelopmental perturbations. *Neurotoxicity Research, 5*, 1–26.

Peyronnet, J., Dalmaz, Y., Ehrstrom, M., Mamet, J., Roux, J. C., Pequignot, J. M., et al. (2002). Long-lasting adverse effects of prenatal hypoxia on developing autonomic nervous system and cardiovascular parameters in rats. *Pflügers Archiv — European Journal of Physiology, 443*, 858–865.

Rao, R. B., de Ungria, M., Sullivan, D., Wu, P., Wobken, J. D., Nelson, C. A., et al. (1999). Perinatal iron deficiency increases the vulnerability of rat hippocampus to hypoxic insult. *The Journal of Nutrition, 129*, 199–206.

Roncagliolo, M., Garrido, M., Walter, T., Peirano, P., & Lozoff, B. (1998). Evidence of altered central nervous system development in infants with iron deficiency anemia at 6 mo: Delayed maturation of auditory brainstem responses. *The American Journal of Clinical Nutrition, 68*, 683–690.

Rose, S. A., Feldman, J. F., McCarton, C. M., & Wolfson, J. (1988). Information processing in seven-month-old infants as a function of risk status. *Child Development, 59*, 589–603.

Sahakian, B. J., & Owen, A. M. (1992). Computerized assessment in neuropsychiatry using CANTAB: Discussion paper. *Journal of the Royal Society of Medicine, 85*, 399–402.

Sesma, H. W., & Georgieff, M. K. (2003). The effect of adverse intrauterine and newborn environments on cognitive development: The experiences of premature delivery and diabetes during pregnancy. *Development and Psychopathology, 15*, 991–1015.

Shevell, M. I., Majnemer, A., & Morin, I. (2003). Etiologic yield of cerebral palsy: A contemporary case series. *Pediatric Neurology, 28*, 352–359.

Siddappa, A. J., Georgieff, M. K., Wewerka, S., Worwa, C., Nelson, C. A., & deRegnier, R. A. (2004). Iron deficiency alters auditory recognition memory in newborn infants of diabetic mothers. *Pediatric Research, 55*, 1034–1041.

Siddappa, A. J., Rao, R. B., Wobken, J. D., Casperson, K., Leibold, E. A., Connor, J. R., *et al.* (2003). Iron deficiency alters iron regulatory protein and iron transport protein expression in the perinatal rat brain. *Pediatric Research, 53*, 800–807.

Stolarova, M., Whitney, H., Webb, S. J., deRegnier, R. A., Georgieff, M. K., & Nelson, C. A. (2003). Electrophysiological brain responses of six-month-old low risk premature infants. *Infancy, 4*, 437–450.

Stover, P. J. (2004). Physiology of folate and vitamin B12 in health and disease. *Nutrition Reviews, 62*, S3–S13.

Thorp, J. A., Jones, P. G., Clark, R. H., Knox, E., & Peabody, J. L. (2001). Perinatal factors associated with severe intracranial hemorrhage. *American Journal of Obstetrics and Gynecology, 185*, 859–882.

Trask, C. L., & Kosofsky, B. E. (2000). Developmental considerations of neurotoxic exposures. *Neurologic Clinics, 18*, 541–562.

West, J. R., Chen, W. J., & Pantazis, N. J. (1994). Fetal alcohol syndrome: The vulnerability of the developing brain and possible mechanisms. *Metabolic Brain Disease, 9*, 291–322.

Yager, J. Y., Armstrong, E. A., Miyashita, H., & Wirrell, E. C. (2002). Prolonged neonatal seizures exacerbate hypoxic–ischemic brain damage: Correlation with cerebral energy metabolism and excitatory amino acid release. *Developmental Neuroscience, 24*, 367–381.

INSTITUTIONAL CARE AS A RISK FOR DECLARATIVE MEMORY DEVELOPMENT

Maria G. Kroupina,* Patricia J. Bauer,[†] Megan R. Gunnar,[‡] and Dana E. Johnson*

* DEPARTMENT OF PEDIATRICS, UNIVERSITY OF MINNESOTA, MINNEAPOLIS, MINNESOTA, USA
[†] DEPARTMENT OF PSYCHOLOGY, EMORY UNIVERSITY, ATLANTA, GEORGIA, USA
[‡] INSTITUTE OF CHILD DEVELOPMENT, UNIVERSITY OF MINNESOTA, MINNEAPOLIS, MINNESOTA, USA

Many researchers have argued that human brain development can be affected by the quality of early experiences (e.g., Greenough & Black, 1992). In recent years, we have learned a lot about the normal course of declarative memory development and associated brain structures (see Chapter 1); however, we know much less about effects of adversity on memory development. Increasing evidence shows that early adverse life experiences appear to have long-term effects on the brain and development. Unfortunately, one of the challenges of studying the effects of early adversity on later development is that most children who experience early adversity also continue to live in adverse environments (e.g., neglectful

137

and abusive families) through their entire childhood. Over developmental time, it becomes increasingly difficult to disentangle the effects of early adversity from the continued adversity to which these children are exposed in their lives.

It has been argued that research with postinstitutionalized children provides a unique opportunity to understand the impact of a clearly demarcated period of early deprivation on later development (Gunnar, 2001; Rutter, 1981). Given that adoption brings a dramatic change in a child's life, it can be considered a major intervention. As such, research with this population also can help us uncover the effects of intervention (i.e., adoption) on children's developmental trajectories. Most of the current research is focused on uncovering the impact of institutional care on development in general cognition. In this chapter, we summarize finding from animal and human studies that declarative memory function may be particularly sensitive to the effects of early adversity such as institutional care. We also argue that studies of cognitive functions such as declarative memory associated with specific brain structures may help us to understand the mechanisms by which early adversity impacts later development. Given that the majority of postinstitutionalized children adopted into families within the first 3 years of their lives, the developmental period associated with the most rapid declarative memory development (see Bauer, 2007, for review), the argument is made in this chapter that studies of postinstitutionalized children may provide us this opportunity to study the impact of early adversity on development of declarative memory. Previously the question of how institutional care might impact declarative memory has not been addressed in humans. In this chapter, we present two experiments addressing this question. At the end of this chapter, futures directions in research in this area are discussed.

I. Postinstitutionalized Children—Cognitive Function

For many years, scientists have been trying to understand the effects of institutional care on the development of children. The first wave of studies demonstrated profound adverse effects on human development (e.g., Rutter, 1981). A dramatic increase in the number of internationally adopted children from institutional care settings has resulted in a new wave of studies of this population (e.g., Ames, 1997; O'Connor, Rutter, & Beckett *et al.*, 2000; O'Connor, Rutter, & English and Romanian Adoptees Study Team, 2000; Rutter, Kreppner, O'Connor, & English and Romanian Adoptees Study Team, 2001). Several studies have shown that children raised in institutional care often reach their adoptive families physically stunted and developmentally delayed (Hostetter & Johnson, 1989; Hostetter *et al.*, 1991; Johnson *et al.*, 1992). The effects are pervasive, impacting physical growth, general intelligence, language, and social–emotional functioning (for discussion, see Gunnar, 2000). Some evidence that early deprivation in institutional care may result in abnormal brain development has recently emerged from studies of postinstitutionalized children and children in Romanian institutions (Chugani *et al.*, 2001; Marshall & Fox, 2003; Parker & Nelson, 2003). A growing number of studies have also demonstrated abnormal functioning of the stress sensitive system in children raised in adverse contexts including institutional care (for further discussion, see Gunnar, 2000). Several studies have indicated that institutional care is associated with disturbances in the normal diurnal cortisol production (Carlson & Earls, 1997; Gunnar, 2000; Gunnar, 2001).

In institutional care, children often are exposed to risk factors such as neglect and poor nutrition. Older children in particular are at risk for physical and sexual abuse (Verhulst, Althaus, & Versluis-Den Bieman, 1990). Some of these risk factors are the same as those experienced by children raised in the context of neglect and poverty. However, a conglomerate of risk factors is common across many institutions, including the lack of stable adult–child relationships, the dearth of individualized care, and deficits in age-appropriate sensory and social stimulation. Different degrees and types of deprivation may be related to different developmental outcomes (Ames, 1997; Gunnar, 2000; Rutter & The E.R.A. Study Team, 1998).

It is been suggested that studies of children from institutional care present us with relatively consistent picture, even though children in different studies potentially were exposed to different degree of deprivation (O'Connor, Rutter, & Beckett, *et al.*, 2000). Rutter *et al.* (2001) proposed that there are several impairments that are particularly associated with early deprivation in institutional care that may persist even many years after adoption. According to their findings, these impairments include attachment problems, difficulty in the ability to control attention and behavior, abnormal social behavior, and a syndrome that mimics autism. Findings from previous studies also suggest that impairment in general cognition constitutes one of the consequences of institutionalization (O'Connor, Rutter, & Beckett *et al.*, 2000; O'Connor, Rutter, & English and Romanian Adoptees Study Team, 2000; Rutter *et al.*, 2001). The duration of institutional care relates to developmental functions (Carlson & Earls, 1997; Kaler & Freeman, 1994), with longer durations associated with more negative impact. In an early study by Provence and Lipton (1962), a group of children in institutional care in the United States were studied over their first years of life. The children experienced high quality institutional care, yet they lacked consistent care giving. Provence and Lipton also followed a group of same-age children who lived with their parents or foster parents. Prior to 6 months of age, the institution-reared and home-reared children did not differ in general developmental level. However, by the end of the first year, a difference in cognitive development was apparent. More recently, it has been reported that by the age of 5 years, children in Romanian institutions are more than 2 years behind normal mental developmental levels (Carlson & Earls).

Effects of the duration of poor quality institutional care are apparent even after adoption. Rutter & The E.R.A. Study Team (1998) found that the age at adoption (which in most cases corresponds with the length of deprivation) was particularly associated with the level of general cognitive functions, as measured by the General Cognitive Index, MacCarthy Children's Developmental Scales. By the age of 4–6 years, children adopted before 6 months of age appeared to have completely recovered. In contrast, children adopted between 6 and 24 months continued to score lower compared to children adopted before 6 months (Rutter *et al.*, 1998; O'Connor, Rutter, & Beckett *et al.*, 2000). Similar results were found in a group of Romanian children adopted into British Columbian homes (Ames, 1997). Children who were adopted at an age older than 24 months were more likely to exhibit significant impairments in general cognitive skills (IQ < 85), relative to children adopted before 24 months. Thus, the older the children are at the time of adoption, the more difficult it is for them to recover cognitive function. The result is that a considerable percentage of postinstitutionalized children continued to show significant impairments in the general cognitive area even many years after adoption (O'Connor, Rutter, & Beckett *et al.*; O'Connor, Rutter, & English and Romanian Adoptees Study Team, 2000). Rutter *et al.* (2001) addressed this possibility that older children spend less time in their new environment, one of the possible explanations of the age factor. However, even when they took into account time of being in a new environment, they found a strong effect of age at adoption on general cognitive functions. Rutter *et al.* (2001) also found that postadoptive environment such parental education does not impact catch-up in the general cognitive domain. The same study found an association between head circumference at the time of entry into the country and cognitive level at 6 years. Postinstitutionalized children whose scores suggested general cognitive impairments also had head circumference 1 standard lower than those with no cognitive impairments. Based on these findings, Rutter *et al.* (2001) suggested that the impact of institutional care on the general cognitive domain can be explained by experience-expectant programming or neural damage models.

In summary, the results from previous studies suggest that the combination of risk factors to which children may be exposed in institutional care negatively impacts the development of general cognitive functions. However, from these studies we cannot draw any conclusions about possible underlying mechanisms of this impact. As Gunnar (2001) points out, the question of how the experience of early deprivation affects the development of specific cognitive areas has not been addressed. It is important that we address this question, given that an assessment of more specific cognitive functions of postinstitutionalized children associated with specific brain structures may be a particularly useful tool that will allow us to investigate the mechanisms of how early adversity translates into later problems. In the next section, we discuss reasons to expect that the specific cognitive function of declarative memory may be affected, in particular.

II. Specific Cognitive Functions: Declarative Memory and the Typical Developmental Course

As reviewed in Chapter 1, there is strong evidence that declarative memory is subserved by a particular brain system including the hippocampus, other medial temporal lobe structures, and surrounding cortices (see Zola & Squire, 2000, for a review). The declarative memory system undergoes substantial development during the first 2 years of life, as the neural structures that support it themselves develop (Bauer, 2004; Carver & Bauer, 2001). Concomitant changes are observed in declarative memory behavior (see Chapters 1–3). Given the protracted development of declarative memory in infancy, there is ample opportunity for the environment in which children are raised to impact its course. A suboptimal environment may compromise the development of declarative memory and underlying brain structures. Evidence consistent with this suggestion is discussed below.

A. EVIDENCE FROM ANIMAL AND HUMAN STUDIES

There is increasing evidence from rodent models of early deprivation that adverse early life experiences are connected with a long-term memory deficit (e.g., Brunson, Eghbal-Ahmandi, Bender, Chen, & Baram, 2001). Gunnar (2004) summarized the evidence from animal studies suggesting that stress early in the postnatal life affects the hippocampus and associated structures that mediate declarative memory. Specifically, receptors for glucocorticoids are widely distributed in different brain structures, and the hippocampus is one of the brain areas that has a particularly high concentration of these receptors (e.g., McEwen, de Kloet, & Rostene, 1986).

Manipulation of maternal behavior in rats early in an offspring's life changes the number of receptors for glucocorticoids in the hippocampus (Liu, Diorio, Day, Francis, & Meaney, 2000; Meaney, Aitken, Van Berkel, Bhatnagar, & Sapolsky, 1998). In addition, administration of a corticotropin-releasing hormone (CRH) to the brains of immature rats (which produces a model of how early stress may affect brain development) is associated with progressive loss of hippocampal neurons (Brunson et al., 2001). The CRH-treated rats exhibited impairments in performance on the tasks that required retaining previously learned information. These animals continued to exhibit impairments in their performance on the hippocampally mediated tasks throughout life. The effects of early deprivation in rodents are similar to those that result from stressful environments (e.g., Brunson et al., 2001; Meaney et al., 1998). However, despite the adversity, rat pups who experience higher quality postnatal care (i.e., their mothers were more involved in such behaviors as licking and grooming) performed at higher levels on the hippocampally mediated tasks later in life (Liu et al., 2000). Overall, the results from the studies with rodents support the hypothesis that the plasticity of the memory system early in life makes this system open to positive effects from the environment; however, it makes this system vulnerable as well (Nelson & Carver, 1998).

The results of studies with nonhuman primates are not as clear as those with rodents. For example, in the series of studies done by Harlow, Harlow, and Suomi (1971), it was found that separation from the mother and peer group rearing did not dramatically impair cognitive functions in monkeys. Sanchez, Hear, Do, Rilling, and Herdon (1998) studied a group of infant rhesus macaques reared in a peer group from 2 to 12 months. They found that it was challenging for these animals to learn stimulus–reward contingencies, however, they did not have problems in performing tasks that required learning stimulus–response association after a 10-min delay. Nevertheless, some studies with nonhuman primates indicated that early deprivation might have an effect on the hippocampus (Siegel et al., 1993). Siegel et al. found that total social isolation early in life in rhesus monkeys leads to abnormal development in the dentate gyrus granule layer of the hippocampus.

Although the experimental work on the effects of stress on the hippocampus has been done with animal models, there also are relevant data from adult humans. Hippocampally mediated memory problems have been found in adults previously exposed to stressful events early in life

(Heim, Owen, Plotsky, & Nemeroff, 1997; Sanchez *et al.*, 1998). Brunson *et al.* (2001) proposed that stress early in life might have a long-lasting effect on the hippocampus in humans. However, the results of the studies that address the question of how early traumatic events affect the hippocampus in humans also present a more complex picture. For example, an early history of severe physical or sexual abuse is associated with a smaller hippocampal volume in women with major depression (Vythilingam *et al.*, 2002). In contrast to these findings, a 2-year longitudinal study of a small group of maltreated children diagnosed with posttraumatic stress disorder (PTSD) did not find differences in the hippocampal volume between the group diagnosed with PTSD and the control group (De Bellis, Hall, Boring, Frustaci, & Moritz, 2001). It is important to note that in both studies, the assessment was done on a small subgroup of people who were not only exposed to an early traumatic event, but had major psychopathological symptoms as well. Therefore, it is difficult to generalize the results of these studies to all people who are exposed to early stress. It is important to consider also the duration, the severity, and the type of stress to which children were exposed (Vythilingam *et al.*, 2002).

Several review articles have summarized how stress and trauma in early development may compromise the normal developmental course of declarative memory (e.g., Nelson & Carver, 1998). The reviews feature consistent evidence that high levels of glucocorticoids associated with stress may damage the hippocampus and associated brain structures (e.g. McEwen, 1998; Sapolsky, 1996). It also has been suggested that during the first years, development of the brain structures underlining declarative memory may be particularly sensitive to the effects of stress and trauma (Nelson & Carver, 1998). There is some evidence from studies with animal and humans to support this argument.

Overall, the results from animal studies suggest that stress and deprivation may lead to a disturbance in the developmental course of hippocampally mediated memory processes. Data from human studies also raise the possibility that the experience of early institutionalization may affect the development of declarative memory. Nelson and Carver (1998) suggested that the first years of life could be a particularly vulnerable time for the development of declarative memory. Critically, as elaborated above, the structures are especially vulnerable to effects of deprivation and stress such as that associated with institutional care; potential effects could be especially devastating during periods of rapid developmental change (Nelson & Carver, 1998). The combination of the impoverished environment and the limited opportunities institutionalized children have to explore may potentially prevent the brain from receiving critical input for normal development of such cognitive functions as declarative memory.

As discussed above, in institutional care, children usually are deprived of normal sensory and motor stimulation. These children are deprived also of normal interactions with adults, the main source of learning in the first years of life. Greenough, Black, and Wallace (1987) suggested that by actively interacting with their environment infants create an environment critical for normal development (see also Chapter 7). Passivity has been recognized as one of the main behavioral characteristics of children in institutional care (Spitz, 1946). As a result, children may become less capable of benefiting from experiences. Infants who are not capable of exploring their environment effectively may be at risk for later learning impairments (Ruff, McCarton, Kurtzberg, & Vaughan, 1984).

Given that most of the internationally adopted children arrive at their new homes during their second or early third year of life, coinciding with a period of especially rapid and important changes in memory development (e.g., Bauer, 2007; Bauer *et al.*, 2000), this group present us with a unique opportunity to address the question of how early adversity impacts declarative memory development.

B. DECLARATIVE MEMORY SKILLS IN POSTINSTITUTIONALIZED TODDLERS

The present research presents a first attempt to test relations between the experience of early deprivation and the development of declarative memory. In Experiment 1, we compared the declarative memory performance of children who had been raised in institutional care for the first months of life and were subsequently adopted into homes in the United States with that of home-reared children in the United States. The children were assessed, on average, 8 months after adoption. In Experiment 2, we compared the performance of children adopted earlier versus later in life. The children were assessed, on average, 6 months after adoption. In both experiments, most of the children had come to their new homes during their second or early in their third year of life.

C. IMITATION-BASED TASKS

In both experiments, the children were tested using imitation-based tasks. We chose to use this method for three main reasons. First, since most of the children come to the adopted families before their third birthdays, we needed a nonverbal test. This method is designed to assess preverbal children. Second, as discussed earlier, the method is accepted as a measure of declarative memory. Third, the method has proven sensitive to declarative memory deficits in children from other special populations, including infants born prior to term (de Haan, Bauer, Georgieff, & Nelson, 2000) and children with Down syndrome (Rast & Meltzoff, 1995).

In both experiments, the children were tested for immediate recall and for recall after a brief delay (10–15 min). As the name implies, in the immediate recall task, performance was tested immediately after presentation of the test sequences. In the delayed recall task, a delay was imposed between demonstration of the sequence and the test for recall. The delays were roughly 10 min and 15 min in Experiments 1 and 2, respectively. As discussed by Bauer (Chapter 1), although relatively brief, delays of this length provide a strong test of the integrity of the declarative memory system.

In the first experiment, we also addressed the possibility that differences between the groups on their performance could be attributed to non-mnemonic factors. Because inattention and hyperactivity have been found to be major areas of concern for this group (Kreppner, O'Connor, Rutter, & English and Romania Adoptees Study Team, 2001), we address the possibility that poor attention skills might affect children's performance on the imitation tasks. To address this question, in Experiment 1, we included a "distraction" in one condition of the imitation task. In this condition, as the multistep sequences were modeled, a musical toy was activated. Consequently, more demands were placed on the child's attention system during encoding of the event. In the second experiment, we tested immediate and delay recall only.

III. Experiment 1

A. METHOD

The present research was part of a large-scale project that investigated the effects of institutional care on the development of children. A group of postinstitutionalized children was recruited from the International Adoption Clinic at the University of Minnesota and through information given to the adoption agencies. A comparison group of family-reared children matched on age and sex was recruited from an existing pool of parents who expressed interest in participating in research at the time of their children's birth. Fifty-two children participated, with 18 females and 8 males in each group. The postinstitutionalized group included children adopted from China ($n = 11$), Eastern Europe ($n = 10$), Vietnam ($n = 3$), and India ($n = 2$). All children in the family-reared group were Caucasian.

The adopted children were assessed at 2 and 8 months after adoption. The measures for the present research were obtained during the second wave of data collection, which took place 8 months postadoption (6 months after the first wave of data collection). Eight months after adoption, children participated in a 75-min laboratory assessment of declarative memory and other specific cognitive domains (i.e., attention). Within 2 weeks after this laboratory session, children participated in a 1-h session during which we assessed general cognitive and motor skills. At the time of assessment, the children's ages ranged from 11.9 to 26.3 months (mean = 18.8 months). None of the postinstitutionalized or family-born children had been diagnosed with any congenital disorder at the time of assessment.

All the children were tested with the three novel event sequences. Children younger than 15 months were tested using two-step sequences; children aged 15 months were tested on three-step sequences (see Bauer *et al.*, 2000; Chapter 2 for discussions of age-related changes in the lengths of sequences that children are able to reproduce). All sequences were temporally constrained by enabling relations, such that in order to reach a goal, the actions had to be performed in a particular order.

For each sequence, the props were given to the child for exploration. The children's performance prior to modeling was a measure of the spontaneous production of the target actions and pairs of actions produced in the target order.

For the immediate recall and 10-min delayed recall conditions, after the baseline period, the experimenter modeled the sequence two times with narration. In the immediate recall condition, the experimenter then returned the props to the child and encouraged imitation with prompts such as, "Now it is your turn! You make a gong, just like I did." In the 10-min delayed recall condition, there was a delay between demonstration of the sequence by the experimenter and imitation by the child. During this time, the children stayed in the same room with their parents and were offered a snack. After the delay, the props were given to the child, and the child was encouraged to imitate the modeled sequence. In the distraction condition, a musical toy animal was turned on for 15 s after each step of the sequence was modeled. The toy was located to the left side of the child. In order to look at the musical toy, children had to turn their heads from the props. After the toy stopped, the experimenter attracted the children's attention and presented her or him with the next step in the sequence. After the modeling, the props were returned to the children, and they were encouraged to imitate the sequence.

Within each group of children, the test sequences were counterbalanced so that each of the sequences occurred equally in each recall condition.

The order of the conditions was also counterbalanced. Primary and reliability scoring was done from videotapes of the sessions. The dependent measures of number of individual actions produced and production of actions in temporal order were derived as described in Burch *et al.* (Chapter 2).

B. RESULTS AND DISCUSSION

Descriptive statistics for performance on the imitation-based tasks (i.e., mean proportions of target actions and mean proportions of pairs of the actions produced in target order) are provided in Table I. We conducted separate 2 (modeling condition: premodeling, postmodeling) × 3 (task: immediate, delay, distraction) × 2 (groups: family reared, postinstitutionalized) mixed analyses of variance (ANOVA) for each dependent measure (modeling condition and task are within-subject factors). There were clear effects of modeling condition. Across tasks and groups, the children produced larger proportions of target actions, $F(1, 42) = 106.1$, $p < .0001$, and pairs of actions in target order. $F(1, 42) = 94.5$, $p < .001$, after modeling than they

Table I

Descriptive Statistics for the Mean Number (and Standard Deviation) of Proportion of Different Target Actions and Mean Number of Proportion of Pairs of Target Actions Produced in the Correct Order

| | | Group | |
| | | Mean (SD) | |
Dependent Measure/Task		Postinstitutionalized	Family Reared
Proportion of target actions produced			
Immediate	Premodeling	.21 (.25)	.40 (.33)
	Postmodeling	.71 (.35)	.80 (.33)
10-Min delay	Premodeling	.19 (.25)	.30 (.32)
	Postmodeling	.63 (.33)	.81 (.27)
Distraction	Premodeling	.17 (.24)	.37 (.30)
	Postmodeling	.71 (.36)	.72 (.33)
Proportion of pairs of actions in the target order			
Immediate	Premodeling	0 (1.70)	.20 (.29)
	Postmodeling	.54 (.42)	.67 (.44)
10-Min delay	Premodeling	0 (.18)	0 (.20)
	Postmodeling	.42 (.43)	.64 (.44)
Distraction	Premodeling	0 (0)	.12 (.25)
	Postmodeling	.56 (.40)	.55 (.44)

had prior to modeling. The analysis did not reveal a main effect of the task for either dependent measure ($Fs < 1.20$). The main effects of group were significant for both dependent measures, $F(1, 42) = 5.6$, $p < .02$ and $F(1, 42) = 5.1$, $p < .03$, for the proportion of target actions and proportion of pairs in target order, respectively. Overall, the performance of the postinstitutionalized group was lower than that of the family-reared group.

Because the main effects of groups were not qualified by interactions with modeling condition, based on this analysis alone, it is not appropriate to attribute group effects to children's recall; the effect may have been apparent even prior to demonstration of the sequences. To examine this possibility, children's premodeling performance was compared in the three conditions. Prior to modeling, relative to family-reared children, the postinstitutionalized children produced fewer target actions in the immediate recall, $F(1, 47) = 4.84$, $p < .03$, and distraction, $F(1, 44) = 6.14$, $p < .02$, conditions, and fewer pairs of actions in the target order in the distraction condition, $F(1, 44) = 4.67$, $p < .04$. There also was a nonsignificant trend of lower performance for postinstitutionalized children on the number of pairs of actions produced in target order in the immediate recall condition, $F(1, 47) = 3.35$, $p < .07$. In contrast, we did not find a group difference for either dependent measure in the premodeling performance in the 10-min delayed recall condition ($ps < .17$ and $.64$).

In light of the difference in premodeling performance in the immediate recall and distraction conditions, to determine whether there were effects on recall, *per se*, we conducted ANCOVAs on children's postmodeling performance with their premodeling performance in each condition covaried. For the immediate recall and distraction conditions, with baseline performance statistically controlled, there was no effect of group on either dependent measure ($ps < .57$). Thus, the groups did not differ in the immediate recall and distraction tasks. Given the lack of group differences in performance prior to imitation in the 10-min delayed recall condition, we did not use premodeling performance in the analysis of groups for the delay recall task. We found that the postinstitutionalized group produced significantly fewer target actions in this condition, $F(1, 46) = 3.96$, $p < .05$. The analysis also revealed a strong trend for group difference in ordered recall, as measured by production of pairs of actions in target order, $F(1, 46) = 3.43$, $p < .07$.

Lower levels of ordered recall performance on the 10-min delayed recall task were also apparent in nonparametric analyses in which we determined the number of children whose performance on the tasks improved after demonstration of the sequences, relative to the premodeling performance, and the number of children whose performance did not improve (Table II). In the 10-min delayed recall condition, comparable percentages of children in

Table II
Number (and percentage) of Children whose Performance Improved and did not Improve after Modeling, Relative to the Baseline

Task/Dependent Variable	Pre/Postmodeling Change	Group	
		Postinstitutionalized	Family Reared
Immediate			
Actions	Was not improved	6 (24%)	4 (17.4%)
	Improved	19 (76%)	19 (82.6%)
Pairs	Was not improved	9 (36%)	6 (26.1%)
	Improved	16 (64%)	17 (73.9%)
10-Min delay			
Actions	Was not improved	6 (24%)	4 (18.2%)
	Improved	19 (76%)	18 (81.8%)
Pairs	Was not improved	15 (60%)	7 (31.8%)
	Improved	10 (40%)	19 (68.2%)
Distraction			
Actions	Was not improved	4 (20%)	6 (28.6%)
	Improved	20 (80%)	15 (71.4%)
Pairs	Was not improved	6 (28%)	7 (38.1%)
	Improved	18 (72%)	13 (61.9%)

the two groups increased their production of the individual target actions of the sequences after exposure to the model: 76% in the postinstitutionalized group compared to 82% in the family-reared group. However, only 40% of the children in the postinstitutionalized group increased their production of ordered pairs of actions, compared with 68% of the family-reared children ($\chi = 3.77, p < .05$). These results suggest that the requirement to defer recall over a delay as brief as 10 min impaired the performance of the postinstitutionalized children. Similar patterns were not apparent in the other two tasks. Specifically, comparable numbers of children in the two groups improved their performance in the immediate recall and distraction tasks.

We also explored the possibility that the disparity in performance between the groups was due to differences in children's overall general cognitive. Consistent with previous studies, we found that 8 months after adoption, the postinstitutionalized children scored significantly lower in general cognitive functioning than did family-reared children (as measured by the Bayley MDI). We found that 86% of the family-reared children had MDI scores at or above 1 standard deviation below the mean ($M = 99.6$, SD $= 11.6$). However, only 68% of the postinstitutionalized children scored within this range ($M = 86.3$, SD $= 14.30$). Analysis of the means revealed that the difference was significant, $F(1, 45) = 12.1, p < .001$. With the difference in overall cognitive level (as measured by the Bayley MDI) controlled, the group difference in children's production of ordered pairs of actions was significant, $F(2, 42) = 3.29$, $p < .05$, and there was a strong nonsignificant trend for differences in the production of the individual target actions of the sequences, $F(2, 42) = 2.85$, $p < .07$.

Given that the two groups of children performed at comparable levels on the immediate recall and distraction tasks, it is unlikely that the children's difficulty was due to problems encoding the event sequences. However, before concluding the alternative, namely, that they encountered difficulty maintaining the information over the 10-min delay, we conducted an analysis in which we statistically controlled the variance associated with immediate recall performance. If the difference at delay was apparent even with individual variability at encoding (as measured by immediate recall performance) controlled, then we are on firmer ground in concluding that the source of difficulty on the delayed recall task was the delay itself. Accordingly, we conducted an ANCOVA in which we controlled for encoding ability, using children's immediate recall performance. Separate analyses were conducted for each dependent measure. With immediate recall performance controlled, a significant group difference was found for the proportion of target actions produced in the 10-min delayed recall condition, $F(1, 46) = 3.47$, $p < .04$. With immediate recall performance controlled, there was a nonsignificant trend for the other dependent variable, namely, the proportion of pairs of actions produced in the target order, $F(1, 46) = 2.54$, $p < .09$. These results suggest that the difference between the groups after the 10-min delay should be attributed to the difference in the children's ability to retain information over time, as opposed to differences in encoding the material in the first place.

Overall, the results suggest that it was particularly challenging for the postinstitutionalized children to retain information over a delay. Similar results have been found in humans with temporal lobe damage and in monkeys with temporal lobe lesions (e.g., Reed & Squire, 1998; Zola, Squire, Rempel, Clower, & Amaral, 1992, respectively).

IV. Experiment 2

A. METHOD

The participants were 35 postinstitutionalized children (26 females and 9 males): 17 adopted from Eastern Europe, 16 adopted from China, and 2 adopted from Latin America. We included children from a wide range of ages (i.e., 17–33 months with a mean age of 21 months), in order to assess the effects of length of institutional care on declarative memory performance. The average age was = 21.4 (min = 17, max = 33). One child was excluded from the data analysis based on evidence of a congenital disorder. The children were assessed 1–3 months after adoption and again 6 months after adoption. The second session included an assessment of general cognitive skills and specific cognitive functions and is the subject of the present experiment.

As in Experiment 1, the children were tested on sequences that were temporally constrained such that in order to reach a goal, the actions had to be performed in a particular order. The children were tested with four sequences, two in the immediate recall and two in the 10-min delayed recall condition. The distraction task was not administered.

B. RESULTS AND DISCUSSION

Across the tasks, the postinstitutionalized children produced a larger number of target actions and pairs of target actions after modeling than they had prior to modeling, $F(1, 33) = 93.3$, $p < .001$ and $F(1, 33) = 98.1$, $p < .001$, for action and pairs, respectively. Descriptive statistics on performance are provided in Table III.

The analyses also revealed main effects of task for both dependent measures, $F(1, 33) = 4.4$, $p < .04$ and $F(1, 33) = 7.0$, $p < .01$, target actions and pairs, respectively. To assess the effect of the delay without the contribution of premodeling performance, we conducted within-subjects t tests

Table III

Experiment 2: Descriptive Statistics for the Number of Different Target Actions and Number of Pairs of Target Actions Produced in Target Order

| | Modeling Condition | |
| | Mean (SD) | |
Dependent Measure/Task	Premodeling	Postmodeling
Number of target actions		
Immediate	1.07 (.52)	2.32 (.70)
15-Min delay	1.07 (.52)	1.96 (.77)
Pairs of actions in target order		
Immediate	.21 (.28)	1.28 (.63)
15-Min delay	.17 (.24)	.97 (.68)

Note: For the analysis, we calculated mean scores of the performance on two tasks in each condition.

comparing postmodeling performance in the immediate recall and 10-min delayed recall conditions for both measures. For both measures, the difference was significant ($t = 2.65$, $p < .01$ and $t = 2.34$, $p < .02$, for target actions and pairs, respectively). These results are consistent with the findings from Experiment 1 and again indicate that for postinstitutionalized children, maintaining information in memory over a brief delay presents a cognitive challenge.

To determine whether, in the present sample, delayed recall performance differed as a function of age, we divided the sample into two subgroups: postinstitutionalized children younger than 20 months ($n = 16$ and mean age $= 18.4$) and older than 20 months ($n = 18$ and mean age $= 24$ months) at the time of assessment.

For the younger group, there was no significant decrease in performance between immediate and 10-min delayed recall performance ($t = 1.2$, ns and $t = .59$, ns, for target actions and pairs, respectively). In fact, some of the younger children actually had *higher* levels of performance after the delay, relative to at immediate recall (25% and 38% on the number of target actions and pairs of actions, respectively). In contrast, in the older group, performance after the delay was lower than performance at immediate testing ($t = 3.07$, $p < .01$ and $t = 2.97$, $p < .01$, for target actions and pairs, respectively). Also, in contrast to the first experiment, we found a negative relation between age at assessment and performance on the delayed recall task. The delay had a greater negative effect on the performance of the postinstitutionalized children who were older than 20 months at the time of assessment. In the older subgroup, only one child produced more target actions after the delay, relative to in immediate recall; two children increased their performance on the number of pairs of actions produced after the delay. These results suggest that the performance after the delay was particularly challenging for children older than 20 months at the time of the assessment.

Based on the studies of typically developing children, we know that by the end of the second year of life, children are able to retain information after delays of 10–15 min with no decrement in performance. For example, in a study by Bauer *et al.* (1999), the performance of a group of 20-month-old children after a 10-min delay was identical to their performance in immediate testing. However, studies of the typical developmental trajectory of declarative memory indicate that younger children (13- to 16-month-olds) are more challenged by a 10-min delay, relative to older children (20-month-olds) (Abravanel, 1991). These results indicate that after 20 months, the effect of institutionalization becomes apparent in the declarative memory domain.

V. Conclusions and Future Directions

Relatively little is known about how early experience shapes the development of declarative memory functions. As discussed previously, data from animal and human studies suggest that declarative memory may be one of the cognitive functions that is particularly vulnerable to the effects of adversity. The question of whether early deprivation affects memory development in humans has yet to be addressed. It is difficult to imagine a more abnormal environment for development than institutional care. The purpose of the two presented experiments was to investigate how institutional care affects the development of the specific cognitive function of declarative memory. The results of both experiments indicated that recall after a delay poses a particular challenge for the postinstitutionalized child. In Experiment 1, the challenge was apparent in the comparison of family-reared and postinstitutionalized children; in Experiment 2, the challenge was apparent in the comparison of performance on immediate and delayed recall tasks.

The postinstitutionalized children apparently suffered from a specific deficit in declarative memory ability. That is, even though the postinstitutionalized children were capable of imitating after modeling an event, they had more difficulty retaining the information over a brief delay relative to the family-reared children. Indeed, when a 10-min delay was imposed for children in the postinstitutionalized group, performance after modeling was not significantly above the premodeling level.

The results of both experiments indicate that the conglomerate of risk factors that postinstitutionalized children experience prenatally and postnatally may compromise the development of declarative memory and its associated brain structures. The problem may exist independent of and in addition to problems with encoding, attention, and general cognitive impairment. However, we need to reiterate that small sample size is a significant limitation of the present research. Replication of the tests using large samples may shed more light on the impact of the institutionalized care on the development of declarative memory in institutionalized children.

In addition to including larger samples, future research should follow samples of postinstitutionalized children over time. The importance of the plasticity of the developing brain has been emphasized (Nelson & Carver, 1998). Even if the experience of early institutionalization may lead to an abnormal pattern of declarative memory development, it is possible that we may see recovery in this domain over time. This possibility can best be addressed with longitudinal research.

In the first experiment, we addressed the question of the possible effect of general cognitive function on delay performance. In future studies, it will be important to address how developments in these two areas are interconnected. Declarative memory is one of the core cognitive areas, and it is logical to expect that its development will affect the development of general cognitive skills. For example, impairments in declarative memory and associated brain structure may prevent children from acquiring new information critical for normal development. It thus may be one the mechanisms that can lead to later general cognitive impairments.

In future studies, we must continue to address the role of other factors that may contribute to the challenge that postinstitutionalized children face in remembering over a delay. We addressed the possibility that attention skills in particular may affect their performance in the delay conditions. Though suggestive, the pattern of findings on the distraction task must be considered preliminary and thus be interpreted with caution. In future studies, it will be important to further explore how development in other domains impact declarative memory skills in postinstitutionalized children. It has been found that it is challenging for postinstitutionalized children to respond and initiate social interaction (Gunnar, 2001). It is import to investigate how potentially social deficit may impact performance on imitation-based tasks.

In the second experiment, we found that performance after a delay was especially challenging for children older than 20 months of age. We also found an association between changes in head circumference and children's performances on the imitation-based tasks in the delay condition (unpublished data). Given the small sample, these results have to be interpreted with caution. Future studies must address the question of the best-fitting model to explain the impact of institutional care on declarative memory development.

Previous studies have revealed a wide range in general cognitive skills of postinstitutionalized children (Ames, 1997; O'Connor, Rutter, & English and Romanian Adoptees Study Team, 2000). In the present research, we found that some postinstitutionalized children performed as well as children in the family-reared group. As it was suggested by O'Connor, Rutter, & Beckett et al., (2000), whereas current models of early experience help us to understand normative developmental course, it is challenging to use them to explain individual differences such as observed in high-risk groups. It has been suggested that individual difference might imply difference in children's genetic background (O'Connor, Rutter, & Beckett et al., 2000). It is also important to consider other prenatal and postnatal risk factors that postinstitutionalized children might be exposed prior to adoption.

The present research also revealed the unexpected finding of superior performance of postinstitutionalized children in the distraction condition (Experiment 1), in which we placed more demands on attention than in the other conditions. This suggests a possible difference in the way postinstitutionalized and family-reared children encode sequences. In future studies, it will be important to investigate how the manipulation of modeling conditions affects children's performance after a delay. It is also possible that it is easy for these children to encode information under certain conditions. This question has very important practical implications. If we find that a certain way of presenting information will help postinstitutionalized children's retention, we can design intervention programs for these children. Lack of appropriate intervention programs is a critical issue in the clinical work with this population.

Rutter & the E.R.A. Study Team (1998) suggested that studies of institutionalized children adopted into families have a number of unavoidable limitations. The present research is no exception. One of the limitations of these studies is that we do not have information regarding biological risk factors that the postinstitutionalized children may have experienced prior to adoption. These include risk factors related to pregnancy and birth, and also potential malnutrition and toxic exposure after birth. There is consistent support from research findings that different risk factors can lead to the same outcome (Cicchetti & Rogosch, 1996). Prenatal exposure to drugs and nutritional deprivation are known risk factors for child memory development (Georgieff & Rao, 2001; Streissguth & Connor, 2001). From the studies of low birth weight children and premature children, we also know that these children have problems in the memory domain later in life (e.g., de Haan *et al.*, 2001; Rose & Feldman, 2000; see Chapter 5).

It is not easy to address the effects of different risk factors and how they interact with the impact of institutional care. As one possible methodological approach, future studies should include children from different areas of the world. Potentially, children adopted from different regions of the world may have been exposed to different prenatal risk factors. For example, children adopted from China are likely at a lower risk of prenatal exposure to drugs, malnutrition, and stress than are children adopted from other regions of the world. Because we had a relatively small sample size in both experiments, we were not able to address the issue of risk factors in the present study. However, it is one of the questions that will be important to investigate in future studies.

Another possibility is that the differences in the quality of the children's postnatal experiences in institutional care prior to adoption may account for the differences in performance. Many parents have very little information about the condition of orphanage care (Gunnar, Bruce, & Grotevant,

2000); however, from what is known, there are some indications that the quality of the preadoptive experience may play a role in the development of cognitive skills (Ames, 1997; Castle *et al.*, 1998; O'Connor, Rutter, & English and Romanian Adoptees Study Team, 2000). Ames found that being a favorite child or not and the number of toys in the orphanage were associated with children's general cognitive scores after adoption. Based on existing studies, we also know that postnatal deprivation of specific micronutrients, such as iron, can lead to abnormal hypocampus development (Georgieff & Rao, 2001). The question of micronutrient deficiency has not been addressed in the population of institutionalized children, and it could be interesting direction for future studies. Higher incidences of vision and hearing problems in postinstitutionalized children compared to the general population were also found (unpublished data). The problems in these domains may potentially impact normal development in the cognitive domains by constraining a child's ability to explore the environment. Overall it is possible that the children who have experienced the greatest number of biological risk factors the most sensitive to the quality of their postnatal environment (Sameroff & Chandler, 1975).

Unfortunately, there are dramatic numbers of children, all over the world living in institutional care. There are ever-increasing numbers of these children adopted into Western countries. We know from previous studies that some of these children continue to exhibit deficits in general cognitive domain years after adoption and many children have learning problems (Gunnar, 2001). This makes studies of postinstitutionalized children critically important from a practical stand point. It will be important in future research to address whether memory skills measured soon after adoption are predictive of later general cognitive functioning. Potentially, assessment of memory skills soon after adoption could be helpful in identifying the children who will benefit from early intervention programs.

In conclusion, in this chapter we argue that studies of more specific cognitive functions such as declarative memory in postinstitutionalized children can help us to understand the mechanism of how early adversity affects later development. These studies also may help us to develop assessment and intervention tools for children at risk.

Acknowledgment

This research was supported in part by the grants from NICHD (HD28425, HD 42483) to Patricia J. Bauer and the NIH (MH59848) to Megan R. Gunnar.

REFERENCES

Abravanel, E. (1991). Does immediate imitation influence long-term memory for observed actions? *Journal of Experimental Child Psychology, 51*, 235–244.

Ames, E. (1997). *The development of Romanian orphanage children adopted to Canada.* (Final Report to the National Welfare Grants Program: Human Resources Development, Canada)Burnaby, British Columbia: Simon Fraser University.

Bauer, P. J. (2004). Getting explicit memory off the ground: Steps toward construction of a neuro-developmental account of changes in the first two years of life. *Developmental Review, 24*, 347–373.

Bauer, P. J. (2007). *Remembering the times of our lives: Memory in infancy and beyond.* Mahwah, NJ: Lawrence Erlbaum Associates.

Bauer, P. J., Van Abbena, D., & de Haan, M. (1999). In for the short haul: Immediate and short-term forgetting by 20 month-old children. *Infant Behavior and Development, 22*(3), 321–343.

Bauer, P. J., Wenner, J. A., Dropik, P., & Wewerka, S. S. (2000). Parameters of remembering and forgetting in transition from infancy to early childhood. *Monographs of the Society for Research in Child Development, 65*(4).

Brunson, K. L., Eghbal-Ahmandi, M., Bender, R., Chen, Y., & Baram, T. (2001). Long-term progressive hippocampal cell loss and dysfunction induced by early-life administration of corticotropin-releasing hormone reproduce the effects of early-life stress. *Procedures of the National Academy of Science, 78*(15), 8856–8861.

Carlson, M., & Earls, F. (1997). Psychological and neuroendocrinological sequelae of early deprivation in institutionalized children in Romania. *Annals of the New York Academy of Sciences, 807*, 419–428.

Carver, L. J., & Bauer, P. J. (2001). The dawning of a past: The emergence of long-term explicit memory in infancy. *Journal of Experimental Psychology: General, 130*(4), 726–745.

Chugani, H. T., Behen, M. E., Muzik, O., Juhasz, C., Nagy, F., & Chugani, D. C. (2001). Local brain functional activity following early deprivation: A study of postinstitutionalized Romanian orphans. *NeuroImage, 14*(6), 1290–1301.

Cicchetti, D., & Rogosch, F. A. (1996). Equifinality and multifinality in developmental psychopathology. *Development and Psychopathology, 8*, 597–600.

De Bellis, M. D., Hall, J., Boring, A. M., Frustaci, K., & Moritz, G. (2001). A pilot longitudinal study of hippocampal volumes in pediatric maltreatment-related posttraumatic stress disorder. *Biological Psychiatry, 50*(4), 305–309.

de Haan, M., Bauer, P. J., Georgieff, M. K., & Nelson, C. A. (2000). Explicit memory in low-risk infants aged 19 months born between 27 and 42 weeks of gestation. *Developmental Medicine and Child Neurology, 42*(5), 304–312.

Georgieff, M. K., & Rao, R. (2001). The role of nutrition in cognitive development. In C. A. Nelson & M. Luciana (Eds.), *Handbook of developmental cognitive neuroscience.* Cambridge, MA: The MIT Press.

Greenough, W. T., & Black, J. E. (1992). Induction of brain structure by experience: Substrates for cognitive development. In M. R. Gunnar & C. A. Nelson (Eds.), *Developmental behavioral neuroscience ed. The Minnesota symposia on child psychology* (Vol. 24, pp. 155–200). Hillsdale, NJ: Erlbaum.

Greenough, W., Black, J., & Wallace, C. (1987). Experience and brain development. *Child Development, 58*, 539–559.

Gunnar, M. R. (2000). C. A. Nelson (Ed.), *The effects of adversity on neurobehavioral development: Minnesota symposia on child psychology* (Vol. 31, pp. 163–200). Mahwah, NJ: Lawrence Erlbaum Associates.

Gunnar, M. R. (2001). Effects of early deprivation: Findings from orphanage-reared infants and children. In C. A. Nelson & M. Luciana (Eds.), *Handbook of developmental cognitive neuroscience*. Cambridge, MA: The MIT Press.

Gunnar, M. R., Bruce, J., & Grotevant, H. D. (2000). International adoption of institutionally reared children: Research and policy. *Development and Psychopathology, 12*(4), 677–693.

Harlow, H. F., Harlow, M. K., & Suomi, S. J. (1971). From thought to therapy: Lessons from a primate laboratory. *American Science, 59*, 538–549.

Heim, C., Owen, M. J., Plotsky, P. M., & Nemeroff, C. B. (1997). The role of early adverse life events in the etiology of depression and posttraumatic stress disorder: Focus on corticotropin-releasing factor. *Annals of the New York Academy of Sciences, 821*, 194–207.

Hostetter, M. K., Iverson, S., Thomas, W., McKenzie, D., Dole, K., & Johnson, D. E. (1991). Medical evaluation of internationally adopted children. *New England Journal of Medicine, 325*, 479–485.

Hostetter, M. K., & Johnson, D. E. (1989). International adoption. *American Journal of Diseases in Children, 143*, 325–332.

Johnson, D. E., Miller, L. C., Iverson, S., Thomas, W., Franchino, B., Dole, K., *et al.* (1992). The health of children adopted from Romania. *Journal of American Medical Association, 268*, 3446–3451.

Kaler, S. R., & Freeman, B. J. (1994). An analysis of environmental deprivation: Cognitive and social development in Romania orphans. *Journal of Child Psychology and Psychiatry, 35*, 769–781.

Kreppner, J. M., O'Connor, T. G., & Rutter, M., English and Romania Adoptees Study Team. (2001). Can inattention/overactivity be an institutional deprivation syndrome? *Journal of Abnormal Child Psychology, 29*(6), 513–528.

Liu, D., Diorio, J., Day, J. C., Francis, D. D., & Meaney, M. J. (2000). Maternal care, hippocampal synaptogenesis and cognitive development in rats. *Nature Neuroscience, 3*(8), 799–806.

Marshall, P. J., & Fox, N. A. (2003). *Electrophysiological indices of auditory novelty processing among institutionalized and community children in Romania. Paper presented at the 70th Biennial Meeting for the Society for Research in Child Development, Tampa, Florida, 2003.*

McEwen, B. S. (1998). Stress, adaptation, and disease. Allostasis and allostatic load. *Annals of the New York Academy of Sciences, 840*, 33–441.

McEwen, B. S., de Kloet, E. R., & Rostene, W. (1986). Adrenal steroid receptors and actions in the nervous system. *Physiological Review, 66*(4), 1121–1188.

Meaney, M. J., Aitken, D. H., Van Berkel, C., Bhatnagar, S., & Sapolsky, R. M. (1998). Effect of neonatal handling on age-related impairments associated with the hippocampus. *Science, 239*, 766–768.

Nelson, C. A., & Carver, L. J. (1998). The effects of stress and trauma on brain and memory: A view from developmental cognitive neuroscience. *Development and Psychopathology, 10*(4), 793–809.

O'Connor, T. G., Rutter, M., Beckett, C., Keaveney, L., & Kreppner, J. M., The English & Romanian Adoptees Study Team. (2000). The effects of global severe privation on cognitive competence: Extension and longitudinal follow-up. *Child Development, 71*(2), 376–390.

O'Connor, T. G., & Rutter, M. English and Romanian Adoptees Study Team. (2000). Attachment disorder behavior following early severe deprivation: Extension and longitudinal follow-up. *Journal of the American Academy of Child and Adolescent Psychiatry, 30*(6), 703–712.

Parker, S. W., & Nelson, C. A. (2003). *Electrophysiological indices of face and emotional recognition in institutionalized and community children in Romania. Paper presented at the 70th Biennial Meeting for the Society for Research in Child Development, Tampa, Florida, 2003.*

Provence, S., & Lipton, R. C. (1962). *Infants in institutions.* New York: International Universities Press.

Rast, M., & Meltzoff, A. N. (1995). Memory and representation in young children with Down syndrome: Exploring deferred imitation and object permanence. *Development and Psychopathology, 7*(3), 393–407.

Reed, J. M., & Squire, L. R. (1998). Retrograde amnesia for facts and events: Findings from four new cases. *The Journal of Neuroscience, 18*, 3943–3954.

Rose, S. A., & Feldman, J. F. (2000). The relation of very low birthweight to basic cognitive skills in infancy and childhood. In C. A. Nelson (Ed.), *The effects of early adversity on neurobehavioral development.* Mahwah, NJ: Lawrence Erlbaum Associates.

Ruff, H. A., McCarton, C., Kurtzberg, D., & Vaughan, H. G. (1984). Preterm infants' manipulative exploration of objects. *Child Development, 55*, 1166–1173.

Rutter, M. L. (1981). *Maternal deprivation reassessed.* New York: Penguin Books.

Rutter, M. L., Kreppner, J. M., & O'Connor, T. English & Romanian Adoptees Study Team. (2001). Specificity and heterogeneity in children's responses to profound institutional privation. *British Journal of Psychiatry, 179*, 97–103.

Rutter, M. L.The E.R.A. Study Team. (1998). Developmental catch-up and deficit following adoption after severe global early privation. *Journal of Child Psychology and Psychiatry, 39*, 465–476.

Sameroff, A., & Chandler, M. (1975). Reproductive risks and the continuum of caretaking causality. In E. M. Horovitz, S. Hethereington, S. Scarr-Slapatek & G. Siegel (Eds.), *Review of child developmental research* (Vol. 4, pp. 187–244). Chicago: University of Chicago Press.

Sanchez, M. M., Hear, E. F., Do, D., Rilling, J. K., & Herdon, J. G. (1998). Differential rearing affects corpus callosum size and cognitive functions of rhesus monkeys. *Brain Research, 812*, 38–49.

Sapolsky, R. M. (1996). Why stress is bad for your brain. *Science, 273*(5276), 749–750.

Siegel, S. J., Ginsberg, S. D., Hof, P. R., Foote, S. L., Young, W. G., Draemer, G. W., *et al.* (1993). Effects of social deprivation in prepubescent rhesus monkeys: Immunohistochemical analysis of the neurogiliament protein triplet in the hippocampal formation. *Brain Research, 619*, 299–305.

Streissguth, A. P., & Connor, P. D. (2001). Fetal alcohol syndrome and other effects of prenatal alcohol: Developmental cognitive neuroscience implications. In C. A. Nelson & M. Luciana (Eds.), *Handbook of developmental cognitive neuroscience.* The MIT Press.

Verhulst, F. C., Althaus, M., & Versluis-Den Bieman, H. J. M. (1990). Problem behaviors in international adoptees. *American Academy of Child and Adolescence Psychiatry, 31*, 481–524.

Vythilingam, M., Heim, C., Newport, J., Miller, A. H., Anderson, E., Bronen, R., *et al.* (2002). Childhood trauma associated with smaller hippocampal volume in women with major depression. *American Journal of Psychiatry, 159*(12), 2072–2080.

Zola, S. M., & Squire, L. R. (2000). The medial temporal lobe and the hippocampus. In E. Tulving & F. I. M. Craik (Eds.), *The Oxford handbook of memory,* (pp. 485–100). New York: Oxford University Press.

Zola, S. M., Squire, L. R., Rempel, N. L., Clower, R. P., & Amaral, D. G. (1992). Enduring memory impairment in monkeys after ischemic damage to the hippocampus. *Journal of Neuroscience, 9*, 4355–4370.

DECLARATIVE MEMORY IN ABUSED AND NEGLECTED INFANTS

Carol L. Cheatham,[†] Marina Larkina,[‡] Patricia J. Bauer,[‡]
Sheree L. Toth,[§] and Dante Cicchetti[‖]*

* NUTRITION RESEARCH INSTITUTE, UNIVERSITY OF NORTH CAROLINA
AT CHAPEL HILL, KANNAPOLIS, NORTH CAROLINA, USA
[†] DEPARTMENT OF PSYCHOLOGY, UNIVERSITY OF NORTH CAROLINA AT CHAPEL
HILL, CHAPEL HILL, NORTH CAROLINA, USA
[‡] DEPARTMENT OF PSYCHOLOGY, EMORY UNIVERSITY, ATLANTA, GEORGIA, USA
[§] MT. HOPE FAMILY CENTER, UNIVERSITY OF ROCHESTER, ROCHESTER,
NEW YORK, USA
[‖] INSTITUTE OF CHILD DEVELOPMENT, UNIVERSITY OF MINNESOTA, MINNEAPOLIS,
MINNESOTA, USA

I. Declarative Memory in Abused and Neglected Infants

Children are a particularly vulnerable population. Unfortunately, according to the National Child Abuse and Neglect Data System (NCANDS) report (U.S. Department of Health & Human Services, 2010), in 2008 in the United States, there were 772,000 substantiated cases (out of 3.3 million reports involving over 6 million children) of child

161

Advances in Child Development and Behavior
Patricia Bauer : Editor

maltreatment. Of the substantiated cases, 70% suffered neglect, whereas 25% suffered physical or sexual abuse. Many children were the victims of both neglect and abuse. Shockingly, in general, 80% of the perpetrators are parents, and 33% of all the cases are children under 3 years of age. Children younger than 12 months had the highest rate of victimization of all age groups at 22%. Maltreatment of children is a deplorable failure in caregiving that continues to be an insidious social issue. In fact, maltreated children experience developmental delays at three times the typical rate (Scarborough, Lloyd, & Barth, 2009). In the research reported in this chapter, we explored the cognitive effect of abuse and neglect by investigating the effects of chronic stress on declarative memory at a time when the neural substrates underlying cognitive development are in the formative stages.

II. Maltreatment Subtype Classification

Although standardized methods for classifying maltreatment subtypes have been developed, they are not utilized consistently (Barnett, Manly, & Cicchetti, 1993; National Center on Child Abuse and Neglect, 1988). A standard method of classification is important because differences between definitions utilized in research and by Child Protective Services continue to make it difficult to interpret the results of research, to determine which children are eligible for services, and to ascertain the effectiveness of services (Aber & Cicchetti, 1984; Cicchetti & Rizley, 1981; Runyan *et al.*, 2005). In the policy arena, each State defines maltreatment and its subtypes differently, but all base their definitions on a set of federal minimum guidelines. The Child Abuse Prevention and Treatment Act (CAPTA) (42 U.S.C.A. §5106g) defines child abuse and neglect as "Any recent act or failure to act on the part of a parent or caretaker which results in death, serious physical or emotional harm, sexual abuse or exploitation; or an act of failure to act which presents an imminent risk of serious harm."

Similar to the error distinction made in Chapter 5, the major difference between abuse and neglect is that abuse is an act of commission and neglect is an act of omission on the part of the caregiver (Connell-Carrick & Scannapieco, 2006; Valentino, Cicchetti, Rogosch, & Toth, 2008). Neglect is often defined as a failure to provide for a dependent child's basic essential needs whether those needs be physical, emotional, or intellectual (Mayer, Lavergne, Tourigny, & Wright, 2007), whereas abuse is an act resulting in physical injury to the child (Scannapieco & Connell-Carrick, 2005). In general, there are four classifications of maltreatment that are recognized by all States: neglect, physical abuse, sexual abuse, and psychological maltreatment.

Classification of types of abuse for research purposes is difficult because different types of abuse occur at different ages and co-occurrence of subtypes is common (Manly, 2005; Bolger, Patterson, & Kuperschmidt, 1998). For example, a child who is physically abused may also be psychologically abused; a child who is physically abused in the early years may be sexually abused as an adolescent. The Maltreatment Classification System (MCS; Barnett *et al.*, 1993) offers a nosological system in which the subtype is identified based on operational definitions. Because children can be classified as having experienced multiple subtypes of maltreatment, a hierarchical standard related to the degree to which the maltreatment deviates from typical caregiving can then be utilized. One method of classifying children based on their experiences involves assigning a primary subtype designation based on the degree of deviation from societal norms. For example, a child who is sexually abused and psychologically maltreated would be classified as sexually abused. Although the hierarchy method cannot accurately portray a child with several maltreatment subtypes, it has been shown to more accurately predict the developmental outcomes of abuse and neglect when compared to the maltreatment characterizations assigned by Child Protective Services in five different states (Runyan *et al.*, 2005). (The MCS also provides other methods for classifying maltreatment that incorporate comorbid subtypes—see Manly, 2005.)

III. Developmental Sequelae of Abuse and Neglect

Maltreatment involves a significant deviation from the average expected environment, and, as such, has consistently been shown to be detrimental to development (for reviews see Cicchetti & Lynch, 1995; Cicchetti & Toth, 2005; Dawson, Ashman, & Carver, 2000; Nelson, 2000; Perlman & Fantuzzo, 2010). Children who suffer abuse, neglect, or both are at increased risk for atypical emotion regulation (e.g., Alink, Cicchetti, Kim, & Rogosch, 2009; Lee & Hoaken, 2007), disorganized attachment (e.g., Barnett, Ganiban, & Cicchetti, 1999), diminished cognitive development (e.g., Porter, Lawson, & Bigler, 2005), and delayed language development (e.g., Eigsti & Cicchetti, 2004; Sylvestre & Merette, 2010). However, it has been shown that neglect and abuse can have differential effects on the developing child (e.g., Shields & Cicchetti, 2001; Smetana *et al.*, 1999) even though the resulting phenotypes may be analogous.

For example, children who have been physically abused develop the ability to identify angry expressions more rapidly than typically developing children (Pollak & Sinha, 2002); neglected children experience difficulty with the identification of emotion from expressions and general emotion knowledge relative to children who have parents who employ harsh discipline and those who have parents who use nonviolent discipline (Sullivan, Carmody, & Lewis, 2010). Abused and neglected children are thus both at risk for atypical socio-emotional development. Abused children are more sensitive than typically developing children to emotional expression changes (Pollak & Kistler, 2002), and their reactions in social situations can be atypical and inordinately aggressive (Manly, Kim, Rogosch, & Cicchetti, 2001; Stouthamer-Loeber, Loeber, Homish, & Wei, 2001). The poor knowledge of emotion found in neglected children also manifests in aggressive behavior due to misunderstandings, especially if their parents neglect to supervise them (Knutson, DeGarmo, Koeppl, & Reid, 2005).

Thus, consistent with the concept of equifinality (Cicchetti & Rogosch, 1996), two very different pathways lead to similar outcomes of aggressive behavior: both an inability to distinguish emotion as seen in neglected children and a sensitivity to emotional changes coupled with a tendency to overidentify anger as seen in abused children. Although the behavioral outcome is similar, abuse and neglect can be linked to different anomalies in brain development.

IV. Maltreatment and Brain Development

Many important neural developments occur during the infancy and toddler periods. For the most part, these developments are driven by experiences in the environment (Huttenlocher, 2002). Certain neurological systems have evolved to be experience-expectant, meaning that stimuli from the environment are anticipated and required for the fine-tuning of these systems; others are experience-dependent in that environmental stimuli enhance development but are not required (Greenough & Black, 1992). Timing of these experiences with the readiness of the underlying neurological bases is integral to successful development. Importantly, species-typical stimuli are required for optimal development: severe deviations from the norm as seen in maltreatment will result in deviations from optimal development (Cicchetti & Lynch, 1995; Cicchetti & Toth, 2005).

Because the brain is most vulnerable to insults when it is rapidly developing, suffering neglect and/or abuse during the first 3 years of life can have particularly deleterious consequences for the hippocampus and the frontal lobe, as well as the functions they subserve (i.e., memory and executive functions). During the first 3 years of life, the human brain undergoes rapid and extensive development. As has been detailed in other chapters in this volume (see Chapter 1), the neural substrates that support memory in humans have a protracted developmental course. In humans, hippocampal development starts around 16 weeks gestation and continues rapidly at least into the third year of life (Zaidel, 1999), not reaching adult morphology until 5 years of age (Seress, 2001). Development of the memory circuit that includes areas of the frontal lobe is even more protracted, with alterations and increases in gray and white matter continuing into adolescence (Tsujimoto, 2008). Thus, the serious deviation from a species-typical environment seen in maltreatment during the first 3 years of life will have a profound effect on specific brain areas, and subsequent development will be atypical.

By this same logic, global postnatal development of the brain involving the pruning of neural connections that were overproduced *in utero* and the myelination of axons (for review see Webb, Monk, & Nelson, 2001) also will be affected by maltreatment. Myelination is the process through which the axon of the neuron is encased in a white fatty substance, the myelin sheath, which facilitates movement of action potentials down the axon effectively increasing processing speed. Myelination progresses rapidly from the prenatal period into adolescence, but continues into adulthood. Importantly, myelination of the corpus callosum, along with other axons, proceeds rapidly between 6 months and 3 years of life (Giedd *et al.*, 1999; Paus *et al.*, 2001; Thompson *et al.*, 2000). The corpus callosum is the white matter pathway between the two hemispheres of the brain as well as to the frontal lobe and parietal lobe, brain areas that are integral to memory and attention, respectively. Myelination is dependent on environmental input such as nutrition (Wiggins, 1982) and stimulation (De Bellis, 2005), and is susceptible to stress (Dunlop, Archer, Quinlivan, Beazley, & Newnham, 1997). Disorders of myelination have been related to developmental delay (Harbord *et al.*, 1990). Thus, in the absence of proper nutrition and stimulation from the environment and/or because of chronic stress, the brains of maltreated children may not achieve optimal myelination, which may contribute, in part, to developmental delay.

Overproduction of axons, dendrites, synapses, and even, neurons is a genetically determined process (Bourgeois, Jastreboff, & Rakic, 1989). However, the pruning of unused connections is an experience-expectant process and as such is dependent on input from the environment (for review, see Webb *et al.*, 2001). Postnatal events such as maternal stimulation, social interaction, and language input are expected. If these species-typical interactions do not occur, as in the life of a neglected infant or toddler, it is possible that many neural connections will go unused and during the pruning period, will be lost.

Some evidence of the loss of neural connections may be found in the research being conducted with Romanian orphans who suffer extreme neglect in institutions. Researchers with the Bucharest Early Intervention Project conducted electrophysiology studies with 7- to 32-month-old institutionalized children to determine whether they could recognize basic human emotions (Parker & Nelson, 2005b) and faces (Parker & Nelson, 2005a). Compared to never-institutionalized Romanian children, the institutionalized children exhibited lower levels of brain activity in the components thought to reflect orienting and attention, whereas the opposite was true for the component thought to reflect the updating of memory: the institutionalized children exhibited higher amplitude in this positive slow wave relative to never-institutionalized children (Parker & Nelson, 2005b). Interestingly, whereas a typically developing child will allocate more resources in the service of encoding a novel face relative to a familiar face, the institutionalized children put more effort into (re) processing the face of their caregiver than the face of a stranger (Parker & Nelson, 2005a). Higher low-frequency activity and lower high-frequency activity were seen in the frontal and temporal areas on the scalp in the same institutionalized children, relative to the never-institutionalized children (Marshall & Fox, 2004). In another sample of Romanian orphans who had been adopted 6 years previously, Chugani et al. (2001) found decreased metabolic activity in several brain regions. Taken together, these results could indicate a dearth of neural resources in that a strong orienting and attention response was not seen (Parker & Nelson, 2005b), memory updating was needed for nonnovel information (Parker & Nelson, 2005a), and glucose was not being utilized at an appropriate level (Chugani et al., 2001). Thus, the lack of stimulation from the environment seen in neglectful situations early on may result in alterations in the architecture of the brain that last at least into childhood.

Whereas abused infants and toddlers may also suffer neglect (Barnett et al., 1993; Runyan et al., 2005), they have atypical, unexpected environmental input that may result in an experience-dependent process in which neural connections are produced as a result of individually determined (i.e., not species-specific) experience with the environment. When those experiences are violent and emotion-laden or stress-provoking, the connections that are developed, strengthened, and maintained will be different than the connections seen in the brain of a nonabused child. Experience-expectant processes will result in the retention and strengthening of pathways related to the abuse. Simultaneously, the experience-dependent processes will result in individual differences with the development of neural connections that are unique to that experience and thus, to that individual. Strengthening of pathways has been evidenced in a study of abused school-aged children who, relative to non-abused children, exhibited greater brain activity in response to an angry face than they did to a happy face (Pollak, Cicchetti, Klorman, & Brumaghim, 1997). For the nonabused children, there was no difference between the brain responses to angry versus happy. These results were replicated in a study of several target emotions (Pollak, Klorman, Thatcher, & Cicchetti, 2001). Moreover, it was found that physically abused children oriented to anger more quickly and required the allocation of more neural resources to disengage from an angry condition, relative to nonabused children (Pollak & Tolley-Schell, 2003).

Thus, whereas a neglected child may suffer a decrease in neural connections due to a general lack of stimulation, the abused child may suffer an abnormal increase in certain connections or the strengthening of one pathway over another. Disorders may also occur in myelination and in the development of the temporal and frontal lobes. With these deviations from the norm in brain development, both neglected and abused children will experience atypicality in subsequent social, emotional, and cognitive development.

V. Stress and the Developing Brain

Maltreatment is thought to exact its largest effect on the brain by way of dysregulation of the neuroendocrine system. Maternal–infant interactions during the first year of life serve to regulate emotional behavior and the neuroendocrine stress response (for review see Gunnar & Cheatham, 2003). Stressors are defined as any perturbations in the system or the environment that threaten to disrupt the organism's optimal functioning, and the stress response is the cascade of biological processes necessary to return the system to homeostasis (Sapolsky, 1992). A complete description of the norepinephrine–sympathetic adrenomedullary (NE–SAM) and hypothalamic–pituitary–adrenocortical (HPA) stress systems is beyond the scope of this chapter. The interested reader is directed to the literature for review (Dedovic, Duchesne, Andrews, Engert, & Pruessner, 2009; Gunnar & Cheatham, 2003; Sapolsky, 1992; Schmidt, 2010). Basically, the stress system exists to insure the survival of an organism that is facing environmental extremes — it is the "fight or flight" system. The NE–SAM system releases epinephrine (adrenaline) and norepinephrine, and the HPA system releases glucocorticoids (steroid hormones such as cortisol), in response to a stressor, whether it is actual or perceived. The two work together to channel energy away from systems that are nonessential to the defense (decreasing growth, digestion, immunity, and reproduction), to mobilize and reassign energy to systems that are important to the "fight" (increasing heart rate, metabolism, pain threshold, and sensory thresholds), and to return the system to homeostasis once the threat has passed.

Certainly, maltreated children face daily, chronic stress. Temperament of the child may determine whether the stress system is activated (e.g., Dettling, Parker, Lane, Sebanc, & Gunnar, 2000). Nonetheless, for the majority of maltreated children, chronic stress will be a factor in their development. Importantly, when the stress system is activated for prolonged periods, the ability of the intrinsic negative feedback system to terminate the production of glucocorticoids is disrupted. Left unchecked, the cascade of glucocorticoids will alter genetic expression and subsequently, will affect the sensitivity of the system to future challenges (Sapolsky, Krey, & McEwen, 1986). Thus, the stress system is literally programmed by experience. Deviations from the typical circadian rhythm of cortisol have been shown to be a risk factor in the development of childhood psychopathology (Schreiber, 2010).

Programming begins *in utero*, and is fine-tuned by early experience. Prenatal exposure to high cortisol levels, as measured in amniotic fluid, has been related to lower performance on the Bayley Scales of Infant Development (BSID)-II (Bayley, 1993) at 17 months of age, even after controlling for socio-economic status (SES) and prenatal risk factors, such as maternal smoking (Bergman, Sarkar, Glover, & O'Connor, 2010). This association was moderated by maternal–child attachment status in that mental development index (MDI) scores on the BSID-II and amniotic cortisol levels were negatively related in infants with an insecure attachment, but showed no relation in those with a secure attachment. In another study, it was shown that parental sensitivity is related to a buffering of the cortisol response to threat, especially for socially inhibited children (Kertes *et al.*, 2009). Thus, sensitive caregiving ameliorates dysregulation of the HPA stress system.

Maternal deprivation also can have deleterious effects on the infant. In a study of maternal touch, Feldman, Singer, and Zagoory (2010) found that infants' cortisol levels increased in situations during which maternal touch was withheld. Whereas in typically developing children, cortisol response levels decrease with age (Jansen, Beijers, Riksen-Walraven, & de Weerth, 2010), basal cortisol levels in low-SES children who are feeling threatened and living in a chaotic family increase with age, when compared to high-SES children (Chen, Cohen, & Miller, 2010). Moreover, it appears that even though the system is susceptible to environmental influence, it has a set point that is related to the length of maltreatment. De Bellis *et al.* (1999) found that, relative to nonmaltreated children, maltreated children had higher cortisol and epinephrine metabolites in their urine at age 11, several years after their lives had improved. These levels were related to the length of the maltreatment. Thus, the evidence indicates that neglected and abused children experience some degree of dysregulation of the HPA stress system, and that the dysregulation may be permanent (see also Cicchetti, Rogosch, Gunnar, & Toth, 2010).

Dysregulation of the HPA axis has profound effects on brain development and functioning. The hippocampus, prefrontal cortex, and corpus callosum are particularly susceptible to insults from early stress (Teicher *et al.*, 1997). Chronically high cortisol is related to cell damage in the hippocampus (Sapolsky, Uno, Rebert, & Finch, 1990), and adult survivors of abuse who have been diagnosed with posttraumatic stress disorder (PTSD) have smaller hippocampal and amygdalar structures as well as impaired cognition relative to comparisons (Weniger, Lange, Sachsse, & Irle, 2008). Neurocognitive deficits arising from atypical development of these brain structures involve attention, memory, language, executive functioning, and global intelligence. Abused children who have been diagnosed with PTSD show deficits in executive functions (Beers & De Bellis, 2002). Neglected children who have been diagnosed with PTSD do significantly worse on tests of immediate and delayed memory for faces than neglected children without PTSD and comparisons (De Bellis, Hooper, Spratt, & Woolley, 2009).

The mechanism responsible for the reported effects may be the disruption of hippocampal neurons by adrenal steroids such as cortisol. Hippocampal pyramidal neurons atrophy in the face of chronic stress, and dentate-gyrus-based production of new neurons is suppressed in both chronic and acute stress (McEwen, 1999). The suppression of neurogenesis as a result of early stress has been shown to perpetuate into adulthood (Karten, Olariu, & Cameron, 2005). The importance of the hippocampus for memory coupled with the serious effects of prolonged increases in cortisol on the developing neurons of the hippocampus leads to the hypothesis that the stress of abuse and neglect will have a measureable negative effect on memory abilities. We further hypothesized that neglect would have a more pronounced effect given that neglect generally begins earlier (Mayer *et al.*, 2007) and is more chronic in nature.

To explore the hypothesis that abuse and neglect will differentially affect memory abilities, 151 children (80 females) from low-SES homes were seen in an investigation of the effects of maltreatment on declarative memory as part of a larger study conducted at the Mt. Hope Family Center in Rochester, New York (Cicchetti & Curtis, 2005; Cicchetti, Rogosch, & Toth, 2006; Valentino, Cicchetti, Toth, & Rogosch, 2006).

VI. Method

A. PARTICIPANTS

Participants were recruited from the local Department of Human Services (DHS). All children resided with their biological mothers and all mothers were named as perpetrators of the maltreatment. Forty-six children had no history of maltreatment, and 105 children were identified as suffering some form of maltreatment. Nonmaltreated low-SES families were receiving public assistance in the form of Temporary Assistance to Needy Families. Nonmaltreatment status was confirmed by an absence of Child Protective Services or Preventive Services records for the family, and by maternal interview (for details see Valentino *et al.*, 2006). Maltreated children were further classified into neglecting or abusing groups using the MCS (Barnett *et al.*, 1993). Any maltreating family in which physical abuse was documented, irrespective of concomitant neglect or emotional maltreatment, was classified into the abusing group ($N=46$). The remaining maltreating families were neglecting ($N=59$); as is quite common, many of the neglect cases also involving emotional maltreatment. Four additional children participated in the memory task but were excluded from the final sample: 3 could not be confidently classified as maltreated or nonmaltreated due to ambiguous information, and 1 child experienced only emotional maltreatment.

Children averaged 21 months of age ($M=21.14$ months, range 18.15–23.93 months). The majority of the participants were nonHispanic (91%). The sample comprised African Americans (58%), White/Caucasian (19%), multiracial (21%), and unknown (2%). Abused, neglected, and nonmaltreated children did not differ on relevant demographics (see Table I). Children were equivalent in age. Distributions in child gender and child ethnicity categories were similar between groups. Groups were equivalent in SES with 78% of the abusing group, 82.2% of the neglecting group, and 77% of the nonmaltreated group falling in the two lowest social strata. Caregivers provided informed consent to participate in the study according to the regulations of the Institutional Review Board at the University of Rochester. Consent also was given by each caregiver to examine the family's records at DHS.

B. PROCEDURE

Children were assessed in the laboratory by trained female research assistants, using an imitation paradigm and the BSID-II (Bayley, 1993). Also included in the following analyses are scores from the BSID-II from

Table I
Demographic Statistics: Mean (Standard Deviation)

Demographic Domain	Group			
	Nonmaltreated ($N=46$)	Maltreated ($N=105$)	Neglected[a] ($N=59$)	Abused[a] ($N=46$)
Mean child age (months)	21.20 (.93)	21.11 (1.05)	21.01 (1.02)	21.25 (1.08)
Child gender (female)	47.83%	55.24%	54.24%	56.52%
Ethnicity (nonCaucasian)	71.74%	80.95%	91.52%	67.39%
BSID–PDI motor (12 months)	100.8 (11.66)	94.0 (16.34)	96.6 (15.78)	90.8 (16.61)
BSID–MDI mental (12 months)	96.2 (10.03)	91.8 (10.89)	91.9 (12.34)	91.6 (8.83)
BSID–MDI mental (20 months)	87.4 (10.41)	80.3 (11.94)	81.0 (12.62)	79.5 (11.12)

[a]The neglected and abused samples are subsamples of the larger maltreated group.

another session conducted when the participants were 12 months of age. All BSID-IIs were administered by individuals unaware of maltreatment status and study hypotheses. The elicited imitation procedure utilized in this study was adapted from Bauer, Wenner, Dropik, and Wewerka (2000). All children were tested on six 3-step sequences with enabling relations (see Chapter 2). Each child participated in three conditions: immediate recall, 10-min delayed recall, and interleaved presentation, the order of which was counterbalanced between the participants. The order of the sequences that were used also was counterbalanced across conditions and participants.

At the start of the session, an experimenter who was unaware of the child's maltreatment status and of our study hypotheses administered a practice sequence that was designed to familiarize the children with the procedure. Then, administration of the immediate and delayed recall task began by offering the child the props that comprised one event. The participant was allowed to manipulate the props in any manner she/he wanted until 2 min had passed or until she/he indicated boredom (baseline). The experimenter then retrieved the props and twice in succession demonstrated the actions necessary to arrive at a fun and surprising end-state. Then, either the child was prompted to replicate the experimenter's actions (immediate condition) or the props were put away until a 10-min delay had passed (delay condition). Verbal interaction was limited to encouraging phrases during baseline (e.g., "that is a good idea") and one explicit verbal prompt prior to the recall period ("Now it is your turn. Can you show me how we use this stuff to make X?").

For the interleaved presentation condition, baseline assessment consisted of the children exploring the props for two sequences simultaneously. During modeling, the tester then demonstrated the two sequences in an interleaved manner (i.e., Step 1 of the first sequence, then Step 1 of the second sequence, then Step 2 of the first sequence, etc.). Immediately after modeling, the child was given the props from the first modeled sequence for recall. Following the recall period for the first sequence in the interleaved condition, the child was tested on the second sequence.

The testing sessions were videotaped and coded later by two experienced research assistants, who also were unaware of the children's maltreatment status and the hypotheses of the present study. For baseline and imitation, two dependent variables were derived as in prior reports in this volume (Chapter 2): the total number of individual target actions produced (maximum=3), and the number of pairs of actions produced in the target order (maximum=2). Thus, for each condition, children's performance was described by four different indices: two baseline scores (target actions and pairs of actions), and two recall scores (target actions and pairs of actions), resulting in 12 scores for each participant.

BSID-II raw scores were converted to standardized scores ($M=100$, $SD=15$), providing an MDI at age 12 and 20 months and Psychomotor Development Index (PDI) at age 12 months. A significant difference emerged among groups for 12-month PDI of the BSID-II. Subsequent pairwise comparisons indicated that abused children had significantly lower PDI scores than nonmaltreated children; neglected children did not significantly differ from any other groups (see Table I). On the 12-month MDI, all maltreated children had significantly lower scores than nonmaltreated children, but a comparison of the nonmaltreated with the two maltreated subtypes (abused and neglected) did not reveal differences among the 3 groups. At 20 months, nonmaltreated children had significantly higher MDI scores than children from abused and neglected groups, which did not differ from each other. In relation to the elicited imitation task, correlation analyses indicated that children's PDI scores were not related to their memory performance. There was a significant relation between children's MDI scores at age 12 and 20 months and their performance on the elicited imitation task. Specifically, the MDI scores at 12 months of age were positively related to children's imitation scores from both the immediate and delay conditions; the MDI scores at 20 months of age were positively related to imitation scores in all conditions ($rs=.17-.33$, $ps<.05$). Thus, the BSID-II MDI scores were entered as covariates in all further analyses.

VII. Results

Descriptive statistics for children's memory scores are presented in Table II. To assess memory performance for target actions and pairs of actions in target order, we first compared nonmaltreated children with all maltreated children (abused and neglected together) by conducting 2 (group: nonmaltreated, maltreated) × 3 (condition: immediate, delay, interleaved) × 2 (phase: baseline, recall) mixed model ANCOVAs, controlling for Bayley mental and motor scores. There was no effect of group either for target actions or pairs of actions. Thus, performance did not differ on the imitation task between maltreated and nonmaltreated children in this sample when the maltreated were analyzed as one group.

Given the evidence that neglected and abused children's early experiences are different and, therefore, have different underlying developmental sequelae, we hypothesized that those differences would be evident in an assessment of declarative memory using a specific hippocampal task (imitation paradigm). Thus, we reran the analyses with the maltreated children separated into the two subtype groups, abused and neglected, submitting target action scores and pairs of action scores, in turn, to 3 (group: nonmaltreated, neglected, abused) × 3 (condition: immediate, delay, interleaved) × 2 (phase: baseline, recall) mixed model ANCOVAs, controlling for BSID-II mental and motor scores.

Table II

Despective Statistics on Three Memory Tasks: Immediate, Delay, Integration: Mean (Standard Deviation)

Condition/ Phase	Group			
	Nonmaltreated ($N=46$)	Maltreated ($N=105$)	Neglected[a] ($N=59$)	Abused[a] ($N=46$)
Immediate	0.83 (.50)—act	.68 (.52)—act	.60 (.51)—act	.79 (.52)—act
Baseline	.09 (.19)—pair	.08 (.19)—pair	.06 (.19)—pair	.10 (.20)—pair
Immediate	2.11 (.73)—act	2.04 (.85)—act	1.93 (.83)—act	2.20 (.86)—act
Recall	1.12 (.67)—pair	1.00 (.65)—pair	.90 (.64)—pair	1.13 (.65)—pair
Delay	.79 (.63)—act	.79 (.56)—act	.75 (.54)—act	.84 (.58)—act
Baseline	.15 (.38)—pair	.11 (.27)—pair	.11 (.26)—pair	.11 (.28)—pair
Delay	1.77 (.83)—act	1.71 (.83)—act	1.63 (.84)—act	1.82 (.82)—act
Recall	.84 (.63)—pair	.71(.65)—pair	.64(.61)—pair	.82 (.681)—pair
Interleaved	.43 (.42)—act	.40 (.45)—act	.34 (.43)—act	.47 (.46)—act
Baseline	.03 (.13)—pair	.05 (.16)—pair	.04 (.13)—pair	.08 (.18)—pair
Interleaved	1.53 (.72)—act	1.44 (.71)—act	1.33 (.72)—act	1.58 (.67)—act
Recall	.45 (.52)—pair	.49 (.48)—pair	.42 (.47)—pair	.59 (.47)—pair

[a]The neglected and abused samples are subsamples of the larger maltreated group.

For production of target actions, the children all evidenced a significant increase in performance from baseline to recall, $F(1, 143) = 641.55$, $p < .0001$, indicating that learning had occurred and that all children were capable and engaged with the task (adjusted means: $M = .65$, $SE = .03$, for baseline; and $M = 1.77$, $SD = .82$, for recall). In addition, their performance decreased commensurate with the level of difficulty of the condition, $F(2, 289) = 40.60$, $p < .0001$: performance on the immediate recall condition was higher than in 10-min delayed recall condition, which in turn was higher than children's performance in the interleaved presentation condition (adjusted means: immediate, $M = 1.42$, $SE = .04$; delay, $M = 1.28$, $SE = .04$; and interleaved, $M = .94$, $SE = .04$). *Post hoc* analyses of a condition by phase interaction, $F(2, 286) = 6.85$, $p < .001$, indicated that during baseline, children performed significantly fewer target actions in the interleaved presentation condition than in the other two conditions (immediate: $M = .73$, $SD = .51$; delay: $M = .79$, $SD = .58$; and interleaved: $M = .41$, $SD = .44$). During recall, children produced significantly more target actions in immediate recall than in delayed recall, which was higher than in interleaved presentation performance (immediate: $M = 2.06$, $SD = .81$; delay: $M = 1.73$, $SD = .83$; and interleaved: $M = 1.47$, $SD = .71$).

Analyses of the scores for production of pairs of actions in target order revealed the same pattern of significance as the analyses for target action scores. The children were engaged and learning, $F(1, 143) = 504.51$, $p < .001$ (adjusted means: $M = .09$, $SE = .02$, for baseline; and $M = .77$, $SE = .02$, for recall), and their performance decreased with increases in task difficulty, $F(2, 289) = 34.37$, $p < .0001$ (adjusted means: immediate, $M = .57$, $SE = .03$; delay, $M = .45$, $SE = .03$; and interleaved, $M = .26$, $SE = .03$). The significant interaction between condition and phase, $F(2, 286) = 26.17$, $p < .001$, provided further evidence that the interleaved presentation task was difficult for the children at baseline (immediate: $M = .08$, $SD = .19$; delay: $M = .12$, $SD = .31$; and interleaved: $M = .05$, $SD = .71$) and during recall (immediate: $M = 1.04$, $SD = .66$; delay: $M = .75$, $SD = .64$; and interleaved: $M = .47$, $SD = .49$).

From these analyses, we can conclude that the assessment was valid. The children all gained in performance as a function of modeling: for both production of target actions and production of pairs of actions in target order, the children had higher scores from imitation after watching modeling than they did when they first manipulated the props. In addition, for both scores, performance declined as the difficulty of the task increased. Further evidence indicated that interleaved presentation was the most difficult. Thus, we are confident that with this paradigm we were effectively assessing the declarative memory abilities in children as has been documented in past research (Bauer, 2004; Bauer, Burch, & Kleinknecht, 2002;

Bauer *et al.*, 2000) and that it is appropriate to utilize this methodology in the testing of maltreated children.

Importantly, the analyses of production of target actions revealed a main effect of group, $F(2, 143) = 7.16$, $p < .001$. The *post hoc* comparisons, using the Tukey–Kramer adjustments, indicated that the abused and neglected groups were significantly different from one another. Across all conditions and phases, neglected children produced fewer target actions than abused children (adjusted means for the neglected group, $M = 1.12$, $M = .04$ and for the abused group, $M = 1.32$, $M = .04$). Moreover, the performance of children from neglecting families was moderately lower than performance of nonmaltreated children (adjusted means $M = 1.20$, $M = .04$, $p = .07$). Surprisingly, the performance of children from the abused group did not differ significantly from nonmaltreated children. A similar pattern of results emerged between groups on scores for pairs of actions in target order, $F(2, 143) = 5.36$, $p < .01$. Children in the neglected group produced significantly fewer pairs than abused children. However, in this analysis of the scores for production of pairs of action in target order, there was no difference between either the abused or the neglected and the nonmaltreated groups (adjusted means $M = .37$, $M = .02$ for neglected group; $M = .49$, $M = .03$ for abused group; and $M = .42$, $M = .03$ for nonmaltreated group).

VIII. Summary and Conclusions

To summarize, all children interacted with the experimenter and actively participated in the imitation task. There was evidence of improvement in performance from baseline to recall as would be expected with attention to, and memory for, the actions that were modeled by the experimenter. All participants evidenced a decrease in performance as the difficulty of the task increased, as would be expected. When the maltreated children were compared to the nonmaltreated children in a 2-group design, there was no statistically significant difference in performance. However, when the maltreated group was divided into two subtypes of either neglected or abused, and performance was compared in a 3-group design, it was revealed that the neglected children experienced deficits in performance relative to abused children. For production of target actions, the neglected children's performance trended toward significance when compared to the nonmaltreated children's performance. However, there was no significant difference between the performance of the abused children and the nonmaltreated children for either production of target actions or productions of ordered pairs.

The children in this longitudinal study were assessed previously at 12 months of age in a mother–child play situation (Valentino *et al.*, 2006). Interactions during structured play between mother and child were evaluated for maternal directives and child responses. Interestingly, the difference in social interactions that was most reliable was the finding that the abused children imitated their mothers more often than did the non-maltreated children. There was no difference between the imitative behaviors of the neglected children and the abused or nonmaltreated children. The researchers note that by imitating their mothers, the abused children might be attempting to prevent further abusive incidents. Limit setting behaviors of the mothers in response to child initiations were positively related to the children's imitative behaviors. Thus, it would appear that maternal negative feedback to child-initiated behaviors is related to an increase in imitative behaviors that are most likely met with positive reinforcement. The continued pursuit of this positivity may impede the development of self-initiated behaviors; delayed development of self-initiated behavior has been linked to disorders of social competence (Landry, Smith, Miller-Loncar, & Swank, 1998).

However, imitation has long been known to be a mechanism of learning (Piaget, 1962) and has become an accepted tool for assessment of declarative memory (Bauer, 2004). Whereas the adaptation to abuse posited by Valentino *et al.* (2006) may be detrimental to social development, our data for this same sample indicate that the reliance on imitative behavior exhibited by the abused children may afford them an advantage at 21 months of age in imitation paradigms. The neglected children are thus at a disadvantage relative to the abused children in the study reported here in that they were not reinforced by mothers for imitative behavior.

It is important to note that all children in this sample were from low-income homes. Scores on these events for both target actions and ordered pairs are higher in samples of higher SES children (e.g., Bauer *et al.*, 2000). Thus, the low SES of the families affected performance across the groups. It is possible that the factor responsible for the difference between the abused group and the neglected group is resilience in the face of poverty. Resilience is the ability to recover following a traumatic event or adversity (Masten, 2001), and has been related to child characteristics, such as general intelligence (Masten *et al.*, 1988). It has been proposed that neural plasticity may be responsible for this recovery (Cicchetti & Curtis, 2006). Alternatively, as has been detailed earlier in this chapter, the advantage afforded abused children could arise from the strengthening of neural pathways. It would be adaptive to develop exceptional event memory so as to avoid the events that lead to abuse. Mechanisms of plasticity are responsible for the laying down of memories

(Aimone, Wiles, & Gage, 2006). Thus, the higher performance seen in the abused group could be related to a preservation of brain plasticity that facilitates resilience in the face of poverty, stress, and/or trauma. Plasticity in the brains of the neglected children may be lost due to the lack of stimulation, leaving them more vulnerable to the stress of poverty and neglect.

In conclusion, maltreated children have often been studied as a single group. However, it is becoming clear from research conducted by our group and others that the subtypes of maltreatment may have different developmental sequelae. It is important that we understand the differential pathways involved in the development of abused versus neglected children. As discussed in other chapters of this volume, the imitation paradigm has emerged as a valuable tool in the identification of at-risk infants and toddlers. With the data reported here, it is evident that data from the elicited imitation procedure utilized herein differentiates between the subtypes of maltreatment. Research must be conducted to further elucidate the correlates of resilience in toddlers who have been abused. A longitudinal investigation would enable investigation of the questions of continuity of the observed increase in imitative behavior and whether increased imitation has a detrimental social effect while exerting a bolstering cognitive effect.

Acknowledgment

Support for this research was provided by grants from the Administration for Children, Youth, and Families; the National Institute of Mental Health (MH54643); and the Spunk Fund, Inc., to Sheree Toth and Dante Cicchetti; and grants from the NIH (HD2425, HD42483) to Patricia J. Bauer. We also thank the research assistants and the infants and mothers who participated in this research.

REFERENCES

Aber, J. L., & Cicchetti, D. (1984). Socioemotional development in maltreated children: An empirical and theoretical analysis. In H. E. Fitzgerald, B. Lester & M. Yogman (Eds.), *Theory and research in behavioral pediatrics* (Vol. 2, pp. 147–205). New York: Plenum Press.

Aimone, J. B., Wiles, J., & Gage, F. H. (2006). Potential role for adult neurogenesis in the encoding of time in new memories. *Nature Neuroscience, 9*(6), 723–727.

Alink, L. R., Cicchetti, D., Kim, J., & Rogosch, F. A. (2009). Mediating and moderating processes in the relation between maltreatment and psychopathology: Mother–child relationship quality and emotion regulation. *Journal of Abnormal Child Psychology, 37*(6), 831–843.

Barnett, D., Ganiban, J., & Cicchetti, D. (1999). Atypical attachment in infancy and early childhood among children at developmental risk. V. Maltreatment, negative expressivity, and the development of type D attachments from 12 to 24 months of age. *Monographs of the Society for Research in Child Development, 64*(3), 97–118. (Discussion 213–120).

Barnett, D., Manly, J. T., & Cicchetti, D. (1993). Defining child maltreatment: The interface between policy and research. In D. Cicchetti & S. L. Toth (Eds.), *Advances in applied developmental psychology: Child abuse, child development, and social policy.* (pp. 7–73) Norwood, NJ: Ablex Publishing Corporation.

Bauer, P. J. (2004). Getting explicit memory off the ground: Steps toward construction of a neuro-developmental account of changes in the first two years of life. *Developmental Review, 24*(4), 347–373.

Bauer, P. J., Burch, M. M., & Kleinknecht, E. E. (2002). Developments in early recall memory: Normative trends and individual differences. *Advances in Child Development and Behavior, 30*, 103–151.

Bauer, P. J., Wenner, J. A., Dropik, P. L., & Wewerka, S. S. (2000). Parameters of remembering and forgetting in the transition from infancy to early childhood. *Monographs of the Society for Research in Child Development, 65* (4, Serial No. 263).

Bayley, N. (1993). *Bayley scales of infant development-II.* New York: Psychological Testing Corporation.

Beers, S. R., & De Bellis, M. D. (2002). Neuropsychological function in children with maltreatment-related posttraumatic stress disorder. *American Journal of Psychiatry, 159*(3), 483–486.

Bergman, K., Sarkar, P., Glover, V., & O'Connor, T. G. (2010). Maternal prenatal cortisol and infant cognitive development: Moderation by infant–mother attachment. *Biological Psychiatry, 67*(11), 1026–1032.

Bolger, K. E., Patterson, C. J., & Kupersmidt, J. B. (1998). Peer relationships and self-esteem among children who have been maltreated. *Child Development, 69*(4), 1171–1197.

Bourgeois, J. P., Jastreboff, P. J., & Rakic, P. (1989). Synaptogenesis in visual cortex of normal and preterm monkeys: Evidence for intrinsic regulation of synaptic overproduction. *Proceedings of the National Academy of Sciences of the United States of America, 86*(11), 4297–4301.

Chen, E., Cohen, S., & Miller, G. E. (2010). How low socioeconomic status affects 2-year hormonal trajectories in children. *Psychological Science, 21*(1), 31–37.

Chugani, H. T., Behen, M. E., Muzik, O., Juhasz, C., Nagy, F., & Chugani, D. C. (2001). Local brain functional activity following early deprivation: A study of postinstitutionalized Romanian orphans. *Neuroimage, 14*(6), 1290–1301.

Cicchetti, D., & Curtis, W. J. (2005). An event-related potential study of the processing of affective facial expressions in young children who experienced maltreatment during the first year of life. *Development and Psychopathology, 17*(3), 641–677.

Cicchetti, D., & Curtis, W. J. (2006). The developing brain and neural plasticity: Implications for normality, psychopathology, and resilience. In D. Cicchetti & D. J. Cohen (Eds.), *Developmental psychopathology, Vol. 2: Developmental neuroscience.* (2nd ed., pp. 1–64). Hoboken, NJ, USA: John Wiley & Sons, Inc.

Cicchetti, D., & Lynch, M. (1995). Failures in the expectable environment and their impact on individual development: The case of child maltreatment. In D. Cicchetti & D. J. Cohen (Eds.), *Developmental psychopathology: Risk, disorder, and adaptation* (Vol. 2, pp. 32–71). New York: Wiley.

Cicchetti, D., & Rizley, R. (1981). Developmental perspectives on the etiology, intergenerational transmission and sequelae of child maltreatment. *New Directions for Child Development, 11*, 31–55.

Cicchetti, D., & Rogosch, F. A. (1996). Equifinality and multifinality in developmental psychopathology. *Development and Psychopathology, 8,* 597–600.

Cicchetti, D., Rogosch, F. A., Gunnar, M. R., & Toth, S. L. (2010). The differential impacts of early abuse on internalizing problems and diurnal cortisol activity in school-aged children. *Child Development, 25,* 252–269.

Cicchetti, D., Rogosch, F. A., & Toth, S. L. (2006). Fostering secure attachment in infants in maltreating families through preventive interventions. *Development and Psychopathology, 18*(3), 623–649.

Cicchetti, D., & Toth, S. L. (2005). Child maltreatment. *Annual Review of Clinical Psychology, 1,* 409–438.

Connell-Carrick, K., & Scannapieco, M. (2006). Ecological correlates of neglect in infants and toddlers. *Journal of Interpersonal Violence, 21*(3), 299–316.

Dawson, G., Ashman, S. B., & Carver, L. J. (2000). The role of early experience in shaping behavioral and brain development and its implications for social policy. *Development and Psychopathology, 12*(4), 695–712.

De Bellis, M. D. (2005). The psychobiology of neglect. *Child Maltreatment, 10*(2), 150–172.

De Bellis, M. D., Baum, A. S., Birmaher, B., Keshavan, M. S., Eccard, C. H., Boring, A. M., *et al.* (1999). Developmental traumatology, Part 1: Biological stress systems. *Biological Psychiatry, 9,* 1259–1270.

De Bellis, M. D., Hooper, S. R., Spratt, E. G., & Woolley, D. P. (2009). Neuropsychological findings in childhood neglect and their relationships to pediatric PTSD. *Journal of the International Neuropsychological Society, 15,* 868–878.

Dedovic, K., Duchesne, A., Andrews, J., Engert, V., & Pruessner, J. C. (2009). The brain and the stress axis: The neural correlates of cortisol regulation in response to stress. *NeuroImage, 47*(3), 864–871.

Dettling, A. C., Parker, S., Lane, S. K., Sebanc, A. M., & Gunnar, M. R. (2000). Quality of care and temperament determine whether cortisol levels rise over the day for children in full-day childcare. *Psychoneuroendocrinology, 25,* 819–836.

Dunlop, S. A., Archer, M. A., Quinlivan, J. A., Beazley, L. D., & Newnham, J. P. (1997). Repeated prenatal corticosteroids delay myelination in the ovine central nervous system. *Journal of Maternal-Fetal Medicine, 6*(6), 309–313.

Eigsti, I. M., & Cicchetti, D. (2004). The impact of child maltreatment on expressive syntax at 60 months. *Developmental Science, 7*(1), 88–102.

Feldman, R., Singer, M., & Zagoory, O. (2010). Touch attenuates infants physiological reactivity to stress. *Developmental Science, 13*(2), 271–278.

Giedd, J. N., Blumenthal, J., Jeffries, N. O., Rajapakse, J. C., Vaituzis, A. C., Liu, H., *et al.* (1999). Development of the human corpus callosum during childhood and adolescence: a longitudinal MRI study. *Progress in Neuropsychopharmacology and Biological Psychiatry, 23*(4), 571–588.

Greenough, W. T., & Black, J. E. (1992). Induction of brain structure by experience: Substrates for cognitive development. In M. R. Gunnar & C. A. Nelson (Eds.), (Developmental behavioral neuroscience ed., pp. 155–200). *The Minnesota symposia on child psychology* (Vol. 24, pp. 155–200). Hillsdale, NJ: Erlbaum.

Gunnar, M. R., & Cheatham, C. L. (2003). Brain and behavior interfaces: Stress and the developing brain. *Infant Mental Health Journal, 24*(3), 195–211.

Harbord, M. G., Finn, J. P., Hall-Craggs, M. A., Robb, S. A., Kendall, B. E., & Boyd, S. G. (1990). Myelination patterns on magnetic resonance of children with developmental delay. *Developmental Medicine and Child Neurology, 32*(4), 295–303.

Huttenlocher, P. R. (2002). *Neural plasticity: The effects of environment on the development of the cerebral cortex.* Cambridge, MA: Harvard University Press.

Jansen, J., Beijers, R., Riksen-Walraven, M., & de Weerth, C. (2010). Cortisol reactivity in young infants. *Psychoneuroendocrinology, 35*(3), 329–338.

Karten, Y. J., Olariu, A., & Cameron, H. A. (2005). Stress in early life inhibits neurogenesis in adulthood. *Trends in Neurosciences, 28*(4), 171–172.

Kertes, D. A., Donzella, B., Talge, N. M., Garvin, M. C., Van Ryzin, M. J., & Gunnar, M. R. (2009). Inhibited temperament and parent emotional availability differentially predict young children's cortisol responses to novel social and nonsocial events. *Developmental Psychobiology, 51*(7), 521–532.

Knutson, J. F., DeGarmo, D., Koeppl, G., & Reid, J. B. (2005). Care neglect, supervisory neglect, and harsh parenting in the development of children's aggression: A replication and extension. *Child Maltreatment, 10*(2), 92–107.

Landry, S. H., Smith, K. E., Miller-Loncar, C. L., & Swank, P. R. (1998). The relation of change in maternal interactive styles to the developing social competence of full-term and preterm children. *Child Development, 69*(1), 105–123.

Lee, V., & Hoaken, P. N. (2007). Cognition, emotion, and neurobiological development: Mediating the relation between maltreatment and aggression. *Child Maltreatment, 12*(3), 281–298.

Manly, J. T. (2005). Advances in research definitions of child maltreatment. *Child Abuse & Neglect, 29*, 425–439.

Manly, J. T., Kim, J. E., Rogosch, F. A., & Cicchetti, D. (2001). Dimensions of child maltreatment and children's adjustment: Contributions of developmental timing and subtype. *Development and Psychopathology, 13*(4), 759–782.

Marshall, P. J., & Fox, N. A. (2004). A comparison of the electroencephalogram between institutionalized and community children in Romania. *Journal of Cognitive Neuroscience, 16*(8), 1327–1338.

Masten, A. S. (2001). Ordinary magic: Resilience processes in development. *American Psychologist, 56*(3), 227–238.

Masten, A. S., Garmezy, N., Tellegen, A., Pellegrini, D. S., Larkin, K., & Larsen, A. (1988). Competence and stress in school children: the moderating effects of individual and family qualities. *Journal of Child Psychology and Psychiatry, 29*(6), 745–764.

Mayer, M., Lavergne, C., Tourigny, M., & Wright, J. (2007). Characteristics differentiating neglected children from other reported children. *Journal of Family Violence, 22*, 721–732.

McEwen, B. S. (1999). Stress and hippocampal plasticity. *Annual Review of Neuroscience, 22*, 105–122.

National Center on Child Abuse and Neglect. (1988). *Study findings: Study of national incidence and prevalence of child abuse and neglect: 1988*. Washington DC: US Department of Health and Human Services, Office of Human Development Services.

Nelson, C. A. (Ed.) (2000). *The Minnesota symposia on child psychology: The effects of early adversity on neurobehavioral development* (Vol. 31). Mahwah, NJ. USA: Lawrence Erlbaum Associates, Inc.

Parker, S. W., & Nelson, C. A. (2005a). An event-related potential study of the impact of institutional rearing on face recognition. *Development and Psychopathology, 17*(3), 621–639.

Parker, S. W., & Nelson, C. A. (2005b). The impact of early institutional rearing on the ability to discriminate facial expressions of emotion: An event-related potential study. *Child Development, 76*(1), 54–72.

Paus, T., Collins, D. L., Evans, A. C., Leonard, G., Pike, B., & Zijdenbos, A. (2001). Maturation of white matter in the human brain: A review of magnetic resonance studies. *Brain Research Bulletin, 54*(3), 255–266.

Perlman, S., & Fantuzzo, J. (2010). Timing and influence of early experiences of child maltreatment and homelessness on children's educational well-being. *Children and Youth Services Review, 32*, 874–883.

Piaget, J. (1962). *Play, dreams, and imitation in children.* New York: Norton.

Pollak, S. D., Cicchetti, D., Klorman, R., & Brumaghim, J. T. (1997). Cognitive brain event-related potentials and emotion processing in maltreated children. *Child Development, 68*, 773–787.

Pollak, S. D., & Kistler, D. J. (2002). Early experience is associated with the development of categorical representations for facial expressions of emotion. *Proceedings of the National Academy of Sciences of the United States of America, 99*(13), 9072–9076.

Pollak, S. D., Klorman, R., Thatcher, J. E., & Cicchetti, D. (2001). P3b reflects maltreated children's reactions to facial displays of emotion. *Psychophysiology, 38*(2), 267–274.

Pollak, S. D., & Sinha, P. (2002). Effects of early experience on children's recognition of facial displays of emotion. *Development and Psychology, 38*(5), 784–791.

Pollak, S. D., & Tolley-Schell, S. A. (2003). Selective attention to facial emotion in physically abused children. *Journal of Abnormal Psychology, 112*(3), 323–338.

Porter, C., Lawson, J. S., & Bigler, E. D. (2005). Neurobehavioral sequelae of child sexual abuse. *Child Neuropsychology, 11*(2), 203–220.

Runyan, D. K., Cox, C. E., Dubowitz, H., Newton, R. R., Upadhyaya, M., Kotch, J. B., et al. (2005). Describing maltreatment: do child protective service reports and research definitions agree? *Child Abuse & Neglect, 29*(5), 461–477.

Sapolsky, R. M. (1992). *Stress, the aging brain, and the mechanisms of neuron death.* Cambridge, MA, USA: MIT Press.

Sapolsky, R. M., Krey, L. C., & McEwen, B. S. (1986). The neuroendocrinology of stress and aging: The glucocorticoid cascade hypothesis. *Endocrine Reviews, 7*(3), 284–301.

Sapolsky, R. M., Uno, H., Rebert, C. S., & Finch, C. E. (1990). Hippocampal damage associated with prolonged glucocorticoid exposure in primates. *The Journal of Neuroscience, 10*(9), 2897–2902.

Scannapieco, M., & Connell-Carrick, K. (2005). Focus on the first years: Correlates of substantiation of child maltreatment for families with children 0 to 4. *Children and Youth Services Review, 27*, 1307–1323.

Scarborough, A. A., Lloyd, E. C., & Barth, R. P. (2009). Maltreated infants and toddlers: predictors of developmental delay. *Journal of Developmental and Behavioral Pediatrics, 30*(6), 489–498.

Schmidt, M. V. (2010). Molecular mechanisms of early life stress—Lessons from mouse models. *Neuroscience and Biobehavioral Reviews, 34*(6), 845–852.

Schreiber, J. E. (2010). *Psychopathology symptoms in middle childhood: Complex associations with cortisol activity.* USA: ProQuest Information & Learning.

Seress, L. (2001). Morphological changes of the human hippocampal formation from midgestation to early childhood. In C. A. Nelson & M. Luciana (Eds.), *Handbook of Developmental Cognitive Neuroscience.* (pp. 45–58). Cambridge, MA: The MIT Press.

Shields, A., & Cicchetti, D. (2001). Parental maltreatment and emotion dysregulation as risk factors for bullying and victimization in middle childhood. *Journal of Clinical Child Psychology, 30*(3), 349–363.

Smetana, J. G., Toth, S. L., Cicchetti, D., Bruce, J., Kane, P., & Daddis, C. (1999). Maltreated and nonmaltreated preschoolers' conceptions of hypothetical and actual moral transgressions. *Developmental Psychology, 35*(1), 269–281.

Stouthamer-Loeber, M., Loeber, R., Homish, D. L., & Wei, E. (2001). Maltreatment of boys and the development of disruptive and delinquent behavior. *Development and Psychopathology, 13*(4), 941–955.

Sullivan, M. W., Carmody, D. P., & Lewis, M. (2010). How neglect and punitiveness influence emotion knowledge. *Child Psychiatry and Human Development, 41*(3), 285–298.

Sylvestre, A., & Merette, C. (2010). Language delay in severely neglected children: A cumulative or specific effect of risk factors? *Child Abuse & Neglect, 34*(6), 414–428.

Teicher, M. H., Ito, Y., Glod, C. A., Andersen, S. L., Dumont, N., & Ackerman, E. (1997). Preliminary evidence for abnormal cortical development in physically and sexually abused children using EEG coherence and MRI. *Annals of the New York Academy of Sciences, 821*, 160–175.

Thompson, P. M., Giedd, J. N., Woods, R. P., MacDonald, D., Evans, A. C., & Toga, A. W. (2000). Growth patterns in the developing brain detected by using continuum mechanical tensor maps. *Nature, 404*(6774), 190–193.

Tsujimoto, S. (2008). The prefrontal cortex: functional neural development during early childhood. *Neuroscientist, 14*(4), 345–358.

U.S. Department of Health and Human Services. *Administration for Children and Families. Administration on Children, Youth, and Families, Children's Bureau. Child maltreatment.* (2010). Available from, http://www.acf.hhs.gov/programs/cb/stats_research/index.htm#can.

Valentino, K., Cicchetti, D., Rogosch, F. A., & Toth, S. L. (2008). Memory, maternal representations, and internalizing symptomatology among abused, neglected, and non-maltreated children. *Child Development, 79*(3), 705–719.

Valentino, K., Cicchetti, D., Toth, S. L., & Rogosch, F. A. (2006). Mother-child play and emerging social behaviors among infants from maltreating families. *Developmental Psychology, 42*(3), 474–485.

Webb, S. J., Monk, C. S., & Nelson, C. A. (2001). Mechanisms of postnatal neurobiological development: Implications for human development. *Developmental Neuropsychology, 19*(2), 147–171.

Weniger, G., Lange, C., Sachsse, U., & Irle, E. (2008). Amygdala and hippocampal volumes and cognition in adult survivors of childhood abuse with dissociative disorders. *Acta Psychiatrica Scandinavica, 118*(4), 281–290.

Wiggins, R. C. (1982). Myelin development and nutritional insufficiency. *Brain Research, 257* (2), 151–175.

Zaidel, D. W. (1999). Quantitative morphology of human hippocampus early neuron development. *Anatomical Record, 254*(1), 87–91.

DECLARATIVE MEMORY IN INFANCY: LESSONS LEARNED FROM TYPICAL AND ATYPICAL DEVELOPMENT

Patricia J. Bauer

DEPARTMENT OF PSYCHOLOGY, EMORY UNIVERSITY, ATLANTA, GEORGIA, USA

The work reported in this collection makes clear that declarative memory develops dramatically during the first 2–3 years of life, and that its course is influenced by a number of different types of early experiences. Study of the typical patterning of development of declarative memory in infancy got underway in earnest in the middle to late 1980s, with the development of means of assessing the capacity in preverbal infants and early-verbal children, namely, elicited and deferred imitation (e.g., Bauer & Mandler, 1989; Bauer & Shore, 1987; Meltzoff, 1985). Use of the technique with many different samples of infants and young children, in different laboratories, has made clear that declarative memory capacity emerges and coalesces over the course of the latter half of the first year and throughout the second year of life (respectively). Description of the course of development of the capacity in typically developing infants was one of the broad purposes of this volume. The second broad purpose was to examine the implications for development of declarative memory of four varieties of early experience. I discuss major findings relevant to each of these goals of the collection in turn.

Advances in Child Development and Behavior
Patricia Bauer : Editor

I. Declarative Memory in Typically Developing Infants

Chapters 1–3 of the collection provided descriptions of the course of development of declarative memory in the first 2–3 years of life in typically developing infants. The reviews contained evidence that over this period, declarative memory changes from being temporally limited to temporally extended, from being vulnerable to disruption and disturbance to robust, and from being less to more specific in the features that are encoded (Chapter 1). Moreover, over the first 2.5 years of life, infants and young children remember more information, in the form of longer sequences of action. Whereas infants 16 months of age reliably reproduce 2- but not 3-step sequences, children 32 months of age reliably reproduce 7-step sequences (Chapter 2). Over the same space of time, declarative memory ability seemingly coalesces, such that stable individual differences emerge (Chapter 3). In terms of production of the individual target actions of multistep sequences, stability is apparent by 20 months of age. At 20 months, within a session, performance on shorter and longer sequences is correlated. Across sessions, performance at earlier time points predicts performance at later time points. In terms of the more demanding task of producing sequences in temporal order, stability is apparent by 24 months of age, as evidenced by both concurrent and cross-lagged correlations.

As discussed in Chapter 1, ultimately, several sources of variance will be implicated in the explanation of age-related changes in declarative memory. A still small, yet growing, body of evidence implicates encoding processes and consolidation processes, in particular, as explanations for developmental changes in declarative memory early in life. The changes presumably are linked to development of the temporal–cortical network that supports declarative memory, aspects of which are especially slow to reach maturity (see also Bauer, 2006, 2007, 2009 for discussions). Examination of some possible implications of the slow course of development was the second broad purpose of the volume.

II. Declarative Memory in Special Populations of Infants

The fact that the neural network that supports declarative memory develops slowly provided strong motivation to examine the impacts of different types of experience on the development of declarative memory in infancy. That is, a system that is slow to develop is a system that is vulnerable to disruption and perturbation. This leads to the suggestion that there may be populations in whom the early development of declarative memory is compromised. This possibility motivated research with each of four special populations in which there was reason to expect deficits in declarative memory associated with early experiences that compromised the declarative memory network: infants of mothers with gestational diabetes, infants born prior to term, infants adopted from institutional care, and infants maltreated by their caregivers. Consistent with this suggestion, deficits in declarative memory were apparent in each of the populations of infants.

A. COMMONALITY IN ASSESSMENT

For each of four special populations, declarative memory was examined using elicited and deferred imitation. In each case, we collected measures of immediate recall and of recall after a 10-min delay. The delayed recall task in particular was expected to test the integrity of the declarative memory network, based on findings of deficits in performance after this delay in humans with hippocampal damage (e.g., Reed & Squire, 1998) and nonhuman animals with hippocampal lesions (e.g., Zola-Morgan, Squire, Rempel, Clower, & Amaral, 1992).

Across the populations and studies, the lengths of the sequences on which the infants were tested varied, based on expectations of age-appropriate sequence length derived from work with typical infants summarized in Chapter 2. In all samples, the same two dependent measures were obtained, namely, the number of individual target actions that the infants produced and the number of pairs of actions they produced in the target order. Thus, there was substantial continuity in assessment technique. In addition to measures of immediate and 10-min delayed recall in common, the studies of infants of diabetic mothers and of maltreated infants featured assessments of performance following interleaved presentation, the study of infants adopted from institutional care featured assessment of performance following presentation in the presence of distraction, and the study of infants of diabetic mothers featured electrophysiological (event-related potential) measures of memory. In each case, infants also were assessed using the Mental Development Index (MDI) of the Bayley Scales of Infant Development, as a measure of general cognitive function.

B. SUMMARY OF MAJOR FINDINGS

Consistent with the suggestion that infants in the four target populations suffered compromised development of the declarative memory network, in all four groups there was evidence of impaired performance on the elicited and deferred imitation tasks. In each case, infants at greater risk showed greater impairment.

1. Infants of Diabetic Mothers

As summarized in Chapter 4, at 12 months of age, infants of diabetic mothers showed impaired performance in the 10-min deferred imitation task, relative to control infants. The pattern was apparent for both the number of individual actions produced and production of pairs of actions in target order. With MDI scores controlled, only the deficit in production of ordered pairs after a delay remained. Since no differences in immediate recall were apparent, the pattern is most consistent with impaired consolidation, a function absolutely dependent on the hippocampus.

At 24 months of age, no differences in behavioral performance were seen between the groups of infants. The absence of differences should not be interpreted to suggest that the effects of maternal gestational diabetes on infants' development are short-lived, however. First, at both 12 and 24 months of age, differences in neural processing were apparent in the infants of diabetic mothers and the control infants. Thus, although differences in behavioral performance were not detected at 24 months, an altered course of development nevertheless was apparent. Second, as summarized in Chapter 4, when larger longitudinal samples from the groups were tested at 42 months of age, differences again were apparent (Riggins, Miller, Bauer, Georgieff, & Nelson, 2009). On a challenging version of the elicited imitation task, differences in behavior emerged in both immediate and delayed recall. In addition, at 12 months of age and again at 42 months, there was evidence that infants at greatest risk for compromised developed suffered the greatest deficits in memory performance. Specifically, there were correlations between the level of iron in the cord blood at birth and memory performance, such that infants with the lowest iron stores performed most poorly (see Riggins *et al.*, 2009 for elaboration).

2. Infants Born Prior to Term

As summarized in Chapter 5, when tested near their first birthdays, infants born very preterm (i.e., gestational ages 28–34 weeks) showed impaired performance relative to infants born at term (i.e., gestational ages 38–41 weeks). Whereas the very preterm infants were tested at roughly 14 months of age (postnatal age), their performance was more similar to that of full-term infants who were fully 2 months younger (i.e., full-term infants tested at 12 months of age). Also, relative to immediate recall, the delayed recall of the very preterm infants was lower, a decrement not observed in the other groups of infants. Infants born very preterm and who suffered additional complications such as larger intraventricular hemorrhage, ongoing infections, and slow-to-resolve hypoglycemia, showed more pronounced deficits on the task.

In contrast to the impaired performance of infants born very preterm, infants born moderately preterm (i.e., gestational ages 35–37 weeks) performed at levels that were roughly comparable to full-term infants tested at 12 and 13 months of age (i.e., infants matched to the corrected and postnatal ages of the moderately preterm infants, respectively). In contrast to the pattern observed for the very preterm infants, in the moderately preterm sample, the presence of greater risk factors (e.g., nutritional deficiencies, oxygen deprivation, infection, and hematoma) did not result in compromised performance. Thus, it seems that the extra *intra*uterine experience that the moderately preterm infants had, relative to the very preterm infants, worked to mitigate any deficit associated with their preterm birth. In contrast, their 1 month of additional *extra*uterine experience did not have a similar positive effect: the performance of the 13-month-old moderately preterm infants was not greater than that of the 12-month-old full-term infants.

3. Infants Adopted from Institutional Care

As summarized in Chapter 6, infants tested several months after adoption from institutional care showed impaired performance on the delayed recall task, relative to control infants. The deficit was apparent both in terms of the number of individual target actions the infants produced after the delay, and in terms of their production of the actions in the target order. The effects remained even after controlling for general cognitive ability, as measured by the MDI. Postinstitutionalized infants did not differ from controls on either of the immediate recall tasks (standard immediate recall and distraction). Thus, similar to the conclusion for infants of diabetic mothers, their pattern of performance is most consistent with impaired consolidation of new memories.

The work of Kroupina and her colleagues (Chapter 6) also provides evidence that greater risk is associated with greater impairment. Compared with infants adopted earlier, infants adopted later—and thus, who spent more time in institutional care—had lower levels of performance. In fact, as reported in Experiment 2, for infants tested when they were younger than 20 months of age, there was no difference in performance on the immediate relative to the 10-min delayed recall task. In contrast, infants tested when they were older than 20 months of age were challenged to retain the information in memory over the brief delay, resulting in lower

scores on the delayed than the immediate recall task. In typically developing infants, brief delays present a challenge for younger infants (13- to
16-month-olds: Abravanel, 1991), but not for children 20 months of age
(e.g., Bauer, Van Abbema, & de Haan, 1999). The differences in patterns
of performance for the early- and later-adopted infants were observed
even though both groups were tested roughly 6 months after adoption,
and the older-at-adoption infants were older at the time of the test (mean
ages of 18 and 24 months, respectively).

4. Infants Maltreated by Their Caregivers

As summarized in Chapter 7, as a group, infants maltreated by their
caregivers did not differ from control infants on the immediate recall,
delayed recall, or interleaved presentation tasks. However, when the
maltreated group was divided into subgroups that were abused by their
caregivers versus neglected by them (based on the Maltreatment Classification System: Barnett, Manly, & Cicchetti, 1993), differences emerged.
In what at first glance may seem a puzzling pattern, infants neglected by
their caregivers performed at lower levels relative to infants who suffered
physical abuse at their hands. The deficit was apparent on all measures of
performance. Although the neglected infants had scores that were lower
than those of nonmaltreated controls, the differences were not significant.

Insight into the seemingly preserved — and even enhanced — performance
of abused relative to neglected and nonmaltreated infants comes from consideration of a finding from an assessment when the infants in this group
were 12 months of age (Valentino, Cicchetti, Rogosch, & Toth, 2008).
In the context of a structured play between mother and their infants, children in the abused subgroup imitated their mothers more often than did
the nonmaltreated children. There was no difference between the imitative
behaviors of the neglected children and the abused or nonmaltreated children. The authors speculated that by imitating their mothers, the abused
children might be attempting to increase the likelihood of positive reinforcement and, thus, prevent further abusive incidents. Regardless of the source
of the difference, the response mode in the elicited and deferred imitation
task seemingly played into one of the strengths in the profile of abilities
(and disabilities) that characterize abused infants and young children.

III. Mechanisms of Declarative Memory Impairment

Each of Chapters 4–7 featured discussion of plausible mechanisms that
could contribute to the patterns of performance observed in the target
populations. In each case, it is clear that there are multiple causal

mechanisms. Although within these populations, any attempt to isolate *the* cause of compromised development will fail, we can examine the pre- and postnatal experiences of the infants for insights into possible causes and consequences.

In the case of infants of diabetic mothers, maternal blood sugar control problems result in a number of metabolic insults, including iron deficiency. Iron deficiency in turn is thought to affect neurodevelopment in general and perhaps myelination in particular (Larkin, Jarratt, & Rao, 1986). For reasons that are not clear at this time, the hippocampus is a region of the brain that is at particular risk for reductions in iron uptake (Erikson, Pinero, Connor, & Beard, 1997). This suggests that infants born to mothers with diabetes may have suffered disruption of myelination in the hippocampus (Chapter 4).

Nutrients and micronutrients also are implicated in the chain of events that may contribute to impaired declarative memory performance in infants born prior to term. As discussed in Chapter 5, premature birth deprives the fetus of support from the placenta and therefore, of expected intrauterine nutrients important for brain development. Specifically, certain nutrients critical for brain development such as oxygen, glucose, proteins, myelin-supporting fats, iron, and growth factors are no longer being supplied by the placenta. The shorter the gestational term, the longer the period of deprivation from the expected—intrauterine—environ-ronment. "Omission" of nutrients, coupled with the error of "commission" that results from events in extrauterine life when the expected environ-ment was intrauterine (Chapter 5), are likely causes of impaired declara-tive memory in infants born very preterm. Outcome is further imperiled when preterm infants suffer insults at or shortly after delivery, such as intracranial hemorrhage, which leads to cell death in the areas of brain where the blood clots form. Another common challenge faced by infants born prior to term is respiratory problems caused by immaturity of the lungs. To hasten lung development, preterm infants routinely are given dexamethasone, a synthetic form of glucocorticoid. Unfortunately, the hippocampus is selectively and permanently damaged by prolonged expo-sure to glucocorticoids (Neal, VanderBeek, Vazquez, & Watson, 2003). Thus, a life-saving treatment also may contribute to later impairments of declarative memory.

Glucocorticoids also are implicated in the sequence of events that ulti-mately may undermine declarative memory development in infants adopted from institution care and infants maltreated by their caregivers. However, unlike infants born prior to term, in whom the source of glucocorticoids is exogenous, in the case of infants adopted from institu-tional care and infants maltreated by their caregivers, the source is endogenous. Work with nonhuman primates makes clear that animals deprived of normal social interaction and stimulation exhibit elevated levels of glucocorticoids in response to stressors (e.g., Higley, Suomi, & Linnoila, 1992). High levels of glucocorticoids are not healthy for hippo-campal neurons. In addition, there is evidence that normal social interaction supports the development of the hippocampus (Caldji *et al.*, 1998). In rodents, "normal social interaction" involves licking and grooming of the pups by the dams. Removal of this source of stimulation results in levels of hippocampal cell death as much as 50% higher than normal (Zhang, Xing, Levine, Post, & Smith, 1997). The combination of these effects could be profound indeed: infants deprived of social–emotional support and stimulation could be expected to mount exaggerated responses to stressors leading to cell death in a hippocampus that already has fewer than the expected number of neurons.

Infants who spend their early lives in institutional care and infants who are maltreated by their caregivers both experience atypical social–emotional support. As described in Chapter 6, in institutional care, ratios of children to staff often are high and the staff frequently turns over (see Gunnar, 2001 for discussion). These conditions virtually ensure that children receive suboptimal levels of social interaction. As described in Chapter 7, infants who are neglected, abused, or both by their caregivers experience conditions that are not unlike those experienced by infants in institutional care. Even when their basic physical needs are met, abused and neglected children are not provided with levels of positive stimulation and support sufficient to ensure normative development. The lack of social–emotional support, coupled with the chronic stress that infants in these populations experience, can be expected to have deleterious effects on the developing brain. Chronically high cortisol levels associated with the stressful environment may contribute to damage and even death of cells in the hippocampus. In addition, as is the case for infants of diabetic mothers, myelination in general, and perhaps myelination in the hippo-campus in particular, may be compromised as well (Dunlop, Archer, Quinlivan, Beazley, & Newnham, 1997). These insults may be expected to contribute to deficits in declarative memory in particular.

Finally, infants adopted from institutional care and infants abused and in particular, neglected, by their caregivers, experience cognitive as well as social deprivation. In the case of institutional care, high children-to-staff ratios mean that staff have little opportunity to engage infants in activities that can be expected to promote cognitive development. Additionally, as a result of concern over their potential to transmit disease, institutions limit the number of toys and other manipulables that are part of the expected environment of infancy. As a result, infants in institutional care learn less about their impoverished environments. The lack of stimulation experienced by infants in institutional care and infants neglected by their caregivers also can be expected to impact postnatal sculpting of the brain. Overproduction of axons, dendrites, synapses, and even, neurons is a genetically determined process (Bourgeois, Jastreboff, & Rakic, 1989). However, the pruning of unused connections is an experience-expectant process (see Chapter 7 for discussion) and as such is dependent on environmental input. In the absence of expected postnatal events such as maternal stimulation, social interaction, and language input, it is possible that many neural connections will go unused and during the pruning period, will be lost.

IV. Interventions in Early Development

In Chapter 6, Kroupina and her colleagues described adoption from institutional care as a "major intervention" that brings a dramatic change in a child's life. Within the space of a few days to weeks, infants adopted from institutional care are moved from suboptimal conditions to conditions that if not optimal for development, certainly are closer to ideal. As a result, adoption from institutional care provides an especially compelling example of early experience unconfounded by later experience. Although less dramatic, the "intervention" provided to infants of diabetic mothers also can be considered major. From the moment of birth, they no longer are subjected to the roller coaster of changes in blood oxygenation and glucose levels that characterized fetal life. Moreover, infants with low ferritin levels at birth are given iron supplementation, further ensuring that the challenging conditions that prevailed during their gestation come to a halt. Yet even though the infants adopted from institutional care and the infants of diabetic mothers experienced major interventions that brought an end to their suboptimal early experiences, and even though testing took place months after the interventions, impairments in their declarative memory performance were observed. This outcome speaks to the enormous power of early experience and the need for further research into early detection of possible impairment and early intervention.

V. Conclusions

Since the 1980s, we have learned a great deal about the typical course of development of declarative memory in infants and very young children. Papers in the present collection represent significant progress in our understanding of some of the factors and conditions that affect the development of this fundamental cognitive capacity. It now is apparent that on the one hand, the capacity is well preserved in the species. Although the performance of many of the groups tested in the research reported here was impaired relative to comparison groups, in all cases, the infants showed evidence of learning and of retention over brief delays. On the other hand, the fact that brief delays had pronounced negative effects on several of the groups speaks to the fragility of the capacity. More research is needed to identify the factors and conditions that both facilitate and interfere with the development of declarative memory. Careful attention to prenatal and postnatal influences will aid in identification of the critical variables and limiting conditions, thereby allowing for construction of a model of declarative memory development that explains the atypical as well as the typical.

Acknowledgment

The research summarized in this chapter was supported by grants from the NICHD (HD28425, HD42483) to Patricia J. Bauer.

REFERENCES

Abravanel, E. (1991). Does immediate imitation influence long-term memory for observed actions? *Journal of Experimental Child Psychology, 51*, 235–244.

Barnett, D., Manly, J. T., & Cicchetti, D. (1993). Defining child maltreatment: The interface between policy and research. In D. Cicchetti & S. L. Toth (Eds.), *Advances in applied developmental psychology: Child abuse, child development, and social policy* (pp. 7–73). Norwood, NJ: Ablex Publishing Corporation.

Bauer, P. J. (2006). Constructing a past in infancy: A neuro-developmental account. *Trends in Cognitive Sciences, 10*, 175–181.

Bauer, P. J. (2007). *Remembering the times of our lives: Memory in infancy and beyond.* Mahwah, NJ: Erlbaum.

Bauer, P. J. (2009). Neurodevelopmental changes in infancy and beyond: Implications for learning and memory. In O. A. Barbarin & B. H. Wasik (Eds.), *Handbook of child development and early education: Research to practice* (pp. 78–102). New York: The Guilford Press.

Bauer, P. J., & Mandler, J. M. (1989). One thing follows another: Effects of temporal structure on one- to two-year-olds' recall of events. *Developmental Psychology, 25*, 197–206.

Bauer, P. J., & Shore, C. M. (1987). Making a memorable event: Effects of familiarity and organization on young children's recall of action sequences. *Cognitive Development, 2*, 327–338.

Bauer, P. J., Van Abbema, D. L., & de Haan, M. (1999). In for the short haul: Immediate and short-term remembering and forgetting by 20-month-old children. *Infant Behavior & Development, 22*, 321–343.

Bourgeois, J. P., Jastreboff, P. J., & Rakic, P. (1989). Synaptogenesis in visual cortex of normal and preterm monkeys: evidence for intrinsic regulation of synaptic overproduction. *Proceedings of the National Academy of Sciences of the United States of America, 86* (11), 4297–4301.

Caldji, C., Tannenbaum, B., Sharma, S., Francis, D., Plotsky, P. M., & Meaney, M. J. (1998). Maternal care during infancy regulates the development of neural systems mediating the expression of fearfulness in the rat. *Proceedings of the National Academy of Sciences of the United States of America, 95,* 5335–5340.

Dunlop, S. A., Archer, M. A., Quinlivan, J. A., Beazley, L. D., & Newnham, J. P. (1997). Repeated prenatal corticosteroids delay myelination in the ovine central nervous system. *The Journal of Maternal-Fetal Medicine, 6*(6), 309–313.

Erikson, K. M., Pinero, D. J., Connor, J. R., & Beard, J. L. (1997). Regional brain iron, ferritin, and transferrin concentrations during iron deficiency and iron repletion in developing rats. *The Journal of Nutrition, 127,* 2030–2038.

Gunnar, M. R. (2001). Effects of early deprivation: Findings from orphanage-reared infants and children. In C. A. Nelson & M. Luciana (Eds.), *Handbook of developmental cognitive neuroscience* (pp. 617–629). Cambridge, MA: The MIT Press.

Higley, L. D., Suomi, S. J., & Linnoila, M. (1992). A longitudinal study of CSF monoamine metabolite and plasma cortisol concentrations in young rhesus monkeys: Effects of early experience, age, sex, and stress on continuity of individual differences. *Biological Psychiatry, 32,* 127–145.

Larkin, E. C., Jarratt, B. A., & Rao, G. A. (1986). Reduction of relative levels of nervonic to lignoceric acid in the brain of rat pups due to iron deficiency. *Nutrition Research, 6,* 309–314.

Meltzoff, A. N. (1985). Immediate and deferred imitation in fourteen- and twenty-four-month-old infants. *Child Development, 56,* 62–72.

Neal, C. R., Jr., VanderBeek, B. L., Vazquez, D. M., & Watson, S. J.Jr., (2003). Dexamethasone exposure during the neonatal period alters ORL1 mRNA expression in the hypothalamic paraventricular nucleus and hippocampus of the adult rat. *Brain Research. Developmental Brain Research, 146,* 15–24.

Reed, J. M., & Squire, L. R. (1998). Retrograde amnesia for facts and events: Findings from four new cases. *The Journal of Neuroscience, 18,* 3943–3954.

Riggins, T., Miller, N. C., Bauer, P. J., Georgieff, M. K., & Nelson, C. A. (2009). Consequences of maternal diabetes mellitus and neonatal iron status on children's explicit memory performance. *Developmental Neuropsychology, 34*(6), 762–779.

Valentino, K., Cicchetti, D., Rogosch, F. A., & Toth, S. L. (2008). Memory, maternal representations, and internalizing symptomatology among abused, neglected, and nonmaltreated children. *Child Development, 79*(3), 705–719.

Zhang, L. X., Xing, G. O., Levine, S., Post, R. M., & Smith, M. A. (1997). Maternal deprivation induces neuronal death. *Abstracts—Society for Neuroscience,* 1113.

Zola-Morgan, S., Squire, L. R., Rempel, N. L., Clower, R. P., & Amaral, D. G. (1992). Enduring memory impairment in monkeys after ischemic damage to the hippocampus. *The Journal of Neuroscience, 9,* 4355–4370.

Author Index

A

Aber, J. L., 166
Aboitiz, F., 117
Abraham, H., 9
Abravanel, E., 154, 192
Ackerman, E., 173
Adlam, A. -L. R., 5
Aicardi, J., 15
Aimone, J. B., 181
Aitken, D. H., 144
Akin, F., 78, 81
Akin, M., 78, 81
Akturk, Z., 78, 81
Algarin, C., 114–115
Alink, L. R., 167
Althaus, M., 141
Alt, J. J., 116
Amaral, D. G., 14, 152, 189
Ames, E., 140–142, 156–158
Andersen, S. L., 173
Anderson, E., 145
Andrews, J., 171
Andrews, N. C., 75
Angulo-Kinzler, R. M., 114
Appenzeller, T., 73
Archer, M. A., 17, 169, 194
Archer, T., 118
Armstrong, E. A., 116
Arnold, S. E., 9
Ashman, S. B., 167
Atay, E., 78, 81
Atay, Z., 78, 81

B

Bachevalier, J., 4, 74
Baerts, W., 15–16
Baillargeon, R., 2
Baldwin, D. A., 5
Bangston, S. K., 7, 28, 50

Baram, T., 143–145
Barks, J. D., 76, 116
Barnat, S. B., 5
Barnett, D., 166–167, 170, 174, 192
Barr, R. P., 6–8, 12, 28, 71
Barth, R. P., 17, 166
Bauer, P. J., 1–12, 14–15, 18, 27–30, 33,
    44–46, 49–52, 59, 68–69, 71, 73, 77–79,
    84–85, 87, 89–92, 94, 98, 100–103, 113, 117,
    122, 132, 139–140, 143, 146–148, 154, 165,
    175, 178–180, 187–188, 190, 192
Baum, A. S., 172
Bayley, N., 124, 172, 174
Beard, J. L., 15, 74, 115, 193
Beazley, L. D., 17, 169, 194
Beckett, C., 140, 142, 147, 158
Beers, S. R., 173
Behen, M. E., 141, 170
Beijers, R., 172
Bender, R., 143–145
Benders, M. J., 118
Benes, F. M., 9
Beninger, R. J., 118
Bennett, F. C., 124
Berger, H. M., 118
Bergman, K., 172
Bhatnagar, S., 144
Bigler, E. D., 167
Birmaher, B., 172
Bittinger, K. A., 28, 44
Bjorklund, D. F., 6
Black, J. E., 139, 146, 168
Bloom, D., 121
Blumenthal, J., 169
Bolger, K. E., 167
Boniface, J., 7, 12
Boring, A. M., 145, 172
Borscheid, A. J., 77
Bourgeois, J.-P., 9, 169, 195
Boyd, S. G., 169
Brazy, J. E., 120, 123, 128

195

Subject Index

A

Abused and neglected infants
developmental sequelae, 167–168
hippocampal task, 177–178
maltreatment
brain development, 168–171
classification, 166–167
participants, 174
procedure
BSID-II, 174–175
elicited imitation procedure, 175
testing sessions, 176
verbal interaction, 175–176
stress and developing brain
effects, maltreatment, 173
HPA dysregulation, 173
intrinsic negative feedback system, 172
maternal deprivation, 172–173
maternal–infant interactions, 171
reassign energy, 171–172
target actions
imitation, 178
immediate recall condition, 178
post hoc comparisons, 179
Atypical populations
adoption from institutional care
children to staff ratios, 16
compromised hippocampal function,
16–17
infants of diabetic mothers
maternal diabetes, 14
prenatal iron deficiency, 14–15
maltreated by their caregivers, 17
prior to term
risk factors, 15
visual perception, 16

B

Bayley Scales of Infant Development,
second edition (BSID-II), 174–175
Brain-derived neurotrophic factor (BDNF),
76
Brain development risk
errors of commission
biological conditions, 118
cerebral palsy and mental retardation,
118–119
intraventricular hemorrhage, 119
errors of omission
fetus and prematurity maldevelopment,
116–117
periconceptional factors, 116
placental insufficiency, 117
fetal and neonatal growth, 114
genetics and environment, 114
hippocampal cell loss and cell death, 116
iron deficiency, 115
regional vulnerability, 115
BSID-II, *see* Bayley Scales of Infant
Development, second edition

C

Cognitive functions, declarative memory
animal and human studies
early institutionalization, 145–146
hippocampus structures, 143–144
memory problems, adults, 144–145
PTSD, 145
rodent models, 143
stimulus–response association, 144
imitation-based tasks, 146–147
postinstitutionalized toddlers, 146

Contents of Previous Volumes